Utterly Amazed

Miriam Davis grew up in the UK in a loving Christian home whose doors were wide open to people from other cultures. Transformed by an encounter with Jesus at university, she set off in some trepidation after graduation to teach English in Japan for two years. Two years became forty-two! In 1986 she left teaching to join OMF International and spent the next 30 years in Hokkaido, in church planting and as advisor to new cross-cultural workers studying Japanese. She is now retired in Gloucester, UK. She volunteers as a mentor and mission presenter on behalf of OMF and is involved in a local church where she has become an Ordained Local Minister.

Welcoming *Utterly Amazed*

In *Utterly Amazed* Miriam Davis enables us to walk with her through the road map of her life. Through a desire to teach English as a foreign language, Miriam finds herself working in Japan. How God leads Miriam to be a church planter is just a part of the story. A story of love and despair, of hardship and joy: Miriam describes the struggles of the Japanese church and her own personal emotional journey with candid honesty. This is not a mission partner holding herself up as the paragon of virtue — this is a godly woman showing us that despite our weaknesses we too can follow God if we are willing to listen. This part of Miriam's story is told but God is still calling and she is still seeking to follow.

Revd Canon Pauline Godfrey
Head of Discipleship & Vocation, Diocese of Gloucester, 2021

In this short memoir Miriam Davis helicopters over her own life story, including 42 years in Japan. There are sadness and surprise in this story; heartbreak, unfulfilled hopes, burnout, depression and struggles with change. There is submission to another culture marked by deference and duty. Miriam had been warned that in another culture, 'all the scum of your nature will rise to the top.' There is also patience and lifelong learning. Many cross-cultural workers and ministers have read many books, but the book they have not read sufficiently is the book of their own life!

Miriam is also a devoted Bible-reader, trusting the guidance of the illuminating Spirit, making space for transcendence, shaping her obedience to the divine Word. And still the jigsaw is unfinished, still she is 'fitting in', thinking of others; and she invites us to share her journey into wisdom, not clinging to old habits, doing what (only) she can do, not making excuses but travelling on. Share her amazement and find your own path made clearer.

Rev. Howard Peskett, author,
former Dean of Discipleship Training Centre, Singapore,
former Vice Principal of Trinity College, Bristol

Having known Miriam since she was a teenager and I was her father's curate, I can't pretend to approach her story in a coolly unbiased way! But allowing for a prejudice warmly in her favour, two things stand out for me from this highly readable book.

The first is the numbers game. Our generation, including myself, has become used to devouring must-read Christian books, and signing up for must-attend Christian gatherings, where the dominant voices are usually those of men who lead congregations of hundreds or even thousands. I can gladly join in praise for blessings on this scale; I have my heroes too! But Miriam reminds us that God is equally present among churches, not only overseas, registering single figures or not many more. Each 'little flock' is the work of the sovereign heavenly Father, alive with the risen Christ, rich with the harvest of the Holy Spirit. While we all rejoice in numerical growth, small churches are not failed big ones, and those who serve and lead them need at least equal faith, skills and wisdom.

The second outstanding factor here is Miriam's double sensitivity. She has to learn to recognise and use the nuances and subtleties of a very different language and culture, the appropriate gesture, turn of phrase and tone of voice, even when to speak at all, and then help others to learn too. But she has also learnt to know the distinctive tones of Jesus, the Good Shepherd. The sheep for whom he died will recognise his voice, sometimes in surprising ways and unlikely situations. He leads them out, and they respond to what he says. Many readers can be grateful to Miriam for honestly sharing these and countless other insights and treasures, with many a tear, many a smile, and many a prayer. Do come and see, and share her own 'utter amazement'!

Christopher Idle, retired pastor, grandfather, hymn-writer, Herne Hill, London

Miriam's story is inspiring and fascinating. It begins by inviting us to step into a different culture and see it through the eyes of a 22-year-old who is no more 'sorted' than anyone else. I would recommend it to anyone who is wondering what God wants them to do with their lives, not because it will tell them what to do, but because it shows again and again how God lovingly (and sometimes perplexingly!) guides his people a few steps at a time.

Becky Chevis, Music Network Staff Worker, UCCF (Universities and Colleges Christian Fellowship)

Utterly Amazed is a wonderful account of an individual's journey into and through a lifetime of service to God and missions. From early encounters and spiritual experiences, Miriam Davis pieces together her calling as it unfolds along her early journey. Then, as she arrives in Japan, her long-term field of service, she documents the many challenges that face a modern mission worker. It's a very open, honest account of her ups and downs through the years, with her joys and celebrations as well as the times of burnout and feelings of wanting to give up. It's missionary life in all of its reality.

We live in a time where the long-term mission worker seems to be a dying breed. Miriam Davis is one of those who has a lifetime's experience of serving God through mission, most of it on the field in Japan. Her book is an up-to-date account giving a valuable window into this diminishing category of Christian worker. All Christians have something to learn from Miriam about having an utter dependence on God and a willingness to follow wherever he leads.

It's a must read for any mission worker going to Japan or anyone going into extensive cross-cultural Bible teaching or church planting, but it also has many details that would be useful for anyone embarking on a life of mission or ministry, or anyone interested in the sacrifices and challenges a modern mission worker faces.

Mike Frith, Director, OSCAR ('One Stop Centre for Advice and Resources' related to mission)

When I went to All Nations Christian College, UK, in the autumn of 1979 I was astonished to be addressed in Japanese by a young English lady. This was my first encounter with Miriam. After we both returned to Japan we had little opportunity to meet. Then in 2015, I spoke at the Keswick Convention in Sapporo. When my eyes fell on Miriam in the audience she beamed all over her face and waved. She now had silver hair — the crown of 40 years of serving in mission in Japan! My heart was full —'Thank you, Miriam.'

Utterly Amazed is Miriam's story of teaching English; of pioneer evangelism and pastoral ministry with OMF; of supervising the Japanese study of new OMF workers. But the story goes much further. It is an utterly amazing account of how the 'I AM' God led Miriam through his living Word and guiding hand. It begins with her surrender to God at Cambridge and her ensuing encounter with the Holy Spirit. Without pretence she paints vivid pictures of the wonder of coming to know Jesus; of life-changing encounters; of seeking God's will regarding marriage; of burnout and depression and of moving out of her comfort zone into new spheres of service for God. Time and again she looks to the Lord and his Word for guidance. You will be nurtured spiritually if you have your Bible to hand to look up references as you read. I praise God for the miracles of grace in Miriam's life and for the publication of this book.

Revd Hiroo Kudo, former Principal of Kansai Bible College and retired pastor of Kagato Church, Nihon Iesu Kirisuto Kyodan (Jesus Christ Church in Japan)

When my wife and I visited churches in Hokkaido, north Japan, before we were sent to Cambodia as OMF workers in 1995, we stayed in the flat of an OMF colleague from the UK who had returned home temporarily. That colleague was Miriam Davis. Through reading this book, I learnt how God used her to share the good news of Jesus with my fellow Japanese through many challenges and painful experiences — the grief of a broken engagement; the experience of different Japanese environments in Nagoya, Osaka, and Sapporo; church planting in a multicultural team; advising newly-arrived mission colleagues on Japanese language and culture; the experience of burnout and re-entry into life in the UK. This is the life story of a Christian woman who dedicated her life to serve the Japanese. It is written with honesty — not glossing over the discouragements — but full of joy and hope. I am deeply moved and utterly amazed!

Shoichiro Sugaya, OMF International Director for East Asia North

Miriam Davis' life story reminds me of the delightful variety of people God chooses to serve him. I thought back to the major prophets in the Old Testament. We are not surprised at God's choice of the richly gifted, golden-mouthed Isaiah. He was such a brilliant person but it comes as something of a shock when we move on to Jeremiah. Diffident, insecure and self-doubting, Jeremiah resisted God's call to serve as a prophet. Ezekiel is radically different again. Perhaps with an artistic temperament, Ezekiel tends to see God's Word in pictorial form and visions. Then we come to Daniel. Living as a Jewish captive in Babylon under an autocratic and amoral leadership, Daniel steadfastly refused all compromise with the ways of Babylon.

Coming now to Miriam and her life-story *Utterly Amazed*. What sort of person is she as someone sent by God to Japan? Miriam presents herself as someone strongly introvert and somewhat lacking in self-confidence but we notice how her quiet humility fits surprisingly well with Japanese culture. Her gentle love for other people is instrumental too in guiding individuals into a new life-giving faith in Jesus. Her deeply spiritual and biblical family background undergirds everything in Miriam's life and service for the Lord. Thank you, Miriam, for your brave sharing even of painful happenings in your life, for opening our eyes to learn more of the open doors for mission in Japan, for encouraging us in our love for the Lord and trust in him. Indeed, we share with you in declaring that the Lord's generous goodness is truly 'utterly amazing'!

Martin Goldsmith worked cross-culturally in Asia before becoming tutor at All Nations Christian College and a prolific writer and speaker about mission

UTTERLY AMAZED

Following the call of God in Japan

MIRIAM DAVIS

**Illustrations and cover artwork
by Mary Grace Sy**

First published in the UK in 2021 by Fabulahula,
(a publishing imprint of E & Q Services Limited),
254 Stroud Road, Gloucester GL4 0AU, United Kingdom.
Tel: +44 (0)7713 637128, email: info@fabulahula.com, website: www.fabulahula.com

ISBN 978-1-9160519-5-9

A catalogue record for this book is available from the British Library.

Every effort has been made to ensure that this book contains the correct permissions and references but, if anything has been inadvertently overlooked, the Publisher will be pleased to make the necessary arrangements at the first opportunity. Please contact the Publisher directly.

Except where shown otherwise, Scripture quotations are taken from the Holy Bible, New International Version (Anglicised edition), Copyright © 1979, 1984, 2011 by Biblica. Used by permission of Hodder & Stoughton Publishers, an Hachette UK company. All right reserved. 'NIV' is a registered trademark of Biblica. UK trademark number 1448790.

Extracts marked KJV are from The King James Bible, the rights in which are vested in the Crown, and are reproduced by permission of the Crown's Patentee, Cambridge University Press.

Scripture taken from the New King James Version ®, Copyright © 1982 by Thomas Nelson is used by permission. All rights reserved.

Scripture quotations marked HCSB are from the Holman Christian Standard Bible ®, Copyright © 1999, 2000, 2002, 2003, 2009 by Holman Bible Publishers. Used by permission. Holman Christian Standard Bible ®, Holman CSB ®, and HCSB ®, are federally registered trademarks of Holman Bible Publishers.

Scripture quotations marked MSG are taken from THE MESSAGE, copyright © 1993, 2002, 2018 by Eugene H. Peterson. Used by permission of NavPress, represented by Tyndale House Publishers. All rights reserved.

The quotations taken from *Passion and Purity* are by Elisabeth Elliot, Copyright © Elisabeth Elliot, 1984, 2012. Used by permission of Baker Publishing Group. www.bakerpublishinggroup.com

The quotations taken from *A Long Obedience in the Same Direction: Discipleship in an Instant Society* are by Eugene Peterson, Copyright © Eugene Peterson, 1980, 1995. Used by permission of Intervarsity Press. www.ivpbooks.com

In memory of my loving parents,
Eustace Bowater and Eva Davis,
whose commitment to Jesus and to
his mission inspired my own.

Miriam

Contents

Foreword

We first got to know Miriam when she was our language learning supervisor in the OMF Japan language school. We soon learnt to value her wisdom and understanding as we grappled with the complex language and culture. Since then, we have been privileged to see her life and ministry up close as we got to know Miriam as a good friend and valued colleague. What we saw in person comes out so clearly in this book—Miriam's first priority is to honour the Lord and share the good news about Jesus with those who don't know him.

Over 42 years of ministry in Japan, Miriam has experienced the joys, challenges and pitfalls of missionary life. She tells the story of those years with honesty and a keen eye for how God was at work sustaining her, changing her and using her for His purposes. We didn't think our respect could go any deeper, but as we have read more of God's story in her life we have been struck by Miriam's humility, faithfulness, ability to forgive and her obedience in her service of our Lord. The way in which she has shared her feelings, weaknesses and struggles gives testimony to God's work in her life, and ultimately gives God the glory. We know that is just what she wants to do! There is so much wisdom and encouragement in this book about a life lived wholeheartedly for the Lord. As we read, we had to stop many times just to jot down verses, quotes and lessons that God was teaching us through Miriam's story.

We hope that this book will encourage you in your faith and challenge you about the need for sacrifice and perseverance if Jesus is to be made known. We hope it will also encourage you to pray for Japan—a nation that needs prayers and workers who will follow in Miriam's footsteps. Thank you, Miriam, for sharing your life with us—like you we stand 'utterly amazed' at God's work in your life and praise him for all he has done in and through you.

Chris and Kesia Pain
Field Directors, OMF Japan

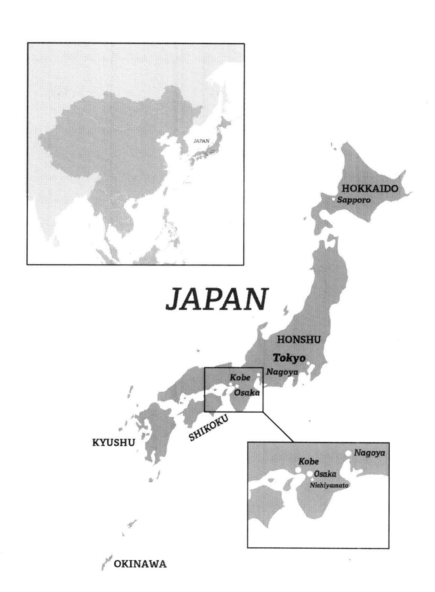

JAPAN

HOKKAIDO
Sapporo

HONSHU
Tokyo
Nagoya
Kobe
Osaka

Kobe
Osaka
Nishiyamato
Nagoya

SHIKOKU

KYUSHU

OKINAWA

Introduction

Why the title *Utterly Amazed*? In the Old Testament book of Habakkuk, the latter accuses God of failure to restrain the evil all around him, and utters a despairing 'How long, O Lord?' In response, God challenges Habakkuk to watch out for the amazing things he is going to do.

> Look at the nations and watch —
> and be **utterly amazed**.
> For I am going to do something in your days
> that you would not believe,
> even if you were told.

> (Habakkuk 1:5)

As I reflect on my life story, I am 'utterly amazed' at how God has led me, and at what he is doing in Japan despite the challenges. Had I been told as a 22-year-old what God would do in my life, I certainly would not have believed a word of it. Mercifully I knew nothing, or I would probably have done a 'Jonah,' and have run away as fast I could, so missing out on a great life-changing adventure with God. I took my first, somewhat fearful, step towards Japan with the promise of John 10:4 lodged as firmly as I could make it in my heart and mind.

> And when he putteth forth his own sheep, he goeth before them, and the sheep follow Him: for they know His voice. (John 10:4 KJV)

Following Jesus one step at a time has brought its surprises and not all were welcome. Sometimes I could not see the road ahead. But Jesus was always there ahead of me, guiding in ways that leave me utterly amazed.

Many Bible passages point to the importance of sharing the wonderful stories of what God has done with future generations. 'One generation commends your works to another. They tell of your mighty acts. They speak of the glorious splendour of your majesty . . . I will proclaim your great deeds' (Psalm 145:4–6).

In *Utterly Amazed* I have attempted to do exactly that — to 'proclaim God's deeds' with the prayer that you, my readers, will be inspired to expect amazing works of God in your own lives.

Note: Where names have been changed for confidentiality purposes I have indicated this by placing an * before the name.

1

主と共に歩みて

Growing up and into faith

It was 28 August 1975. I sat in a noisy cafeteria at Heathrow airport fighting back tears that threatened to overwhelm me. I should have already boarded my flight and been on my way. Instead, the flight indicator shouted out interminably — 'Delayed'. As the wait lengthened to five hours, the strain of the impending goodbye to my mum and brother, there to see me off, became almost unbearable. It was likely to be two years before I saw my family again. Not only that, but the thought of flying for the very first time terrified me. A journey to what, in those days, lay far beyond the extremities of my limited world — the country of Japan.

Only six months before, I'd agonised over the blank future that stared me in the face as university finals and graduation loomed in June. I'd pushed various doors, but all had slammed in my face, and I was deeply discouraged. I was not to know that just 10 weeks after graduation, God would lead me on an amazing journey to a country I knew next to nothing about on the other side of the world. Sudden as this departure from life as I knew it was, it was the consequence of a rich tapestry of experiences woven into the first 22 years of my life. I was born in rural Wiltshire in March 1953, a year history remembers for the coronation of Queen Elizabeth II and the climbing of Mount Everest. I was the youngest of five children and the only girl. My missionary parents had survived 18 months of house arrest, and the tensions of the Communist takeover in China, to arrive back in the UK with three of their boys in 1951. How they must have been looking forward to seeing my eldest brother after two years of separation. Even so, when brother number three first set eyes on his older sibling, he asked in all sincerity, 'Who's that boy?'

Unlike my siblings, I had a tranquil childhood. The world was a safer place then. As a baby, I slept through Sunday morning services in my pram outside St Mary Wingfield where my father was vicar. Just as well the window by the pulpit was plain, not stained glass, so he could keep an eye on me as he preached! My mother, no doubt, had her hands full with four lively boys.

Four years later, in 1957, realising that our family would be unable to return to China with *The Bible Churchman's Missionary Society* (now called *Crosslinks*), my father took on the job of Overseas Secretary in the *BCMS* office in London. We lived in Bromley in Kent, but my mental horizons stretched far beyond life in suburbia as we prayed daily for cross-cultural workers in East Africa, Ethiopia, Burma and India. Marsabit, Karomoja, Dodoma, Pokot and the Maasai — these exotic-sounding place names in East Africa were part of my early vocabulary, and still rise rapidly to the surface of my childhood memories.

Nationals and mission partners from various countries were regular visitors to our home, so Christian faith with a global vision was as natural as the air I breathed. When asked what I wanted to be when I grew up, I replied 'I want to work overseas.' When I was nine, I was given a silver autograph book with coloured pages, and I pressed our guests to write in it. I'm fascinated now to see that Bishop Yohana Madinda, of the Anglican Diocese of Central Tanganyika, wrote in both

English and ChiGogo, a language spoken around the city of Dodoma. Another visitor from Uganda wrote a blessing in Karamojong, the language of the Karamoja people of North Eastern Uganda. Thrilled as I was with this my first brush with foreign languages, my craze for autographs was short-lived. Although I still have the book, two-thirds of its pages are sadly bare.

I loved school and church, and I eagerly absorbed all I was taught. However, I was also keenly aware that mental assent to biblical truth was not changing me as it should. I was competitive, and easily jealous of others. At times I could not control my temper despite the longing to do so. One incident I remember all too clearly, and with shame. In my first year of secondary school at Bromley High, I was overjoyed that I'd won the class prize for academic excellence, and I secretly gloated over the fact that my best friend had not. I assumed the prize would be mine the next year too. It never occurred to me that my friend might win it instead of me. That made the shock all the greater when she did. I may not have shown it outwardly, but I could not rejoice in her success, and I was intensely jealous. I didn't like the ugly 'me' this incident revealed but, throughout my teens, I ignored my unease in an all-absorbing drive for academic achievement.

Asylum Road, Peckham

In 1965, my Dad returned to parish ministry, and took on a struggling Anglican church, opposite the massive gas works on the Old Kent Road in Peckham, South East London. The Old Kent Road was familiar to fans of the board game Monopoly, while drivers knew it as the A2 route from London to Dover, and historians as the Roman Road, Watling Street. My family, however, were not just passing through. They'd left behind the comfortable middle-class suburbia of Bromley to settle in a very different environment.

I was 12 when home became the vicarage at 79, Asylum Road, Peckham, an address that was the source of considerable teasing from Bromley High School friends. Our road was one of a few with private houses in a sea of council housing ranging from gloomy, five-storey post-war blocks to modern, but just as unappealing, concrete tower blocks. I spent many a Saturday afternoon trudging up and down stairs in the older blocks (only the tower blocks had lifts), delivering leaflets for jumble sales or special services. These had been churned out on the church's clattering duplicating machine, which left its inky mark on both the unfortunate operator and the distributor of leaflets!

In Peckham, I absorbed multicultural influences of a different kind to those of the overseas visitors of Bromley days. Throughout my teens I helped in Sunday School at 3:00 p.m. every week. We set out several rows of chairs in our echoing church hall, and waited the often-late arrival of our regulars — West Indian children dressed exquisitely in their Sunday best. My mother often sent me to buy bread at our local Greek Cypriot corner shop. I loved the smell of the freshly baked, large round loaves. There was a sudden influx of Vietnamese boat people, then Uganda Asians and Nigerians. You name it, we had them in the parish.

School and home were worlds apart as I journeyed 50 minutes each way on foot and by train to school in Bromley. One day, I was nearing home on my long walk from the station, in my maroon and grey uniform which marked me out as different from the local teenagers. I was wary of the group of girls lounging towards me along the pavement, and I'd noticed one girl smoking a no-doubt forbidden cigarette. But I anticipated no more than the usual snide comments. When the red-hot cigarette end suddenly collided with my cheek, the emotional impact was far greater than the actual physical pain. I'd been made to feel an outsider in a 'foreign' culture.

While my father struggled to build a church community in a largely unchurched working class area, I grappled in secret with issues of faith. I desperately wanted to believe, but I had no assurance that God really existed. It didn't help that there were no young people of a similar background or interests to befriend. As a vicar's daughter, I had a head packed with knowledge of the Bible, but I could not mention the name of God or Jesus without embarrassment. Doubts came to a head as I left school in 1971 to spend a gap year working and travelling.

I loved my job in the local library. There was lots of time to dip into books as I tidied the shelves. One of the librarians encouraged me to read books that challenged the faith I'd been taught. In January 1972, I set off with a school friend for Israel to work for three months on a kibbutz (a collective community traditionally involved in agriculture). We travelled by coach, train and ship to the port of Haifa, and then on to upper Galilee. Looking back, I'm amazed that my parents let me go. My mum said, 'If I were you, I would want this adventure too,' and bravely entrusted me in her prayers to the God who was so real and dear to her. Her parting words at Victoria coach station in London were, 'Miriam, never forget God is with you.'

Israel impacted me both positively and negatively. I stepped outside my cabin at night, and was overawed by the brilliance of the star-studded sky. Having been brought up in inner London, I'd never seen the like. Acutely aware of my own insignificance I could not but think, 'Someone must be behind this amazing and immense universe.'

Then there was the 'Wow!' of seeing places I'd heard and read about since childhood. Here I was in Nazareth and Cana and Capernaum, to mention just a few familiar names. It was not hard to imagine Jesus out and about in the towns and countryside.

About to begin a degree in history, I was also staggered by the archaeological evidence for the reliability of the Bible. I only had to walk out of my kibbutz, Ayelet HaShachar in Upper Galilee, and across the road to explore Tel Hazor. This was the largest archaeological mound in the whole of Israel, and today is a UNESCO World Heritage site. I discovered that Hazor is mentioned 17 times in seven Old Testament books. Though disputed by some scholars, there is good evidence to back up the biblical account of Joshua's burning of Hazor during the conquest of Canaan by the Israelites in the fifteenth century BC.[1]

On the negative side, I hated the commercialism of famous sights like the Church of the Nativity in Bethlehem. The early 1970s was the era of the hippy trail, and kibbutz volunteers came from a variety of countries. 'Why are you going straight back to the UK? We're just making a stopover here on the way to India. Why don't you do the same?' they asked.

Although I'd not the slightest desire to head off to India and beyond, the encounter with very different lifestyles and values from what I'd known up to this point was profoundly unsettling. It distressed me to meet people who were searching for heightened awareness or mystic experiences in Eastern religions and the recreational use of drugs. Their apparent aimlessness accentuated my growing need to be sure of where I was heading in life.

Have you fallen in love?

Back home in the UK and in church, I was once again playing the part of a model vicar's daughter, but the gap between outward behaviour and inner reality was widening. I felt a terrible hypocrite, and was thoroughly miserable.

---

[1] https://www.academia.edu/28629736/Hazor_Archaeology_and_the_Bible
Accessed 9 February 2021.

Things came to a head some months later in my first term at Cambridge University. I knew I had to sort myself out with God, or there was no point in living. I began to learn about the work of the Holy Spirit in a way I'd not done before. 'There's a meeting at St Matthew's vicarage tonight all about a dead church coming to life. Anyone is welcome to go,' said one of our college Christian Union members.

I didn't know the church; the only way to get there was to cycle and it was pouring with rain. I had a headache, and would know no one there. But I felt a strange compulsion that was not quenched, even by the policeman who stopped me at the bottom of the hill near my college, and sternly warned me of the dangers of cycling in the rain with a faulty front lamp! God took me to St Matthew's that night against all odds.

The group gathered in the vicarage was small and knew each other. I was both ill at ease, and mesmerised as I listened to the story of how God had brought renewal to the church. I longed for the same transforming reality of Jesus in my own life.

'Would you like us to pray for you to be filled with the Holy Spirit?' someone asked at the end.

'Yes,' was my trembling response.

I was disappointed that nothing changed that night and, for several days, I could not settle to my studies. Instead, I bought every book in the Christian bookshop I thought might help. One pointed me to the account of Jesus on the road to the village of Emmaus (Luke 24:13–35). I read how Jesus came alongside two of his grieving disciples. It never for a moment occurred to them that the stranger joining them on the long walk home could be their dear, dead friend, Jesus. They had seen him crucified as a criminal on a cross, and sealed away in a garden tomb. No way could he be alive. But their hearts were set on fire as they listened. Inviting him into their home, they suddenly recognised him for who he was, and inconsolable grief turned into uncontrollable joy. I identified with these disciples. Like them, I didn't yet recognise Jesus, but was much comforted to think that maybe he was already walking beside me and I would know him soon.

A couple of nights later my room-mate was out. I knelt down by my bed, and bargained with God. 'Show me you're real and I'll do anything you want!' I prayed recklessly. I so longed for the transforming presence of God I'd seen in others, that I was willing to hand my life over to him completely.

Next morning in the toilet, I discovered that God had graciously given me a new prayer language, the supernatural gift of tongues, something I could never have conjured up. This rapidly became a vital part of my private prayer life, and it still is — a wonderful aid to praise and worship when I run out of words of my own, and a way to align myself with God's will when confronted with situations beyond me. I was walking on air. 'God really IS alive and he really DOES care about me!'

This confidence transformed everything. For some days, the joy was overwhelming, and God's words shot off the pages of my Bible straight into my heart and mind. People noticed I was different.

'Have you fallen in love?' asked a student I hardly knew.

I don't remember how I replied. But in a way, the answer was actually 'yes'. It was not that I'd formed an entirely new friendship. It had been there in some form before. But now, for the first time, my relationship with Jesus was joyful, vibrant, all-absorbing and life-changing. I found myself largely freed from a crippling fear of what people thought about me and the need to seek approval—I was able to say the name of Jesus without embarrassment. In future years, there would be dark times when I could not sense God's presence. I would question what he was doing. But, after that first transforming encounter with the Holy Spirit, I never once doubted the reality of God, or that he was alive and at work in my life. With the disciples from Emmaus, who rushed back on the long dusty road to Jerusalem to share their excitement with their friends, I too longed to share the good news I'd found with others.

I had no idea the fulfilment of that longing would take me right across the world.

2

主と共に歩みて

I can stick anything for two years!

'Show me you're real, God, and I'll do anything you want!'

Little did I know what I was letting myself in for when I spoke that reckless prayer in November 1972, on my knees in my split-level shared room at New Hall College, Cambridge. The following spring I asked for guidance, 'Lord, how do you want me to spend my summer vacation?'

Part of the answer was to join a UCCF (University and Colleges Christian Fellowship) student team for several weeks. We hosted a variety of events for overseas students who flocked to Cambridge to study at English language schools and, at one event, I met Melida, a round-faced, friendly, chatty young lady from Venezuela. She was not part of the transient population of language students, but worked as an au pair with a local Venezuelan family who demanded much of her. She attended language school in the week in a few spare hours, but had no English friends or opportunity to expand her already considerable English ability. We hit it off immediately, and I found her curiosity and frankness refreshing, except when she hastened to tell me after I'd been home for Christmas that I'd put on weight! Melida was nominally Catholic but, as she had Sundays off, she happily joined me during my second and third year for church and the rest of the day.

A passionate student of English her questions came thick and fast on those Sunday afternoons in my college room. 'What does this mean?' she would ask, a bewildered look on her face. 'Please explain the rules for the present perfect tense,' or 'Miriam, how can I know when to use the indefinite article "a", and when the definite article "the"?'

Questions about grammar completely threw me, as like most native speakers I'd never thought about how I used my native tongue. However, I was soon hooked. Phrasal verbs, for one, fascinated me. These were verbs combined with prepositions like 'on' or 'in' or 'at'. I made the astonishing discovery that there were 70 phrasal verbs using the verb 'put' alone, and no two were alike. Just think of the differing meanings of 'put on,' 'put out' 'put down (a thing),' 'put down (a person),' 'put off,' 'put aside' and 'put through'.

It was no wonder then, that Melida often had a furrowed brow! I began to consider the possibility of a career in Teaching English as a Foreign Language (TEFL).

Had I got my guidance wrong?

However, the doors to postgraduate teacher training courses were firmly closed — I had neither of the necessary qualifications: two years' teaching experience, or a degree in foreign languages or English. 'OK,' I thought. 'I'll get the two years.'

I interviewed for jobs at language schools. All turned me down. This was discouraging, though not surprising since I had neither qualifications nor experience. But a greater blow came from the interviewer who said bluntly, 'We don't think you are at all suited to TEFL teaching.'

I had no training in interview technique and no idea how to put myself across. I agonised in prayer 'God, have I got your leading wrong?' But I couldn't think of anything else I wanted to do.

People suggested Voluntary Service Overseas (VSO). They replied, 'Apply again when you have some experience.'

This left only one option — a short-term appointment with a Christian mission organisation. The Church Mission Society (CMS) were willing to interview me. I, on the other hand, was quite reluctant to proceed. I was under the impression that short-term volunteering with CMS meant either teaching all subjects in a rural bush school in East Africa or helping out in an orphanage in Iran. I couldn't imagine myself in either context. But in spring 1975, trusting God to close the door if it was not right, I caught the bus from my parents' home in Asylum Road, Peckham to the CMS offices on busy Waterloo Road just south of the Thames. No harm could be done, I reasoned, since I'd come to the end of all other options.

The Short-Term Mission Co-ordinator came across as a somewhat unapproachable lady who did little to put me at my ease. She jumped straight to the point, 'If you want to teach English as a Foreign Language, I think Japan would be the best place for you.'

Her words turned my inner world upside down in an instant. Nothing could have been farther from my thinking than Japan. I was not aware that CMS worked in Japan, and nothing so far had piqued my interest in that country. I had mixed with a variety of nationalities but, to my knowledge, I'd never met a Japanese person. The suggestion itself was way outside my comfort zone.

My interviewer, however, had served through CMS with the Anglican Church in Japan. She knew first-hand that there was a great demand for English teachers. 'I'll write to the church leaders and see if any church will take you on,' she said decisively. 'But, you'll have to commit for two years as the culture is a difficult one to adjust to. You'll have to pay your own fare too.'

I thought these were demanding conditions, especially as the commitment for Iran and East Africa was only one year, and travel to Japan was much more expensive. Nevertheless, I resolved to take the next step of attending a CMS selection conference.

The God who goes before

The decision was made! I would be on my way to Japan in a few weeks' time. Travelling home from the conference weekend other passengers jostled me as we surged forward to board the bus. But it was my jostling and jumping thoughts that held my attention. Apprehension warred with excitement and threatened to win the battle. 'How would I find the airfare?' I was a student with no savings. 'How would I cope with a very different and totally unknown culture? And with two years away from my family?'

I let myself in the front door of my parents' house. Just inside, a calendar jutted out bulkily from the left-hand wall. Three hundred and sixty-five days' worth of tear-off Bible verses had created a thick block of paper. I rarely gave the daily verse a passing glance, but that day was different. Something compelled me to stop. I read:

> And when he putteth forth his own sheep, he goeth before them, and the sheep follow Him: for they know His voice. (John 10:4 KJV)

Jesus here describes himself as the Good Shepherd. I had the extraordinary sense that he was speaking to me; it was as though he were saying, 'Miriam, you never in your wildest dreams imagined going to Japan, but don't worry because it's ME that's behind all this. I am the one giving you a gentle shove from behind. And, because I am, I will prepare everything you need before you get there. You just keep on getting to know me and listening to my voice.'

What a comfort this word was. As I clung to the promises God gave me, everything fell into place in a remarkable way, and confirmed the rightness of this step. CMS had suggested a month-long TEFL training course at International House in London. But with 10 short weeks between graduating from university and heading off to Japan, there was only one course I could possibly attend. I rushed to get my application in, only to receive a disappointing letter informing me the course was full. I realised I would have to go to Japan in utter ignorance of how to go about teaching English.

But some weeks later, the phone rang. It was International House. 'Someone has dropped out. The place is yours if you still want it!'

Of course, I did. The course was just what I needed. We had plenty of opportunity to practise on groups of non-native English speakers, as well as learning teaching technique and theory. I worked on my preparation late into the nights, but enjoyed myself immensely. It seemed I'd not been wrong in my choice of career.

Following the teacher-training course, I took a job for just four weeks in a Soho language school. I'd not imagined anyone would employ me, young and inexperienced as I was. This was yet another reassuring sign from the God who goes before, particularly as I needed the money to help pay my airfare. I mostly sat at the reception desk, answering the phone and dealing with endless questions from students, but the school principal kindly let me loose to teach a few classes some afternoons, and I gained valuable experience.

And so, I found myself in the cafeteria at Heathrow Airport, fighting back tears as I waited for my delayed flight. What a long way I'd come with Jesus in the five brief months since my interview at CMS and the first mention of Japan.

It was 28 August 1975. My thoughts were somewhat negative as I finally boarded the plane. 'Well, here we go. I know this is what God wants so I guess I can stick anything for two years.'

Was God disappointed that I was not more eager to embrace the adventures and blessings he had in store for me?

3

主と共に歩みて

Japan—here I come

A brusque welcome

'Why are you late?' I was taken aback by these abrupt and accusing (or so I felt) words from my new boss, Reverend Higuchi, as I wearily dragged my suitcase into the arrival lounge at Osaka airport. I was to discover that this short and stocky gentleman was a man of few words, even in his mother tongue. An occasional transforming smile broke the solemnity of his demeanour, but I was to remain shy in his presence for the next two years. All I remember of this first meeting were the above words. I do know that I failed miserably to make conversation with him on the long drive to his home in the town of Nishiyamato, Nara Prefecture, as I could not keep my eyes open!

I flew on Pakistani Airlines because it was the cheapest option. It turned out to be the worst choice for my first experience of flying. We had to leave the plane with hand luggage at each stop on a very roundabout journey — Frankfurt, Bahrain, Teheran, Karachi, Manilla and Taipei. Sleep was impossible, and anxiety mounted when we were told to change to a different aircraft in Karachi. The reason given, ongoing engine trouble, was the same that had delayed us five hours at Heathrow!

As expected, I missed my ongoing flight from Tokyo. It was a busy Saturday, and the airport was bulging with unfamiliar Asian faces. Internal flights took off constantly without a spare seat on board, and my wait seemed interminable. I longed to stretch out my aching limbs but instead, alternatively slumped or wriggled on a hard plastic seat before, hours later, boarding a plane for the 45-minute flight to Osaka. Possessing only the address of my hosts, I could not contact them directly. I begged the airport desk to contact someone in Osaka airport to page Rev. Higuchi, but I never knew if a message got through to him or not. I saw few Western faces that day in the airport, and mine was the only one on the flight south. Exhausted from travelling for 48 hours without sleep, I felt very alien.

I arrived in Osaka many hours behind schedule so it was not surprising that Rev. Higuchi should be put out. But I felt criticised for no fault of my own, and again I struggled to hold back my tears. Later I realised that as a non-fluent, non-native speaker of English, Rev. Higuchi was probably unable to phrase things differently, or use a softer tone.

Cultural blunders

The limitations of language on both my part and Rev. Higuchi's were only too apparent on other occasions. One incident occurred three weeks after my arrival when I accompanied him to the ancient capital of Kyoto for the installation of a new bishop. Practically the whole diocese of around a thousand Christians were there. At the tea party following the service I was the only foreigner, and I was ill at ease. I didn't understand a word of what was going on so I sat rigidly, trying not to attract attention to myself, or look as bored as I felt.

| Guests: | *Omedeto gozaimasu. Yoroshiku onegai itashimasu.* (Congratulations. I beg your kind favour.) |
| Bishop: | *Kochira koso. Yoroshiku onegai itashimasu.* (Please give me your kind favour too.) |

The bishop was doing the rounds of the people at the tea table. One by one they bowed their heads graciously to him, then he to them, and they exchanged the set phrases appropriate to the occasion. The bishop eventually approached my chair. Completely insensitive to the cultural cues around me and, through sheer fright and ignorance, my head stayed firmly up and my mouth firmly closed. Suddenly, I felt a hand on the back of my head pushing it down in the expected bow of respect. Rev. Higuchi had realised that I was about to offend the bishop deeply, and he'd hastened to remedy the matter in the only way he could! He hadn't found the English words in time to tell me what to do. Did the bishop notice the hand on the back of my head? Perhaps not, but I was mortified that I'd failed to read the cultural cues, and had to be rescued from a major blunder in such an embarrassing way.

Caught by the police

Language deficiencies also got me into trouble with the police. One day I set off from Nishiyamato to explore Kyoto by car. Looking back, it seems a foolhardy thing to have done when I could not read Japanese road signs, and I was totally unfamiliar with the layout of this large city. Bewildered by the traffic, I attempted to turn left at traffic lights in front of Kyoto railway station, only to find myself facing lines of stationary cars head-on! Obviously, I'd turned the wrong way into a one-way system, and I was blocking the exit from one lane. Right on the corner beside me stood a group of stern-looking Japanese policemen. No chance of reversing with no one noticing! Trembling I wound down my window as one of the policemen rushed to my side. As soon as he realised we had a communication problem, he gestured for me to clamber over the gear box to the passenger side, plonked himself in the driver's seat, and headed off for I didn't know where.

Our destination turned out to be the police box round the corner. He parked, took me inside and, with others crowding round, he said repeatedly *'Ippoo tsukoo, ippoo tsukoo.'* I had no idea what the words meant, and I was too shaken to do more than stare back in blank incomprehension. He started to draw on a piece of paper and, as a diagram of the railway station appeared with one-way arrows on the entry and exit roads, it dawned on me what *'ippoo tsukoo'* meant — 'One-way traffic.'

It was hardly a useful addition to my vocabulary either then or later, but it was certainly a phrase I never forgot! My international driving licence evoked a great deal of discussion amongst the police officers who crowded around me like bees attracted to a honey pot. My guess was they'd never seen one before. I was fingerprinted. (I'd already experienced that when applying for my alien registration card, so I understood I was not being treated as a criminal!) Subsequently I was allowed to go without the fine I was expecting.

Sticking out like a sore thumb

Japan in 1975 was not used to Western faces and, as far as I knew, I was the only foreigner in the modern dormitory town of Nishiyamato in Nara Prefecture. I'm of average height in the UK, but there I towered over the petite Japanese. (Forty years later I no longer stood out with regard to height. Many young people were now as tall or taller than me — a result, no doubt of the gradual westernisation of the traditional diet.) Even in the big city of Osaka (population of 16 million-plus and bigger than London in 1975) where I travelled a couple of times a month, it was rare to see a non-Japanese face. On one occasion, I was so excited to see a young Western couple on a busy train platform that I acted totally out of character for my introvert self, and I initiated a conversation.

Small children would point at me as I walked along the road. 'Look, there's an American!' Anger boiled up inside, and I wanted to scream out loud, 'But I'm NOT American'. I discovered it mattered to me that I was British. Even more infuriating was having teenagers shout 'Zis is a pen!' — the first sentence of English they learnt in school. Experiences like these pierced right into the core of my identity, and made me only more aware of being an outsider.

Adapting to a Japanese style of living, in contrast, was something I'd expected to do. It cost me nothing to sit on the floor at a low table to eat and prepare classes, or to sleep on the floor. Rolling my futon mattress up, and storing it away in the built-in cupboards during the day was a great way to utilise space in tiny Japanese rooms. It became second nature to point to my nose to refer to myself rather than to my chest. Even bowing became second nature as I discovered when I finished a phone call one day to find a Western friend trying hard to restrain her giggles, 'Do you realise, Miriam, you were bowing to the person on the other end of the phone at regular intervals as you spoke?' I'd been totally unaware!

Of course, some things puzzled me. Why did my landlady, on setting eyes on me one Sunday at church, suddenly say *'Senshu arigato gozaimashita'* (literally translated, 'Last week, thank you')? I only understood the words 'thank you', and I couldn't imagine what on earth she was thanking me for. My bewilderment evidently showed, and Rev. Higuchi hastened to explain that she was thanking me for the lift home I'd given her the week before! I learnt that, even if you thanked a person on the spot for something they had done, you had to remember to thank them again when you saw them next. And that could be weeks or months in the future! Strange as this practice seemed at first, it became so instinctive that, on visits to the UK, I felt something missing, or even that people were rude because they didn't behave as a Japanese person would!

In Nishiyamato, few spoke English to any degree. Most of the kindergarten teachers had none, or they were too shy to use it. I was dependent on the daily meeting with Rev. Higuchi when he would explain the notes his wife had written in Japanese about what I was to do and where I was to be, at what time. Even then, I was prone to making mistakes, and turned up too early or too late on occasion. Fortunately, Mrs Higuchi was the exact opposite of her husband, a roly-poly chatterbox, who talked to me regardless of my incomprehension. Though initially exhausting, this stream of speech was of immense value in training my ear. Gradually I began to pick out words that were repeated. Dictionary searches were hit-and-miss. Time and time again, I failed to find the word I thought I'd heard, because I couldn't accurately distinguish where one word ended and another began. But I supplemented my learning by ear with a text book and cassette tapes, and I gradually began to join up more pieces of the language jigsaw puzzle.

I put on weight as I comfort ate in my first year. This only made me stick out more amongst the slim petite Japanese women. I experienced a seesaw of emotions — crying one day when I failed to communicate, then on a high when I achieved a simple task such as asking for stamps at the post office. I had no phone for two years, and I wouldn't have dreamt of phoning overseas even if I had. The internet was still a long way into the future. The only contact with home was through sending and receiving a weekly aerogramme. So unusual was it for people to send letters overseas, the post office did not even stock these blue aerogramme letters before I turned up in town.

Everyday tasks were a challenge. I put off having my hair cut for weeks until I couldn't wait any longer. I could have asked Rev. Higuchi to teach me some suitable phrases, or asked him if someone could go with me, but I was too shy or embarrassed to do so. Instead, I pushed open the door of the hairdressers with no idea of what to say. It felt more like going to have my head cut off than my hair. No doubt the hairdressers were just as nervous as I was. On a number of future occasions, I went into shops, only for the shop assistant to disappear rapidly into the back premises. When I called out in Japanese, they would emerge sheepishly and apologise for assuming that I spoke no Japanese, and for panicking because they had no English.[2]

On that first visit to the hairdressers however, they rose to the occasion. One asked, *'Shampoo desu ka? Katto desu ka?'* ('Would you like a shampoo? And a cut?')

I'd not realised that the vocabulary of hairdressing consisted mainly of English words pronounced in a Japanese way! What a relief! On subsequent visits we communicated through gestures and pictures in magazines until my Japanese improved.

Although a supermarket meant that shopping was not the problem it could have been, I had to get used to many strange foods. One day I was at the Higuchis' house when the postman delivered a large cardboard box. They often received gifts of biscuits or sweets so I thought nothing of it, until Mrs Higuchi removed the paper, and began to lift the lid. I was shocked to see a leg extend itself, and begin to wave around. Mrs Higuchi hastily slammed the box lid down on the occupant, which turned out to be a live *Ise ebi* or spiny Japanese lobster. We subsequently ate this great delicacy after

---

[2] I think the last time this happened to me was in the mid to late 1980s. In more recent years, foreigners have become commonplace in Japan. No longer did people turn to stare and, rather than assume I was American, Japanese would politely ask 'Which country are you from?' Japan has become increasingly foreigner-friendly with romanisation of road signs, English, Korean and Chinese on ticket machines in stations, and with multi-language leaflets for tourists and residents alike.

she'd dumped the creature live into a pan of boiling water! This action took my appetite away, and I remember nothing of the taste.

4

主と共に歩みて

I will bring you back to this place

'The month when even monks run'

'*Shiwasu*' written 師走 is the ancient Japanese calendar name for December. The first character means 'monk' or 'teacher', and the second 'to run'. Even calm and serene Buddhist monks rush around in the busy run-up to the main holiday of the year which starts on 1 January.

Traditionally, in late December, housewives cleaned the house from top to bottom. They spent hours preparing special New Year dishes to serve on the first three days of the New Year in exquisite two-to-three-tiered lacquered boxes. [3] Business people were frantically tying up ends at work, and drinking to excess at year-end parties.

---

[3] Japan is moving away from some of these traditions. Working mums have less time to prepare special foods, and are more likely to buy them ready-prepared, while many young Japanese do not like the traditional New Year dishes. Many restaurants and shops, that would have traditionally been shut for at least the first three days of New Year, now open from 2 January.

First Christmas away from home

I was not chasing my tail in December 1975 as those around me were. But that first Christmas in Japan was nevertheless a big shock. In 1975 most Japanese barely gave Christmas a passing thought. But I discovered that stores and businesses were already poised to make the most of Christmas as a commercial opportunity. The now established custom of buying Kentucky Fried chicken to celebrate on Christmas Eve had been introduced the year before with a forceful advertising campaign called 'Kentucky Christmas'. The kindergarten kids were wild with excitement when Santa Claus visited their classrooms. Schools often broke up on 25 December and, elsewhere, it was just an ordinary working day. That year, however, schools finished on the 24th. Christmas morning found me busily preparing hamburgers for the Sunday school party instead of going to church and helping my mother prepare a turkey dinner for a large family gathering!

With so few Christians in Japan, I'd not expected to come across anything familiar in Christmas celebrations. Shops played 'Jingle bells' and 'I'm dreaming of a white Christmas' ad nauseam. So, one day, I was caught unawares as I walked through a large department store and heard 'Silent Night' wafting from the speakers. The familiar melody and words were my undoing, and tears rolled down my cheeks as a wave of homesickness engulfed me. I was 22, and I'd never spent Christmas away from home.

Friends and family helped to ease the ache. One brother recorded a cassette tape that first Christmas. On it, he shared his news as he prepared his evening meal. I can still hear in my memory the sounds of chopping and his words 'I'm doing the onions now.' His voice brought tears again, but the time and effort put into that tape meant a great deal. Four months earlier when I left England, a close friend from university pledged to write to me every week. For two whole years, those letters, along with the loving, prayerful support they expressed, were very precious.

Closer to home, three CMS missionaries working in Osaka, an hour or more away by train, took me under their wing, and their house became a home away from home. Here too I found the spiritual fellowship I longed for in a twice-monthly missionary fellowship. I heard from experienced missionaries of different nationalities and church backgrounds of how God was at work in non-Anglican contexts and about the challenges of long-term mission and church planting.

'May I go to the toilet?'

My main brief was to teach English to 260 children aged four to six, in a kindergarten run by the Anglican Church (*Nippon Sei Ko Kai* or NSKK). Rev. Higuchi was principal and priest in charge of the tiny church that met in one of the classrooms on Sundays. His wife was responsible for the everyday running of the school and supervising of teachers. In the afternoons I taught classes of 6- to 8-year-olds and 9-to 12-year-olds from the primary school across the road and, a couple of evenings a week, I had small classes of adults ranging from teenagers to seniors in their 70s. For a year I also taught four classes of college students (18–20s) in nearby Osaka for one day a week.

All of this was excellent preparation for a career in teaching English as a Foreign Language, but without a word of Japanese I struggled to control large classes of boisterous primary school children on my own. Before I could introduce myself properly, 'Be quiet!', 'Sit down!' and other indispensable classroom commands became an active part of my vocabulary.

Well I remember a lad coming up to me and repeatedly asking me a question I simply could not understand. Eventually he had to physically demonstrate that he needed to go to the toilet. I suddenly acquired a new item of vocabulary — *oshikko*!

In case you are wondering why I'd not acquired the ability to ask for the toilet as a first priority for myself, I had! But children used different words from adults, and the equivalent of English 'I need a wee' didn't feature in my beginner's textbook! The toilet, I discovered, was also one of many objects expressed by one or other of two words depending on gender. Men would refer to the toilet as *benjo*, but for a woman to do so was the height of rudeness. Their word for toilet was either *toire* from the English or the polite *tearai*, which literally means 'hands wash'. Adding the polite prefix *o* (*otoire, otearai*) upped the politeness level a further notch.

Now, with increasing Western influence, the words *benjo* and *tearai* are rarely used. Both men and women say *toire*, but women tend to add the polite *o* not required of men. Other differences in male language remain unchanged. Men are entitled to say either *kuu* or *taberu* for 'to eat', but women may only use the politer *taberu*. The differences widen further in the phrase 'to have a meal.' Men may say either *meshi o kuu* or the politer *shokuji o toru (lit. To take a meal)*, but women only the latter.

The local dialect further complicated my communication with the children as it had different verb endings from the patterns in my standard Japanese textbook. Fortunately, the kindergarten teachers stayed with the younger children and helped as interpreters, while I taught in the mornings. Japanese preschool was also more formal and regimented than in the UK, so the first half of my day was peaceful compared to the stormy afternoons with primary pupils.

'We don't need Bible studies'

With the last months before my move to Japan dominated by university finals, an intensive one-month course in TEFL and a few weeks' work in a language school to earn sufficient money for my airfare, I'd had little time to read up about the country. If I hadn't already been aware that less than 1% of Japan was Christian, my first Sunday service alone would have been enough to impress me with its spiritual need. The average congregation was five to six, including myself and Rev. and Mrs Higuchi. At Christmas and Easter there might be 20 mainly older people. An 80-year-old granny accompanied our singing on a wheezy old harmonium. Other than visitors staying with me, there was one newcomer to church in the whole two years I was there, and he only came for a few weeks. I seriously wondered what the future held for St Peter's Church.

The kindergarten children heard Bible stories every week and, by the end of my two years, I was able to identify and understand a good percentage of these. However, Sunday sermons read word for word by Rev. Higuchi remained a total mystery. There was also a healthy Sunday school, but most children dropped out by the time they were 12. Gruelling entrance exams for each stage of education (Junior High at 12, Senior High at 15 and University entrance) meant many children attended *juku* or cramming schools after their regular school day finished. Participating in the myriad of after-school clubs or English classes or music was not just popular, but an essential part of a child's life. Teenagers had no time to be involved in church, even had they been so inclined.

Most teachers in the kindergarten were not Christians, so one small positive step forward in my two years was the introduction of weekly staff prayers. With the enthusiasm of a 22-year-old, I suggested to Rev. Higuchi that perhaps we could invite interested mothers to study the Bible with me in English. Few women in 1970s Japan went out to work, and we had contact with the mothers of 260 children. Here surely was a great opportunity? I was shocked by Rev. Higuchi's answer, 'Oh, we don't need Bible studies. Japan has Buddhism.'

I grieved over his response, while realising I had no right, as a newcomer to Japanese culture and church life, to criticise or expect to be listened to. Reviewing my two years in a report for CMS in 1977, I did however write, 'What concerned me about the situation was not so much the smallness of numbers, but the defeatist attitude of the church — "Japan is difficult", and not "God is Mighty"'.

Nearly 40 years later in September 2016 I made a farewell visit to Nishiyamoto where my life in Japan had begun. St Peter's church no longer had a resident minister, and the kindergarten was about to close. But weekly services continued and on Sunday morning the tiny congregation of eight welcomed me warmly. To my astonishment, one lady remembered me (sadly I didn't remember her!) and dug out of a dusty cupboard an ancient photo album in which we both featured. At her invitation I joined her for a tasty bowl of noodles after church in a local restaurant. It was an even greater joy to share our stories, as we noisily slurped our food, of what God had done over the intervening years. God in his mercy was still at work in Nishiyamato.

Japan—Not just for two years

Remember the 'I know it's what God wants so I can stand anything for two years' attitude with which I got on the plane at London Heathrow? Forty-two years later I was still working in Japan though now about to retire home to England. How did that all come about? While open to seeking God's will for my life, I had no thought of spending more than two years in Japan until some words in my daily Bible reading struck me forcibly. 'This is what the LORD says: "When seventy years are completed for Babylon, I will come to you and fulfil my good promise to bring you back to this place"'(Jeremiah 29:10).

I was not particularly asking God to show me his future plans. My next steps—a Masters in Linguistics at York University and a TEFL course in Manchester—were already mapped out. Neither had my situation anything in common with the Jews to whom the words were originally spoken. They were about to experience an uncertain and potentially unending exile in Babylon. They must have been immensely comforted by God's promise that in 70 years he would take them back to Jerusalem. But I was not in exile. Nor, fortunately, was a period of 70 years relevant!

God, however, spoke to me clearly through the words 'I will bring you back to this place.' No doubt I can be accused of taking Bible verses out of context but, somehow, I knew unmistakably that God was calling me to serve him in Japan long-term. I learnt too of the importance of regular times of prayer and reading the Bible that opened up my heart and mind to hear God, even when I was not specifically seeking a word from him.

People sometimes ask, 'What took you to Japan?' I can only say, 'God did'. It was God from start to finish, and it was God who kept me there through all the ups and downs.

Japanese friends often want to know what I like about Japan. As with any culture there is much to like and some things to dislike. I can only fully explain my passion for Japan by acknowledging God's hand in bringing to life in me a deep love for its people.

Japan is home to one of the biggest megacities in the world. I never lived in Greater Tokyo whose population borders on 40 million people. But in my early years in the crowded cities of Nagoya and Osaka I sometimes longed to escape the intense pressures of Japan's claustrophobic, over-busy urban society. When I did, I was overawed by God's amazing handiwork in nature—steeply soaring, snow-topped mountains, smoking volcanoes and hot springs; rice paddies evolving from the bare brown earth of winter through the light green of growing seedlings in spring to the waving, golden-glowing mature plants of autumn; the iconic plum blossom, cherry, chrysanthemums and flaming maples that decorate the changing seasons.

Society runs like clockwork as does the intricate train network (that is, barring an earthquake or a suicide on the line). Travelling to an interim train station alone with no knowledge of Japanese, one anxious overseas visitor asked, 'How will I know when to get off?' The reply was reassuring. 'When the train stops at 14:42!' Service is second-to-none although you are no longer welcomed by an immaculate bowing young lady when you board an elevator in a department store. People are polite and quiet if reserved. Streets and public places are litter-free, crime rates are low and it's very safe. 'I just can't get over seeing all these small children going to school unaccompanied,' said my brother Murray, repeatedly, when he visited in 2014.

I love many types of raw fish and, now I'm living in the UK, my yearning for Japanese rice can only be satisfied by shopping on the internet. On the other hand, an allergy to soya means that many Japanese dishes disagree with me. Some things are done better by the British, and some by the Japanese. Japanese culture will never cease to fascinate me, and there is always more to learn. But much as I loved the country and its people, a few cultural traits never ceased to frustrate me as a Westerner. I was a teacher, and I worked hard to encourage meaningful interaction. But Japanese people were used to rote learning, and deferring to the teacher's superior knowledge. It was not culturally appropriate to express personal opinions freely, and I was often left wondering what people really thought. I cannot adequately explain my passion for Japan and love for its people as anything other than God-inspired and God-given.

Two years in Nishiyamoto New Town was only the beginning. I had no inkling of the many more 'utterly amazing' things God had in store for me in the years to come.

5

主と共に歩みて

Further studies

My heart leapt as I spotted an Asian face. Could she possibly be Japanese? It was October 1977, and I was one of an international group of 14 students about to start an MA course in Linguistics at York University. As soon as orientation finished, I made a beeline for this young lady on the far side of the seminar room.

'Hallo, my name's Miriam. Where are you from?'

'Hi, I'm Makiyo from Japan.'

'Fantastic! I've just come back from two years there.'

And so began a precious friendship that continues to the present day. In 1977, students from Japan were still relatively few and, the probability of one of our group being Japanese was so remote, it had not occurred to me that I might find such a friend in York. Thrilled to bits, I felt it was another confirmation of my call to Japan. God had yet again 'gone before'. Our friendship was mutually beneficial—I helped Makiyo with English corrections to her essays, and she allowed me to practise my Japanese. Thirteen years later, when I became Language Advisor for the OMF language school for missionaries in Sapporo, Makiyo was teaching Japanese as a Foreign Language to Asian students in a large school in Tokyo. Her background in writing Japanese language textbooks for Asians and knowledge of their linguistic problems was a great help as I advised the increasing numbers of Korean and other Asian OMF missionaries on how to learn Japanese. Their approach to learning and the linguistic issues they faced were very different from those from a Western background, and new in my experience.

Makiyo was one of the few Japanese friends I could discuss anything with, and in the language of intimates rather than the everyday polite language used for most conversations.[4] Before her marriage to Brendan from Glasgow in Scotland, a futon on the tatami (rush straw) mat floor of her Tokyo flat was always available to me. It was so good to know I could make a stopover in Tokyo on the one or two occasions I had to fly to the UK for a family emergency.

Manchester

Following my Linguistics course, I moved to the Department of Education at Manchester University for a year. This resulted in a Diploma in Teaching English Overseas and a PGCE (Postgraduate Certificate of Education). The latter qualified me to teach at schools in the UK although I never did. My sights were set on Japan. I gained valuable experience in the first term through teaching at a College of Adult Education. The classrooms were packed with angry young Iranian students whose emotions would shortly reach boiling

---

[4] A key feature of the Japanese language is its system of honorifics. Verb forms, as well as actual words, change according to how your listener relates to you in terms of status—very formal, polite language for those of higher status, everyday polite language for those of a similar status and casual language for close friends, children and pets!

point with the January 1979 Islamic Revolution in Iran and the overthrow of the Shah.

A second term of teaching practice at a boys' secondary school in Barcelona, Spain, added to my experience of ability levels, educational background and teaching contexts. I enjoyed Spain, but here again the political situation was volatile. Sitting one day by the ceiling-to-floor window of a café on Las Ramblas, the pedestrianised centre of Barcelona, I was startled by the abrupt arrival of an armoured police van on the pavement outside. The van's back door opened, and men with guns flooded out onto the street, while I hastily moved away from the window. Another day I turned up at school to find the gates barred by students on strike. I enjoyed the extra day off!

Spain fascinated me, but I realised that it was a culture into which I didn't naturally fit. A high introvert, I already felt much more at home in Japan than I ever would with the emotionally volatile Spanish. The lifestyle of a long siesta in the afternoon, then working into the evening and eating late, did not suit me. God in the infinite variety of his character confirms his purposes for us in all sorts of ways. Sometimes he speaks through ordinary life experiences. Through the simple realisation that Spain and I were not a natural fit, I felt again God's reassuring leading in the direction of Japan.

I learnt another important lesson through feedback from my university professor who came to observe me teaching a class of teenage Spanish boys. I put my heart and soul into the class, and thought I'd been lively and animated. I was therefore shocked to be told, 'You have a soporific effect on your students. You send them all to sleep!'

A nice way of telling me I was boring perhaps? As negative comments often do, these words burrowed themselves into my mind, and I don't remember if there was any positive feedback. I was indignant at first, but over the years I found

this criticism helped me, not just in English teaching but in preaching too. I recognised the need to make a conscious effort to use the dynamics of my voice, and to present in as lively and creative a way as I could.

'If you were my daughter . . . '

With an MA in Linguistics, a TEFL qualification and some experience, I thought I was now all set to look for a teaching job at any level in Japan. But unexpectedly, God had another year of training in store for me. At the end of 1978, I went to a weekend mission conference run by OMF International[5] for

---

[5] OMF was founded as the *China Inland Mission* (CIM) by James Hudson Taylor in 1865. The door to China closed in the mid twentieth century with the Communist takeover and, in 1951, CIM moved its international headquarters to Singapore, and expanded ministry to other countries of South East Asia including Japan. It changed its name to *Overseas Missionary Fellowship* (OMF) in 1964 and to OMF International in 1993. Today OMF is made up of around 1,400 workers from 40 countries serving East Asians around the

the under 30s. It took place at All Nations Christian College, a mission training college in the beautiful Hertfordshire countryside. On Saturday evening, the college principal, David Morris, spoke about the kind of training available, and its value in preparing for cross-culture ministry. I was fascinated, and went to speak to him afterwards.

'I'm doing a TEFL course and believe God is calling me to serve him in Japan through English teaching,' I told him. 'Until tonight, I hadn't thought about mission studies as I don't intend to join a mission organisation. How would you advise someone like me?'

'If you were my daughter, I would very definitely encourage you to study here,' said David. 'Even a year's study would be very helpful to you in your profession. But if you are interested in applying for September you will have to get on with it.'

The deadline for applications was fast approaching. There was a great demand for places but, within weeks, I'd been interviewed and accepted for the one-year Diploma in Mission. Once again, God had clearly gone before me in an unexpected way.

It was a wonderful year. I lapped up the biblical and mission studies, and gained valuable practical experience on church placements and with small groups. I forged precious friendships which lasted a lifetime. It was a joy to study alongside several Japanese, and write assignments on Japanese religion and the history of Christianity in Japan.

At the time, I saw my year at All Nations as a wonderful, but still optional, experience. Great for my personal development as a Christian, but not essential professionally. Little did I realise that six years later, when I left full-time teaching to become a career missionary, it meant I did not

---

world. https://omf.org/about-omf/history/ Accessed 22 March 2021.

have to do further theological training. God was preparing me for a future I was as yet completely unaware of.

'You don't need to pay'

One condition of studying at ANCC was to have at least enough money to pay the fees for the first term. Depending on God for financial provision has always been one way of testing a missionary call. I'd been a student for the past two years, but I actually had funds in hand for term one. I trotted along to the bursar's office with my cheque book.

'Who do I write the cheque out to?' I asked.

'You don't need to,' said the bursar with a smile. 'Your fees have already been paid for this term.'

I was stunned. Someone had made an anonymous gift on my behalf to the college and, to this day, I have no idea who it was. When he puts his sheep out, he goes before them.

Mission or secular employment?

Most of the 150 students at college were accepted candidates of overseas mission organisations or planning to join one. In this environment, I naturally questioned whether I should join a mission organisation rather than returning to Japan to teach. I talked to tutors and mission leaders. OMF was my top candidate for missions working in Japan. I got as far as a preliminary application, but then OMF UK told me there was no guarantee that I could teach English—I could only apply to do church planting as this was the focus of OMF's work in Japan.

I was drawn to the OMF ethos, and had been involved in monthly OMF prayer meetings during the previous two years in York and Manchester. But I was unforgiving of what looked to me like inflexibility; a stubborn refusal to recognise the very obvious opportunities for ministry that English teaching opened up. My pride was hurt that the mission was not rushing to accept me as an ideal candidate. After all, I'd already lived and worked in Japan, and had the qualifications to teach at university level. I could not visualise myself in full-time church planting, and I was sure I did not have the gifts for it. For the time being at least, God was very definitely steering me in a different direction as I began to scan The *Times Educational Supplement* for secular employment in Japan. One job looked ideal. I applied and sailed through my interview so, when an official looking envelope landed in my college pigeon-hole, I tore it open eagerly.

British Council, London

May 29th 1980

Dear Miss Davis,

I am sorry to inform you that you have not been selected for the post of teacher of English at Aichi Shukutoku Educational Institution.

I was stunned. I hadn't anticipated rejection. But then a second letter followed hard on the heels of the first.

British Council, London

June 4th 1980

Dear Miss Davis,

I am pleased to tell you that the selected candidate for the post of teacher of English at Aichi Shukutoku has withdrawn. We are advising our representatives in Japan that your papers should be immediately forwarded.

And so it was that I returned to Japan in August 1980 to teach English at a private girls' high school in Nagoya, reassured of my calling to serve as a 'tentmaker' [6], and

---

[6] 'Tentmakers are Christian workers, usually missionaries, who work full-time to support themselves rather than draw support or a salary from a church or mission organisation. Tentmaking is so-

determined to share my faith through whatever opportunities presented themselves in my school life. I barely slept a wink that first night in the two-room apartment rented for me. I tossed and turned on the futon laid out on the floor, not because the newly laid, fresh-smelling tatami mats were not comfortable, nor primarily because of jetlag. No, what I remember of that first night in Nagoya in 1980 is the overwhelming sense of joy at being back in Japan for at least the next two years. This was where God wanted me to be for now!

---

called because the apostle Paul was a tentmaker by trade, and relied on that trade to support himself in Corinth on his second missionary journey.'

https://www.gotquestions.org/Christian-tentmaking.html
Accessed 23 January 2020.

6

主と共に歩みて

Shukutoku and Poole

The sharp click of the letterbox, announcing the arrival of *The Japan Times* English newspaper, drags me to consciousness around 7:00 a.m. By 8:20, I'm at my desk in the Shukutoku Senior High School staffroom, along with 60 other teachers. The remaining 40 teachers have their own staffroom in the adjoining junior high school. I'm the only foreigner, and teach around 300 pupils a week in classes of 45 or 50 in both parts of the school. Promptly at 8:25 the bell rings, and the headmaster stands up to begin the five-minute daily staff meeting. All the teachers stand, we bow and exchange greetings, announcements are made and another school day begins.

This became the pattern of my life in term time for four years. I immersed myself in teaching and curriculum development, while wondering how to share my faith in a secular school environment, where religion had, it seemed, no place at all. To my surprise, the principal, and at least one other member of staff turned out to be active, though part-time, Buddhist priests. The principal was a remote and forbidding person, and I was hesitant to approach him with my limited Japanese, but anything I did needed his permission.

Most pupils were involved in club activities after school. I asked an English-speaking teacher to make an appointment and accompany me to see the principal. 'Could I run an English Bible club?' I asked tentatively.

Back came the ready and surprising response, 'Go ahead and do as much as you like.'

So I started an after-school English Bible club for the 15- to 18-year-old pupils. My abiding memories are of frustration, rather than fulfilment. I never knew who would turn up. Some girls were keen on extra English for free, but there were many demands on their time. I poured out my woes in a prayer letter.

> Last week, the girls had to practise after school for a sports tournament so we cancelled. The week before, only the teacher who is helping me turned up. My keenest and longest-standing member told me she can no longer come, as she has to take supplementary classes for university entrance exams, several times a week. Today, I had one girl and my teacher help, at opposite extremes in English ability. We translated back and forth, and I wondered if either of them really learnt anything at all. I long for a more stable and committed group.

If nothing else, this experience did spur me on to renewed efforts in learning Japanese. I'd been made only too aware of the limitations of introducing Jesus through the medium of English.

I also ran an English Bible study group at church. Yuka, one of my pupils, graduated from Shukutoku High School and, like the majority of pupils, moved on to the two-year college next door. She was planning a three-month study trip to Los Angeles, and started attending church at my invitation.

'How do you find church and the Bible?' I asked, after a few weeks.

'Well, I've never thought about the meaning of life before,' she said, with a shake of the head. 'I don't think I will be able to work out a meaning anytime soon.'

This somewhat ambivalent response was typical of many Japanese then, and still is today. Brett Rayl, a Mission to the World member working cross-culturally in Japan, explains that the busyness of their lives means 'there is no space for transcendence' — no time or opportunity to ask the bigger questions of life.[7]

Brett believes that preaching the gospel in secular Japan 'must begin with making space for transcendence,' and suggests that 'sports, art, travel, counselling, nature, community and more can create space for transcendence. They beckon us to look up and out, stirring a longing inside of us that cannot be satisfied by anything in this world.'

Back in the early 1980s, it would not have occurred to me to think about outreach in such terms, but practice came before theory, as I realised when I had an unusual opportunity to introduce biblical stories.

'Do you know anywhere I could study the Bible in English?'

After the frustration of the English Bible Club, you can imagine my delight when Mrs Ota, one of the Japanese English teachers, asked me this question.

'If we can find a suitable time, I'd love to read the Bible with you,' I replied, offering up a silent prayer of thanks.

Not all teachers were able listeners, or fluent English speakers, but years of rote learning meant they had a high level of vocabulary and reading comprehension. There was real potential for exploring the big questions of life together.

---

[7] https://japanharvest.org/making-space-for-transcendence-in-secular-japan/ Accessed 26 August 2020.

Mrs Ota and I put our heads together and discovered a period a week when we were both free. Amazingly, two other teachers were also free at the same time. For two terms from late 1983 and spring 1984, the four of us borrowed an empty classroom, and the Japanese love of art and music became a way to present biblical truth.

Mrs Ota had been to a Rembrandt exhibition and bought an illustrated souvenir book. 'Many of the paintings are based on stories from the Bible,' she said. 'I don't know the stories, so I can't appreciate the artwork. Can we read the stories with you?'

As Christmas approached, we listened to parts of Handel's *Messiah* and discussed the meaning of the words.

'What next?' I wondered. Then the teachers asked, 'Can you suggest a book for us to read?' I chose *The Lion, the Witch and the Wardrobe* by C.S. Lewis. They read a chapter in preparation, and in class we discussed the links to biblical themes such as sin and sacrifice.

To my knowledge, none of these ladies became Christians. In fact, one told me plainly at the outset, that she did not want to be the target of Christian propaganda. We remained friends and, 30 years later, I was on a visit to her home near Tokyo. She opened an old exercise book with yellowing pages. 'Do you remember this?' she asked.

Inside, she'd pasted all the handouts I'd prepared years before in Nagoya. I was greatly encouraged to see how she'd treasured these notes. Visible results or not, my task was to be faithful in providing the opportunity for Japanese to hear the good news of Jesus. The rest was up to them and God.

A red-letter Christmas present

Only in eternity will we know the full extent of God's work in the lives of people who have crossed our paths. But on Christmas Day 2011 I got a wonderful glimpse of how, unknown to me, God had been at work in the life of one Shukutoku student I'd taught 28 years before.

By this time I was in cross-cultural mission with OMF in the city of Sapporo, two hours by plane to the north-east of Nagoya. I was on the staff of a Japanese church and, early on Sunday 25 December, headed out in the snowy conditions, typical of a Sapporo winter, to spend my day in church. I shook the snow off my boots as I entered, unburdened myself of anorak, scarf and gloves, and went to my pigeonhole to collect the notice sheet. Tucked alongside it was a large, bright red envelope. Obviously, a Christmas card but, when I turned it over, I didn't recognise the sender's name or address. Intrigued, I opened it, and read the letter inside.

> This is *Asami. You taught me English at Shukutoku High School in Nagoya. I didn't know if you were still in Japan, so I googled you, and you popped up on the Hokuei Church website. I wanted to tell you that I started going to church with my two daughters in February, and I am going to be baptised on Christmas Day! You were the first Christian I ever met.

I had no recollection of Asami at the time of receiving the card, and certainly couldn't lay claim to having had much, if anything, to do with her becoming a follower of Jesus. She hadn't even attended the English Bible Club, as far as I could recollect, but her card was the most wonderful Christmas present I could have had. When we later spoke on the phone, Asami reminded me that she'd visited me at Wakaba Church in Hokkaido, in the late 1980s and again in Gloucester, in 1991. I dug out my old photo albums, and there she was! We'd lost touch soon after the Gloucester visit, when she moved to Indonesia to work.

In January 2015, I flew from Sapporo to Nagoya to meet Asami. What a joy it was to attend church with her, and to meet her son and two daughters — three teenagers actively involved in church life. It's just as well God doesn't forget people who have slipped from my memory!

'You went white as a sheet!'

My four years in Nagoya were not just about teaching and tent making. I was learning a great deal about Japanese life and culture. Some experiences were more agreeable than others. One day I sat at the back of a classroom on the top floor of our school building along with a number of staff. We were observing a demonstration lesson with about 50 girls. Suddenly the building shook violently. The girls scrambled to shelter under their desks. It was a quake — was this the BIG one? Terror squeezed my heart and glued me to my seat. The whole building moved. Was it swaying side-to-side, or shunting up-and-down? I don't remember — each quake is different. The higher you are the worse it is, not simply because there's further to go to safety, but because modern buildings purposely sway with the movement of the earth. The quake seemed to go on forever, but the other staff took it all in their stride.

Back in the staffroom, the vice-principal teased me, 'Don't you have earthquakes in England? You went white as a sheet, and I thought you were going to faint!'

Psalm 46:1–3 took on a deeper meaning:

> God is our refuge and strength, an ever-present help in trouble. Therefore we will not fear, though the earth give way and the mountains fall into the heart of the sea, though its waters roar and foam and the mountains quake with their surging.

The shaking and quaking of the mountains were no longer a metaphor for anxiety or disruption caused by life-events. I'd come face to face with a real threat to physical life from an unstable earth crust. I could only pray that, if I was ever personally caught up in a life-threatening natural disaster,

God would give me faith and freedom from fear when I needed it.

Training in perseverance

It was at Shukutoku that I ran my first and only 'marathon' called in Japanese, 'cold weather training,' as it took place at the coldest time of year in January. The course was actually only 4.3 kilometres long, so not a marathon at all, but it was extremely hilly. Two thousand girls and a handful of teachers set off at staggered intervals. I puffed and panted up and down the hills with the inevitable stop here and there to catch my breath. I somehow made the final summit, and seeing the finishing goal in the school ground below gave me that extra spurt of energy for the last downhill run. My time of 28 minutes was far off the fastest time of 16, but I was proud of my achievement. One teacher told me the purpose of this marathon was to teach the girls to 'gambaru', an oft-used Japanese expression meaning 'to persevere, to stick it out, to grin and bear it', to do your best, however hard or even meaningless it might be. To give up is to be shamed in the sight of the group. I recalled the words of Paul in Hebrews

12:1b–2: 'Let us run with perseverance the race that is set before us, looking to Jesus the pioneer and perfecter of our faith, who for the joy that was set before him endured the cross.'

I reminded myself that I could only *gambaru* or persevere with language and culture learning as I kept my eyes firmly fixed on him, my motivation and strength.

Osaka 1984 to 1986

After four years in Nagoya it was time to move on, and I accepted an invitation to take up a teaching post at Poole Gakuin where I'd taught from 1976–1977. By now, the two-year college for girls aged 18-20 had expanded, and had a beautiful new campus in the city of Sakai, Osaka Prefecture.[8] The Anglican missionaries, who founded the attached high school in 1879, named it after Arthur William Poole, the first Anglican bishop of Japan.

If I'd thought this 'mission school' background would make it easier to share my faith than it had been in Shukutoku Gakuin, I was firmly mistaken. If anything, it was more difficult. Although there was chapel every day, classes in Bible and an active group of Christian students, a clear testimony to the gospel was often lacking. One day I returned to my office in tears following a poorly presented, largely incomprehensible chapel time. Where was the relevance to the lives of these 18- to 20-year-olds who had to attend whether they liked it or not? I longed for meaningful services that would draw them to Jesus, rather than the more likely outcome — that they would be put off Christianity for life.

---

[8] Subsequently it gained accreditation as a four-year university and added a graduate school as well.

Orientation camp in a Buddhist temple?

At one departmental meeting, we faced the tricky question of where to accommodate 250 new students for an overnight orientation camp.

'We have only one option left—a Buddhist temple!' said the principal, who was an ordained Anglican clergyman. He didn't look up as he waited for a reaction.

No one spoke up. I was the youngest there, and one of only two foreigners. The other had no Japanese. Culturally, I was well aware that speaking out would be seen as inappropriate, but it was an issue too important to let go. If none of the Christian staff would protest, then I had to. Taking my courage in both hands and, in far from adequate Japanese, I suggested that it surely was inappropriate for a Christian university to run a camp in a Buddhist temple. Especially for new students who knew nothing about Christianity. If nothing was available, could we not run orientation on the college campus?

The principal turned on me, and said abruptly, 'You're a foreigner. You don't understand our culture and way of thinking.' That hurt, but the meeting concluded with no decision taken.

One staff member spoke to me on the way out. 'Thank you for saying what you did. You could do that because you are a foreigner. I agreed with you, but I could not speak out against the principal.'

I was grateful for the encouragement, but saddened at this instance of culture overriding personal conviction. In the strong group culture of Japan, as a well-known proverb says, 'The nail that sticks out, gets bashed down'. In other words, it is more important to show respect for one's seniors and to maintain the harmony of the group, than to express a personal opinion, however strong one's convictions.

This was perhaps the aspect of culture I found most difficult throughout my years in Japan. I was often unsure what people really thought. In later years, I discovered that even mature Christians in church leaders' meetings rarely came out with anything unless specifically asked for their opinion.

In church circles, sometimes individuals would air a grievance against someone else to me; I would, if appropriate, encourage people to speak directly to the person they had an issue with, rather than talk behind their back. Gossip is present in all societies, but it seemed far more damaging amongst Japanese, trained from childhood to fit into the mould, and not to voice opinions in public. Discontent could rumble on for a long time underground, only suddenly to erupt in a major blow-up. How often I thought, 'We would never have got into this mess if things had been tackled earlier.'

Interestingly, we never did take those 250 new students to the Buddhist temple. The two days of orientation were held on campus, so perhaps the Lord in His graciousness used my intervention after all.

7

主と共に歩みて

A bolt from the blue

When I first laid eyes on the letter, I had no idea it was going to completely change the direction of my life. It was 10 February 1984. I'd just arrived home at the end of a busy school week, thankful for the weekend ahead. The thin blue airmail form was from a Japanese friend I'd met over four years previously in the UK. *Hikaru had long felt God calling him to share the love of Jesus with a particular Asian people group. After theological training in Japan and experience as assistant pastor in his home church, he spent a year studying in the UK, and then left for Asia in 1981 to work with OMF International. By this time, he was based at a refugee camp on the border between two South East Asian countries. I'd visited his home in Japan in December 1980, and met the family, but we'd had sporadic contact since then, apart from an exchange of general newsletters. I carefully unstuck the gummed edges of the folded aerogramme, and spread it out. Words jumped off the page. 'Miriam, would you pray with me about the possibility of marriage?'

I was nearly 31 years old. I'd entered my fourth decade with reluctance as I'd faced the increasing likelihood of never getting married. Now my heart responded eagerly. Hikaru was someone I could see as a life partner. I deeply respected Hikaru's spirituality and passion for mission. I remembered being challenged when he showed me his personal prayer diary. Although his request was a bolt from the blue, I was so excited I found it difficult to keep my news a secret for the next few weeks, while waiting for his next letter.

Communication difficulties

Little did I know the challenges that lay ahead, the least being the reality that letters from the refugee camps often went astray. A postal service was non-existent, so Hikaru entrusted his letters to acquaintances travelling to the capital. On one occasion the 'postman' simply forgot to post the letter, and other letters never arrived. For the year before Hikaru arrived back in Japan on home assignment, communication was never easy.[9] Even had Hikaru answered immediately, which was unlikely, I could not expect a reply to a letter of mine for at least two weeks. Every day over that, I was on tenterhooks. My hopes were all too frequently dashed, and I began to appreciate the agonising emotion of the psalmist: 'Hope deferred makes the heart sick, but a longing fulfilled is a tree of life' (Proverbs 13:12).

A binding contract

When Hikaru's letter arrived in February, I was already committed to teaching for two years at Poole Gakuin in Osaka from September 1984. The college was setting up a new department. But if I was to marry Hikaru, I would need to become an OMF mission worker myself, and that would take

---

[9] After a four-year term of service, Hikaru was due a year's home assignment in Japan. The purpose of this was to be refreshed, to re-connect with family and churches, to report back to supporters and to share the missionary vision in churches wherever possible.

time. Blissfully unaware that our plans would not progress as fast as we would have liked, I thought, 'Perhaps I can withdraw from the contract – I haven't signed anything yet.'

In April, not anticipating a problem, I took the train to Osaka for an appointment with the college principal. Short and slim, this gentleman was already past retirement age by Western standards. But he was energetic and, as he had lived in the US for some years, I found him easier to talk to than many Japanese gentlemen of his generation. Now, however, our interaction was tense.

'Your commitment is binding,' he said abruptly, leaving no room to negotiate. 'We've already submitted your name to the Education Ministry. If you back out, they might even withdraw their approval of the new department!'

In the end, I wheedled out of him permission to knock six months off my planned two-year contract. I would teach until the end of the college year in March 1986. Even so, I returned home to Nagoya very discouraged. The two years to March '86 stretched endlessly before me. This disappointment turned out to be only the first in a series in which I had to learn to wait patiently for God's perfect timing when, humanly speaking, it seemed far from perfect.

Severe culture shock

After six years in Japan, I was well adjusted to Japanese life and culture, wasn't I? I certainly thought so, but I was soon to find out that working in and enjoying Japan as a teacher was a very different matter from marrying into a traditional Japanese family, especially one in which the non-Christian dad already strongly disapproved of his second son leaving to serve God overseas. The family had lived in the same village high in the mountains for 300 years. Dad was a pillar of the local Buddhist temple, and there were religious traditions to maintain. Would Dad ever come to terms with the idea of an international marriage? Hikaru had written to his family, and to his home church pastor in early March, but then had waited weeks for an answer. When three letters did arrive—from his mum, dad and pastor, the content was shockingly negative, and ruined Hikaru's sleep. He wrote, 'I spent an hour in the middle of the night worshipping the Lord, and eventually found peace.'

The pastor's letter contained a cassette tape—40 minutes of recorded discussion between *Pastor Suzuki, his wife and a lady from another mission organisation, who was on the staff of the church. Their topic—our proposed marriage! I began to realise that marriage in Japanese culture was a very different thing from that in the West, where two individuals made the decision, and simply announced it to family and friends as a fait accompli. I'd been prepared for opposition from the Japanese family. It was natural, particularly as some of the family did not share our Christian faith and vision. What took me aback, however, was that church leadership needed to be involved; indeed, in order to proceed, they had to give their blessing.

'He's forgotten what it is to be a Japanese'

A quick summer trip to the UK in 1984 between jobs enabled me to visit Hikaru in Asia, briefly on the way there and back. We boarded the long-distance bus for the border. Vehicles tearing past in the opposite direction seemed dangerously close to us on the hot and dusty two-lane highway out of the capital.

'We always try to sit on the right-hand side,' said Hikaru. 'There are lots of fatal accidents on these roads so it is safer not to sit on the side closest to the oncoming traffic.'

I nodded my agreement, thinking, 'What a far cry from my physically safe and secure life in Japan!'

The refugee camps were hot, dusty and overflowing with suffering humanity. Row upon long row of wooden huts were packed together, stretching as far as the eye could see. Despite my best efforts to avoid eating any food offered, I had the inevitable diarrhoea. I didn't understand a word as I watched Hikaru with a group of refugees. They sat under a canvas awning which, although it kept the sun off, did nothing to relieve the stifling heat. But God was drawing many of these traumatised, stateless people into relationship with himself, and I was thrilled to see at first hand the discipling of new believers.

Conditions were even worse for refugees in a detainment centre in the capital, but here too I met Jesus-followers and seekers after truth. This time they gathered for a simple service in a roofed-over cavernous space, open to the elements on all sides. We sat on the bare concrete floor, and sang hymns to the accompaniment of a violin. Were there books or Bibles? I don't remember. But I was acutely aware these were brothers and sisters in Christ who were likely to be deported, perhaps for crimes they hadn't committed.

In the capital I also got to meet some of Hikaru's OMF colleagues. One Japanese couple told me, 'Hikaru has forgotten what it is to be a Japanese.'

I did not expect such bluntness, but they continued to emphasise the importance of the home church relationship. They told me that it wouldn't be right to approach the OMF Japan Home Council regarding my application to OMF, before we had support from Pastor Suzuki.[10] They urged us to wait until February 1985 when Hikaru returned to Japan, before taking any further steps.

'How do you feel?' asked Hikaru later. I struggled to restrain my tears.

However, nothing could be resolved that night because Hikaru needed to get back to his accommodation. A tropical downpour typical of the rainy season was flooding the road outside. Hikaru rolled up his trousers, removed his sandals and nonchalantly waded off down the road through a foot of water. This was evidently no unusual occurrence as far as he was concerned, but I shuddered to think of what his feet might encounter in that dirty flood water!

Back in my concrete-floored room on the third floor of the house where I was staying, my tears fell with as much intensity as the drumming of the rain on the window shutters. The noisy ceiling fan barely moved the air, and the oppressive humidity was a fitting, though decidedly unwelcome, backdrop to my distress. I barely slept, and failed completely to distract myself with a book or by praying.

From my new teaching job in Osaka, I wrote to my parents:

---

[10] As I was living in Japan, it had been suggested by OMF UK staff that I might be processed as a candidate by the Japan OMF Home Council rather than in the UK. This Council was a group of Japanese pastors responsible for selecting and sending out all Japanese candidates with OMF. The Council Chair had by this time heard in a roundabout way (because of the non-arrival of a letter from Hikaru) of our desire to be married, and had warned that Japanese were very conservative about international marriages. He himself expressed surprise at our intentions, but gave no clear opinion.

I was reassured by Hikaru's confidence and encouragement, but was only able to come to terms with the idea of waiting after praying a good deal for peace and willingness to be obedient. I am sure it is the right thing to do — my first major cultural adaptation. It is good to know that it is not ultimately men who are in control of our lives, but God. 'He will be the sure foundation for your times' (Isaiah 33:6) — has been my motto verse these last few days (5 October 1984).

This resolution was tested severely, even after Hikaru's arrival home in Japan more than four months later on 8 February 1985, as Pastor Suzuki dragged his feet about allowing Hikaru to meet me. While at the college ski camp in the Japanese Alps, God challenged me through six commands in Psalm 37: 'Do not fret' (repeated three times); 'Trust in the Lord' and 'Trust in him'; 'Take delight in the Lord'; 'Commit your way to the Lord'; 'Be still ....wait'; 'Refrain from anger'.

The last was particularly difficult. Why did we need the pastor's permission to even meet? 'I think the Lord wants me to share a text with you,' said a missionary friend in May. 'Let everyone be subject to the governing authorities' (Romans 13:1).

Others told me it was very common for Bible schools and denominations in Japan to have strict rules regarding the marriages of their students or pastors. How much more so then for a Japanese missionary wanting to marry a foreigner. It helped a little to see that Pastor Suzuki's attitude stemmed from his Japanese church culture, and was not purely idiosyncratic.

I wrote to my parents on June 30th 1985:

There is no question of trying to force our plans against Pastor Suzuki's opposition. That would not be the way of love although I don't believe he actually has any authority to interfere. I need constantly to pray that I may have the right attitude towards him.

Could I forgive?

I preached my first sermon in Japanese from notes in May 1985 on 'learning to be content whatever the circumstances' (Philippians 4:11).[11] I was a bundle of nerves, despite the loving receptivity and acceptance of my small Japanese church family, but a far greater trial was living out the words I was preaching. How hard it was to be content when frustration boiled over at the lack of progress. I was deeply hurt by what felt like total rejection by a pastor who did not even try to get to know me. I had no desire to forgive, but set myself to pray, 'God, bless Pastor Suzuki and his family, and use him as he pastors his church.'

I could not harbour unforgiveness and simultaneously pray a blessing on Pastor Suzuki, so my hard heart would soften as I prayed. But before long, the anger came rushing back, and I had to bend my will repeatedly to offer up that sacrifice of prayer for Pastor Suzuki. By mid-September 1985, the pressure was so great that I wrote to Hikaru asking if we should call it all off as I could not take much more.

The book *Passion and Purity* by Elisabeth Elliot helped me greatly during those difficult months. She wrote of her struggles in her relationship with her first husband-to-be Jim Elliot.

> . . . waiting on God requires the willingness to bear
> uncertainty, to carry within oneself the unanswered

---

[11] Up to that point for any formal talk, I'd produced a complete script that had been thoroughly checked in advance. I wrote to my parents, 'I feel that's quite a big milestone passed in my Japanese language. I practised preaching aloud three times at home during the week!' NB this milestone was not passed until I'd been immersed in Japanese for nearly seven years! It is a fascinating, but not easy language. Explaining spiritual truth is possibly one of the most difficult of linguistic tasks in a foreign language.

question, lifting the heart to God about it whenever it intrudes upon one's thoughts . . . The things we feel most deeply we ought to learn to be silent about at least until we have talked them over thoroughly with God. (Elliot, 2013, pp. 61-2)

Her prayer became mine, hard as it was to wait for the Lord himself, rather than his answers to my problems.

I wait

Dear Lord, Thy ways
Are past finding out,
Thy love too high.
O hold me still
Beneath Thy shadow.
It is enough that Thou
Lift up the light
Of Thy countenance.
I wait—
Because I am commanded
So to do. My mind
Is filled with wonderings.
My soul asks "Why?"
But then the quiet word,
"Wait thou only
Upon God."
And so, not even for the light
To show a step ahead,
But for Thee, dear Lord,
I wait.

(Elliot, 2013, p. 72)

8

主と共に歩みて

On the move at last!

'The Japan Home Council can't process you here. You must apply to OMF through OMF UK. If you are accepted, we will give you and Hikaru our blessing,' said the Japan Home Council Chairman when I finally met him in Tokyo.

It was November 1985, and 21 long months since Hikaru had asked me to pray about marriage but, at last, things were on the move. Hikaru and I had met a handful of times since February, and once together with his pastor back in April. This latter meeting was not a success. In November, my own Japanese pastor in Osaka stepped in, and arranged a second meeting between myself and Hikaru's pastor. Pastor Ikeda's warm presence broke the tension, and the four and a half hour meeting ended with Pastor Suzuki giving the go-ahead for me to meet the chair of the Japan OMF Home Council about applying to OMF. I owed so much to the love, prayers and practical support of friends like the Ikedas. Prior to that crucial November meeting, I told a dear Christian friend that Hikaru and I had set aside a day to fast. Her immediate response—'I'll join you'—touched me deeply. Now I'd come to meet the Japan Home Council Chairman at his church in

Tokyo. 'May we be officially engaged before I leave Japan in March?' I asked hopefully.[12]

The Chairman shook his head. 'No, that's not possible. You might not be accepted by OMF UK.'

But, at least, the next step was clear. In March 1986, as my teaching contract came to an end, I packed up my belongings, sent a trunk to Hikaru's home, and set off for five months in the UK. At the end of an inspiring three-week orientation course in July, I was accepted as an OMF candidate. What a relief! The last obstacle to my marriage to Hikaru had been cleared away, or so I thought. Little did I know what still lay ahead.

The next step was the 10-week Orientation Course at the OMF International Centre in Singapore from October to December 1986. Hikaru's plans to return to refugee work in June were on hold, so I booked flights to Singapore via Japan hoping to make engagement and even wedding plans in person.

Storm clouds gather

Clouds that had already been hanging over Hikaru's family darkened in intensity. In March 1985, Hikaru's mother was diagnosed with stomach cancer which had already spread to her liver. The whole family was shocked, as Hikaru's elder brother had only just returned to work after a major operation for cancer of the rectum five months earlier.

By spring 1986, there were signs of recurring cancer in both, and in August two phone calls to the UK brought the sad news we'd been anticipating. On 12 August, 'My brother's gone' and, on the 24th, 'My Mum's gone'.

---

[12] Engagement in Japanese churches is a solemn ceremony almost as binding as a wedding itself. No simple exchanging of rings and announcing to all and sundry that you are engaged.

Hikaru told the story in a circular to English-speaking friends on 3 October 1986.

> Thank you very much for your prayers over these long three months. My brother (38) and my mother (74) went to be with the Lord on 12 and 24 August respectively. From June on, the rest of the family took turns in caring for them 24 hours a day. My brother was in hospital, my mother at home ... My brother had been busy working at a company, and didn't have any faith. But during his illness he gradually became more open to the Bible, and to our prayers for him. Towards the end, he made an open confession of faith. My mother received the sad news, on her own deathbed, that my brother had already gone to be with the Lord. But she was kept in peace by the assurance of a reunion with him in heaven. As she grew weaker, my mother spoke of meeting us too in heaven, and planned the details of her own funeral. We children (Hikaru and his elder sisters) appreciated her desire for a Christian funeral, but my father's inherited position as a leader in the village Buddhist temple was a great barrier. However, when we read my mother's will together before she died, my father agreed to everything, and promised ... that he would allow a Christian funeral ... My father's attitude was truly miraculous and a work of God's grace, as well as a proof of their love for one another.

> My mother's funeral was the first Christian funeral ever to have taken place in this country village and, therefore, was a great testimony to God. According to my mother's wishes, more than 700 New Testaments were given out, and we pray that they will be read. The death of two loved ones in a month is a great loss, but God's grace and comfort are enough. We pray for my father (80), my brother's widow and their two children, a five- and a three-year-old, that they too will come into faith, and be able to believe in a reunion with their loved ones in heaven. My father was deeply moved by the funeral, and is more open as a result.

On 16 September, I arrived back in Japan for a brief visit. I visited Hikaru's home for a few hours before moving to the tiny apartment of the missionary from his church.

When Hikaru dropped me off, she sat me down and said, 'Miriam, this is very hard to say, but Hikaru's dad has just been on the phone. He does not want you in his home again. In his bereavement, he just can't cope with the idea of "losing" Hikaru to marriage with a foreigner.'

I couldn't believe my ears. This was despite the fact that Hikaru would not return to Asia for at least the foreseeable future. Hikaru's church group had offered him the chance to work in a new local church plant so that he could support his father, widowed sister-in-law and her two young children.

She went on, 'Hikaru's dad has threatened to commit suicide if you go ahead with marriage plans.'

I knew this was no idle threat. For Hikaru, as the younger of two sons, an international marriage would not have affected the family's reputation much. But now he must take the eldest son's place in the family. Traditionally this meant caring for the ancestors according to Buddhist rituals, and supporting elderly parents and other family members. Hikaru's family had lived in the same place for 29 generations. It was impossible for his father to contemplate one of his sons-in-law in Hikaru's place. He would hardly let Hikaru out of his sight.

The slimy pit

I was devastated. It was not easy to get time alone. There was no privacy in a tiny Japanese home with sliding paper doors between the rooms. I did not know what to do with myself. In desperation, I hid in a bamboo thicket, prey to the many mosquitos which found me so delicious. I cried out in despair to God. 'How could this happen after all the difficulties we have come through?'

I read Psalm 40 over and over:

> I waited patiently for the LORD; he turned to me and heard my cry. He lifted me out of the slimy pit, out of the mud and mire; he set my feet on a rock and gave me a firm place to stand. He put a new song in my mouth, a hymn of praise to our God (Psalm 40:1–3).

David could praise his God for rescue, but I felt I was being sucked deeper and deeper into a slimy pit, drowning in its thick mud and mire. Troubles without number surrounded me (Psalm 40:12). Would I ever get out of this mess, and stand on firm ground again? I never met Hikaru's dad, or entered his house again.[13]

---

[13] In January 1990 I received news that Hikaru's father had died on 8 December 1989. He never made an open confession of faith, and the funeral ceremony was Buddhist, but Hikaru and others felt sure he had believed in Jesus.

Hikaru was struggling with many issues. 'Unless Dad becomes a Christian, I don't see how we could ever be married while he is still alive.'

Hikaru's sisters, church and Japan OMF Home Council members were all surprisingly supportive of me, given the rocky history we'd been through so far. This was some comfort as I set off for OMF orientation in Singapore, and an unknown future beyond December 1986.

The welcome and encouragement from International Centre (IC) staff could not have been warmer. All were deeply concerned for our situation, but opinions were divided. Some thought I should go to the country where Hikaru had been working, others to the OMF area in the north of Japan. Hikaru needed to renew his visa for refugee work. IC leaders encouraged him to visit Singapore on the way. When he arrived in early December, he was emotionally exhausted, and weighed down by his two warring responsibilities – to his dad and to me. OMF leadership felt he was in no state to make important decisions regarding our future, and asked him to return at the end of the month on his way back to Japan. I had to wait some weeks longer.

I wrote to my parents on 14 December 1986:

> We have now reached a point where we have to decide whether we are to continue with our unofficial engagement in the light of the uncertainties, or break it off . . . I know now that whichever way the decision goes, I will go to Japan . . .

I had been reading Psalm 121 several weeks before, and was impressed by the fact that the word 'keep' comes six times. At the weekly Tuesday night IC meeting the speaker chose the same passage, and emphasised that very word. The

General Director of OMF, Dr Taylor[14], spoke to me afterwards. 'I thought of you and Hikaru when we got to verse 8 — "The Lord will watch over your coming and going both now and for evermore".' The next day I received a letter quoting the same words. Isn't it lovely how the Lord repeatedly reassures us?

I shared the following quote with my parents:

> When we keep our gaze focused on the unseen and the spiritual, for us life will not be a reluctant slipping down the slope into the tomb but a glorious ascent into the immediate presence of God. (Saunders, 1984 p. 43)

The likely death of my hopes for marriage was a dark experience — an inexorable descent into tomb-like blackness. But it was one that, if I allowed it, would draw me into a deeper experience of God. I wrote some quotes from Eugene Peterson's book *A Long Obedience in the Same Direction* in my journal.

> Faith is not a precarious affair of chance escape from satanic assaults. It is the solid, massive, secure experience of God who keeps all evil from getting inside us, who keeps our life, who keeps our going out and our coming in from this time forth and for evermore. (Peterson, 1989, p. 41)

Here were echoes of my life verse — when he puts his sheep out he goes before them.

Peterson again:

> We are secure not because we are sure of ourselves but because we trust that God is sure of us. (p. 86)

And also:

---

[14] This was James Hudson Taylor III, 1929–2009, great-grandson of J. Hudson Taylor, founder of the China Inland Mission that became OMF International. I owed much to his loving concern and wise advice to Hikaru and me at that very difficult time, along with the fantastic support of many other OMF leaders, too many to name.

All suffering, all pain, all emptiness, all disappointment is seed. Sow it in God. He will finally bring a crop of joy from it. (p. 95)

Mistake or mystery?

On 26 December, Hikaru returned briefly to Singapore, his mind made up. 'I feel God is saying my family is my priority.'

He shared a Bible verse with me, 'Anyone who does not provide for their relatives, and especially for their own household, has denied the faith and is worse than an unbeliever' (1Timothy 5:8).

My heart was breaking, but I saw that this was the right course of action for Hikaru as a Japanese Christian with a traditional family background. Hikaru's passion was, above all, to see Jesus glorified in the context of his family and community. In a less hierarchical and highly individualistic society like the West, the 'right' and 'godliest' decision would have been different. When non-Christian culture is clearly out of line with biblical teaching, cross-cultural missionaries need to speak God's Word into the culture to transform it. But where the issue is not one of disobedience to God's revealed will, we need to be prepared to give up preferred ways of doing things from our own cultural backgrounds, however hard it is. In the words of Paul, we are to, '. . . become all things to all people so that by all possible means [we] might save some. [We] do all this for the sake of the gospel that [we] may share in its blessings' (1 Corinthians 9:22–23).

The decision to bring our relationship to an end was a joint one, and I felt a sense of relief at an end to the uncertainty of nearly three years. But I had to deal with unanswerable questions and turbulent emotions for years to come. Had we made a mistake? We'd been so sure of God's leading. How could we have got it all so wrong? When I expressed these agonising doubts to the OMF Personnel Director, John Miller, his wise response became an emotional anchor for the rocky years ahead. 'No, not a mistake, but a mystery.'

9

主と共に歩みて

Stars in the dark

My four months in Singapore were traumatic but, in the midst of it all, God graciously encouraged and blessed me. Stars shone in my darkness.

The Japanese Christian Fellowship (JCF), which met on Sunday afternoons at St George's Anglican Church, welcomed me with open arms, and I made many friends in a short time. In November, I shared my testimony at a service, and was invited to talk to around 20 at the weekday ladies' meeting. I spoke on Psalm 40 which had imprinted itself in my mind and heart, since my time in the bamboo thicket two months before. The Japanese community in Singapore was large, and I felt privileged to be a part of the vibrant outreach of one of several Japanese churches for four months.

A large part of the Orientation Course at that time consisted of lectures on linguistics, particularly phonetics. When the Linguistic Consultant realised I had a degree in Linguistics, she immediately said, 'Miriam, you don't need to come.' I was able to spend time with God, and read many books. I took up a suggestion from one of working through the Psalms, and writing down every attribute of God I found. I still have that notebook with different words underlined in red.

Several times a week I took the bus to swim in a beautiful open-air pool where the water was as warm as a bath! I could at least pump out some of my stress and anxiety as my arms and legs propelled me through length after length of the 50-metre pool.

As Christmas approached other opportunities to serve came my way. 'Would you play the piano for my Bible study for Jewish ladies?' asked Sheila, the wife of the OMF Personnel Director.

Leone, wife of the General Director, was singing a solo at the 8:00 a.m. Sunday service at the Dynasty Hotel. 'Could you accompany me?'

This luxurious hotel was run by Chinese Christians and, with OMF help, ran a service every Sunday for around 40 people. I gained insight into some of the multitude of different Christian ministries that even the busiest of staff at OMF made a priority. Singaporean churches of all nationalities were thriving.

The Medical Advisor kept a firm eye on me, took me for walks, lent me great detective stories, and moved me to a single room when she discovered I was having trouble sleeping. In December, when all the other participants on the Orientation Course left, an OMF worker from New Zealand offered me her flat for several weeks, while she was away. I appreciated the greater privacy and comfort of a 'real' home to retire to, with restful green curtains and a view of trees from the window.

So many OMF colleagues reached out to me in countless ways with invitations to concerts and carol services, presents of home-made cookies or invitations for meals — especially over Christmas. Others wrote notes to assure me of their prayers. When Hikaru and I made the decision to part, the Personnel Director said, 'Miriam, you are under no obligation to stay in OMF. You are free to return to the UK, to go back to teaching English in Japan, or to join OMF Japan in Hokkaido. It's completely up to you.'

I had no hesitation. This wonderful OMF family was one I very much wanted to be a part of. It was clear to me that having got this far, God must have a purpose in wanting me in OMF, and it would be a backward step to think of anything other than moving forward, scary as it was, to work in Japan with OMF.

As the Orientation Course progressed, I'd started to pray that God would confirm to me his calling to be a mission worker. I was much in need of this reassurance as it looked more and more likely that I would end up as a single missionary in Japan, which had not been part of the plan. It was likely I would be involved in church planting and evangelism, and I wasn't too sure I was any more up to this challenge than I'd been back in 1979 when I first explored joining OMF. I had no idea how God might answer my prayer but, when he did, it was a very bright star shining in the dark sky.

As the Japanese Christian Fellowship met on Sunday afternoons, I was free in the mornings to visit Singaporean churches of different denominations. One Sunday I joined a couple from the Orientation Course who were assigned to an English-speaking Tamil church. After the service they introduced me to a Tamil lady.

'Ann, this is Miriam,' one of the couple said. 'She has been working in Japan.'

Interest sparked immediately in Ann's eyes. 'Do you speak Japanese?'

'Yes, reasonably well,' I replied cautiously, wondering what this introduction would lead to.

'I am teaching English to a young Japanese mum, and she seems really interested in the Bible. I got a Japanese Bible for her, and I have been trying my best to explain things, but she just doesn't have enough English to understand. Can you help?'

Well, of course I was delighted. Ann's student was a Mrs Mayumi Koizumi, and she had three small children aged five and under. Her husband had a three-year contract as a primary teacher at the Japanese school in Singapore. Ann got permission from Mayumi to give me her telephone number. I plucked up courage to phone, and arranged to visit her at home. Would we hit it off, and could I share anything useful with her in the few short weeks left to me in Singapore?

After shyly introducing myself, I followed Mayumi into her living room, and was astonished to see her Japanese Bible lying open already on the table. Her questions came at me thick and fast. Up to now, I'd tried to build relationships with Japanese so that they felt free to talk about personal or spiritual matters. To reach this stage usually took a great deal of time. But God had prepared Mayumi's heart, and drawn alongside her a young Tamil teacher of English and a fledgling mission worker, buffeted by waves of uncertainty regarding the future!

It was no easy matter to answer Mayumi's questions, then or on future occasions. The baby was crawling round our feet, and the five- and three-year-old girls were continually interrupting. My language abilities were fully stretched too. Many questions were common to all Japanese exploring Christian faith. 'What's grace? Repentance? Baptism? Why did Jesus have to die? Am I really sinful?'

But one memorable question caused me some embarrassment, and Mayumi must have wondered why I struggled to answer. She'd been reading the account of Jesus' birth and early life, and pounced on me with the question 'What's circumcision?' I was stumped. I knew the Japanese word, but did not have the vocabulary to explain what it was. This was before the days of language apps on smartphones or Google searches, and my dictionaries were in storage in Japan.

After meeting Mayumi, I could see another reason for being excused the phonetics lectures. I often had only two lectures a day, which gave me time to visit her, and take her to the Japanese Christian Fellowship's ladies' meetings. On 23 November, I wrote to my parents:

> Yesterday I visited Mayumi, and had a marvellous time despite the distractions of three small children. She is so open and spiritually hungry. She said she understood the cross for the first time when I explained it to her. This was a big encouragement to me at this time of uncertainty, and a confirmation that this new phase of my life as a 'full-time' missionary is right.

The Japanese ladies lent me books to share with Mayumi, and gave her a warm welcome at their meetings. They assured me they would do all they could to follow her up after I left Singapore.

On 14 December, I wrote of another visit.

> The baby was asleep, and the two older children were at kindergarten so we had a more peaceful time than usual. It was lovely to see how the Holy Spirit had been working in her life since our last meeting. We'd talked about Peter walking on the water, and beginning to drown when he

took his eyes off Jesus. She then found the same story in a Japanese children's book I'd given her. I told her of my experience during the week with Psalm 121:8[15], how the Bible is a living Word and the way God speaks to us.

A day or two later, I had a memorable letter, in which she wrote, 'I'm just a baby Christian. I can't do anything, but I will try to crawl!'

On the Sunday before Christmas 1986, Mayumi and her two older children came with me to the Christmas outreach for children. The church was packed with around 200 Japanese including 100 children. The Koizumi children were restless, so I didn't know how much Mayumi took in. Nana (5), sitting on my knee, kept pointing to the figure of Jesus in a stained-glass window.

'Who's that?' she asked.

'It's Jesus,' I said.

'I don't know Jesus,' she replied.

For this little girl Christmas was Santa Claus, goodies and presents. For me, she was a poignant reminder of the spiritual need of Japan.

On 25 December Mayumi, with baby, made it to the JCF Christmas, just in time for the message based on the words of Handel's *Messiah*. The service was a beautifully crafted mix of testimony, message and music. Many non-Christians were there — altogether around 140 compared to the usual attendance of 35. One group played Christmas carols on mandolin guitars and, at the end, the choir from the Japanese club, along with the JCF Christians, gave a very creditable performance of the 'Hallelujah' chorus. My personal highlight was Mayumi's excitement at discovering the meaning of the word 'Christmas'. As she pointed out, in Japan

---

[15] See previous chapter.

it is usually written 'Xmas' when Roman lettering is used. She'd not realised that Christmas was actually about Christ.

I spent a final day at Mayumi's house before leaving for Japan on 26 January 1987. Mayumi also invited two of the Christian Japanese ladies. My contribution was complete, and God would now use these dear ladies to encourage Mayumi further in her Christian journey. Almost a year to the day in January 1988, she sent precious photos of her baptism in a Singapore swimming pool.

The Koizumi family returned to Japan in spring 1988. Their home in Yamanashi prefecture was far from my new one in Sapporo. Over the next 30 years the number of times Mayumi and I met could be counted on one hand. But I spent a wonderful weekend in her home in November 2017 before leaving Japan for retirement. I got on well with her not yet Christian husband, and visited the tiny church she attended. What a lot we had to talk about! And such an encouragement to me to see her still walking hand-in-hand with Jesus, despite some very tough times over those 30 years.

When we first met, Mayumi had just said goodbye to her parents-in-law who'd been on a visit to Singapore. Mayumi had married into a very traditional Japanese family in a small village in the mountains. Living with in-laws and trying to conform to their expectations was too much to bear. Some nights she escaped to sleep in the family car, with one or more of the children. Singapore was a welcome release from the pressure, but a parental visit had brought things to a head again. How was she going to cope when the family returned to Japan!

'When I met you I was on the verge of committing suicide,' she said.

My emotions were too raw to reciprocate at that time with my own story but, 30 years later, I did. God in his wonderful mercy had allowed me to be God's timely provision for her — and for her to be his provision to me! I'd asked God to confirm my call to full-time church ministry. Mayumi was his answer. As I set off again on the next stage of my life with OMF to Japan, it was with the comforting reassurance that God could, and would, use me even in the daunting task of church planting.

10

主と共に歩みて

Wakaba ('Young Leaf') Church

Trying to appear relaxed, I clutched the sides of my car seat as my new OMF colleague Mary drove down narrow roads with six feet of snow on either side, blocking the view at junctions. 'What happens if we meet something suddenly?' I wondered. There was no room to manoeuvre, apart from driving into the snow banks on both sides of the road. Mary handled the tiny car with confidence, but a little too fast for my liking! It was scary—this new world I'd been catapulted into, steamy tropical Singapore already a distant memory. Nara, Nagoya and Osaka, my previous homes in Japan, were all about two hours away by air. Sapporo felt very different. This had nothing to do with size—Osaka and Nagoya were the third and fourth largest cities in Japan, and Sapporo in fifth place was close behind. (In 2021 a Shell city comparison tool indicates that Sapporo's population at 2.6 million was not far behind the UK's second city Birmingham at 2.69 million.)[16]

---

[16] Shell: 'Compare Cities' https://www.shell.com/energy-and-innovation/the-energy-future/future-cities/compare-cities Accessed 19 February 2021.

No, the difference was the harshness of the climate, this far north on the island of Hokkaido. I'd never seen so much snow.

My suitcase had decided not to accompany me on the flight from Singapore and, having to borrow warm clothes until it caught up with me, only added to the strangeness of it all. Initially I was to stay at the home of Mary Alexander, the OMF Japan Field Nurse. We'd lived opposite each other in the dorm at All Nations Christian College in 1979, and she knew something of how my life had recently been turned upside down.

I enjoyed a few weeks of Japanese study at the OMF Japanese language centre—one-to-one classes with two different teachers for two hours a day. I met some of my many new mission colleagues,[17] visited a number of churches and discussed with mission leaders where I might fit in.

'We would love you to join us especially as you are an experienced English teacher,' said Wolfgang and Dorothea Langhans from Germany. 'We have seen people coming to faith through English here in Hanakawa, and we really want to make the most of this opportunity for evangelism.'

This couple with their four young children were church planting in North Hanakawa, a large housing development adjacent to Sapporo.[18] The church had started from zero in the home of Tony and Pat Schmidt from South Africa in October

---

[17] At this time, there were around 100 OMF missionaries in Japan, mainly involved in church planting and student ministries. Sixty-five were in Hokkaido, and a large proportion of these were in Sapporo where the language school and OMF Japan Headquarters were at the time. OMF was also working in Aomori prefecture in the north of the main island of Honshu, and in Tokyo and Yokohama.

[18] This area later became a city in its own right, the city of Ishikari. The population of over 58,000 in 2017 was probably little changed from 20 years before.

1980. By spring 1987, it had a core of 13 members with a Sunday worship attendance of up to 20. The average church size in Hokkaido was around 30, and elsewhere in Japan 50, so, by comparison, this was a healthy church plant.

After much discussion and prayer, everyone agreed that Wakaba ('Young Leaf') church was the best fit for me. I would use my English teaching skills and experience. I would also conduct services, preach, work with the young teenagers and teach Bible studies. Ironically, these activities were the very things I'd baulked at eight years previously, when I first knocked at OMF's door!

This new life was not something I'd planned. I'd joined OMF to get married, and support a husband in his ministry. So, stress levels were high as I joined the Wakaba Church team at the end of March 1987, in time for the start of the new school and business year. We had 80 English students on the books of whom 25 were adults. I was to teach two adult classes, one senior high students' class (15- to 18-year-olds) and one class of 25 primary school children aged 9–12. Each class ended with a 10-minute Bible talk or story in Japanese, so there was much to prepare.

Ten days before moving to Hanakawa, the phone rang. 'You've got the job you applied for at Hokusei University! You start in four weeks' time!'

This was so last minute I'd almost abandoned hope of getting the two-days-a-week teaching job. Life would be very full. I had much to learn about OMF, about church planting and working in a team. But I was at least familiar with teaching English to college students, and knowing I was competent in this one area of my new life helped me cope with the challenges of the rest.

Constantly in motion, only more frequently

OMF was founded as the China Inland Mission in 1865 by James Hudson Taylor. The Communist take-over forced the

CIM to leave China in 1950. The following year, after much prayer, leaders concluded that God was leading them to start work in other countries of East Asia, including Japan. CIM became OMF.

I soon discovered that OMF members joked about these initials. CIM was 'Constantly In Motion' and OMF 'Only More Frequently.' Change is a given in a cross-cultural ministry overseas. In Japan, new OMF workers spent the first two years in full-time language study in Sapporo followed by two years in a church plant or other ministry. After a year's home assignment, they usually returned to a different area and ministry. Unexpected family or medical emergencies at home or overseas could leave a hole in a key ministry that had to be plugged by moving someone. We were impacted not just by our own moves, but by the constant comings and goings of others too — some who'd become close friends, but whom we might not see again for a long time — or even this side of heaven.

In 31 years with OMF in Japan, I moved far less than most of my colleagues but, even so, I did not thrive on change. It was an immense privilege to share deeply with OMF colleagues of varied nationalities and backgrounds. Korean colleagues gained rapid fluency in Japanese, but sometimes struggled with English, the common language of business and fellowship in OMF. As I met regularly with several Korean couples to help them with English, I discovered the delights of ginseng tea and kimchi (spicy pickled cabbage). Their passion for prayer challenged me although, on one overnight stay, I didn't enjoy getting up at the crack of dawn to pray with one family. I also struggled to focus on my own prayers when we prayed Korean style at a meeting — all out loud at the same time!

The joy of fellowship with Korean colleagues was just one example of how life with an international and inter-denominational mission enriched me. But, as the years went by, the constant comings and goings of colleagues for one reason or another, and the reality that some friends went and never came back, took its toll on me. At times, I struggled with a strong reluctance to put time and energy into relationships with mission colleagues, only to have to say 'goodbye' yet again. I would happily have spent all my time with my far more stable community of Japanese friends.

By the time I joined the Wakaba team, I'd already been living a nomadic life for 12 months. I struggled when my temporary stay with Mary extended to three months. This was due to a series of ups and downs over plans to buy a house for Wakaba Church, which had been meeting in rented property till then. 'Constantly in motion' and 'only more frequently' summed up the story of my life at that time.

We looked at several different houses, only to have hopes dashed for one reason or another. Buying was a massive challenge for a membership of a dozen. Miraculously, funds came through loans from the Evangelical Churches Association Building Fund and three OMF-related churches. Also, we had income from our English teaching. Finally, we found the building of God's choice. It had three small adjoining rooms downstairs with tatami mat floors, kitchen, bath area and toilet. As numbers grew, we removed the sliding doors between the three rooms and, eventually, even the wall closing off the kitchen. At Christmas 1988 we broke our attendance record with 44 squeezed into what was still a small space with all four rooms opened up.

Up a narrow wooden staircase was my new home – two small rooms. I trotted up and down frequently to let people in, and to use the toilet and bathroom. Thankfully, the addition of a sink upstairs gave me some privacy. I moved in on 29 June and the building was dedicated on 12 July 1987. The great bonus of the three-month stay with Mary was our deepening friendship and prayer partnership, but it was a relief to unpack properly at last and set up home.

There were constant pressures living upstairs in a small house where children and adults came in and out every day except Mondays, our day off. Our small space downstairs was multipurpose. 'How do I need to set up the room next?' was my constant thought. Several times a day I would put up or put away tables and chairs for different types of meetings. Children sat on the floor at low tables for English. Adults used tables and chairs. For services I put out chairs in rows. We did our own cleaning.

Wolfgang, who headed up our church planting team, was keen to attract men who worked very long hours. One year he decided to hold a weekly men's class at 6:00 a.m. 'I'll open up and get everything ready. You just ignore us, and sleep on till your usual time,' he said.

That was easier said than done. As I slept on a futon[19] on the floor above the meeting room, I could hear doors open and voices rumbling. I found it impossible to relax with others in the building. It was not until I moved out in January 1990 that I realised how great the pressure had been, living in a home open to all.

Adjustments

I also had to adjust to working in a team. Wolfgang was in overall charge of the children and youth work. At one point, he wanted to pass this responsibility to me, to free himself up for other things.

---

[19] I slept on this mattress on the tatami mat floor. During the daytime I rolled up my bedding, and put it away in a cupboard with sliding paper doors, thus freeing up space in my small living room. I didn't buy a bed until 2008 when I moved for the first time into a flat with hard floors. By then, Japan was becoming far more westernised, and few flats were built with tatami mat rooms in the traditional style.

'I'm so sorry, but I don't feel that is my gifting or calling,' I said.

'But if something needs to be done, and there is no one else to do it, God will enable you to do it,' said Wolfgang.

I agonised over the decision. I wanted to pull my weight, but I was out of my comfort zone in many areas. I felt that to do something so very obviously not my gifting would be personally detrimental. Wolfgang graciously accepted my position, although he didn't agree. I can't have been an easy person to work with in those early days, as I struggled with anxiety, grief and being stretched to the limit.

Preaching was something, however, that I grew to love. I was long-winded at first, even in Japanese. In September, after my second Sunday morning sermon, I wrote in a letter to my parents, 'Whoever would have thought that I could preach for 45 minutes in Japanese!' Of course, that was too long for a small group of new Christians and not yet Christians. One morning I was in full swing when Wolfgang held up his arm, and tapped his watch. I deflated like a pricked balloon!

Wolfgang helped me hone my developing preaching skills by making comments after the service. 'Miriam, try to make your points clearer and have more illustrations.'

Having preached my heart out, I was emotionally drained, and sensitive to criticism. In the end, I said 'Wolfgang, could you keep your comments till later in the week when I'm better able to receive them?'

In international mission teams, adjustments have to be made for different personalities, nationalities, background and ways of thinking. I appreciated both Wolfgang's directness and his flexibility.

Danger in a dictionary!

Mrs Tamura was a new Christian in our congregation. She was also a teacher at the OMF language centre. She was passionate that missionaries did not discredit the gospel with poor Japanese language skills. I depended on her and others for language help. In our small space there was no raised area for the pulpit, and we lined the chairs right up under the speaker's nose. One Sunday, I was attempting to expound the characteristics of Abraham's prayer for Sodom and Gomorrah in Genesis 18:16–33. As I talked about persistence in prayer, I used the word I'd looked up in a dictionary. Mrs Tamura was sitting directly in front of me, and I heard her take a sharp indrawn breath. Whoops! I'd clearly said something wrong, so I hastily tried to find another way of expressing what I meant.

Later she explained there are two words for 'persistence' in Japanese. I'd used the one that has strong negative connotations and, in doing so, obscured the meaning of my point! I must have made many far more serious errors over the years, but it was unusual for Japanese to point them out. I was fortunate to have someone who did, although it added to my nervousness in the early days.

Through the back door into OMF

I felt as though I'd got into OMF Japan by the back door. As I'd been accepted with marriage in mind, I had no supporting churches in the UK, no financial supporters and few prayer partners. Now OMF has an individualised system of support but, until the year 2000, donations from around the world went into one pot, and were shared out equally.

'I feel as though I'm a burden to you all,' I told our OMF Hokkaido leader.

'Don't worry your head about that,' he said. 'Look at all the money you are bringing into OMF through your university teaching and church English classes.'

My salary went into the general pot, and our English class income was helping fund church planting. I was relieved to realise that I was not, after all, a drain on the mission financially.

The 'Arctic' of Hokkaido

Hokkaido literally means 'North Sea Road'. From the northernmost tip of the island on a clear day you can see the Russian island of Sahkalin. The fresh water of the Amur River flowed from Siberia mixing with the sea off the east coast, to form thick ice floes that stretched as far as the eye could see. One unforgettable experience was a trip on an icebreaker in brilliant sunshine, seeing eagles perched on ice hills. I could hear, and feel, the crackle and crunch of ice splitting as the boat slowly forged a way ahead.

Winter had many compensations. A harsh, grey world would suddenly be transformed into a sparkling fairyland by a fresh fall of snow and sunny blue skies. I was warmed by the thoughtfulness of the ladies' group in my previous church in Nagoya. Concerned lest I suffer from the cold in the Arctic of Japan, they sent a scarf, gloves and hand knitted socks by special delivery. But I had lots to learn that first winter living in the church.

On many a freezing winter morning, I was reluctant to leave my cosy futon for the back-breaking task of shovelling snow yet again. Freshly fallen snow was light and fluffy, and easier to shift but, on other days, the snow would be wet and heavy, or frozen so solid it had to be chipped away. Sundays that were already long, became even longer, as the missionary team had to clear the parking area in front of the church before people started to arrive at around 8:30 a.m. It was all do-it-yourself as the fledgling church had no money to pay for snow removal. We were delighted to receive the present of a small snow-blowing machine, but I found it difficult to operate. It depleted my energy almost as much as tossing shovelfuls of snow onto banks of snow that, as winter progressed, were higher than my head.

It was rare to have an uninterrupted night's sleep as I was shaken awake by the flashing orange lights and ponderous rumblings of snowploughs. These cleared the roads, but left a barrier of hard packed snow between the road and the parking space in front of the house. Half-asleep, it was sometimes hard to tell if the shaking was the result of an earth tremor or the snowploughs. A glance to see if the light suspended from the ceiling was swinging or not would give me the answer. At other times, the heavy thud of snow sliding off the triangle-shaped roof was, in itself, enough to drag me unwillingly back to consciousness.

The first job of each morning was to run downstairs and check the water. Sometimes I had to pour hot water from an electric kettle over the frozen taps before I could even turn them on. If the water still didn't run (despite being turned off at night, and the pipes emptied), I collected as many heaters as I could to thaw out the boiler room and church kitchen.

One Sunday night, I forgot to take the vase of flowers from the church room to my living room upstairs. Neither vase nor flowers survived the freezing night. I came down to find the vase shattered to pieces, and the flowers limply decorating the carpet!

One Sunday morning despite rising at 6:00 a.m. for pipe warming and snow shovelling duties, the water still had not come through when the service started at 10.30. Halfway through, we were all startled by the sound of rushing waters. Realising the taps had at last unfrozen, I hastily rushed around closing each of the 12 taps upstairs and down. Would that it had been a new kind of Pentecost, and not simply a common experience of winter in Hokkaido! This church building was on a corner, and so especially exposed to the elements.

I learnt a useful tip that day from a church member. 'Use your hair dryer to warm the taps.'

It worked! But I still struggled with water frozen in the toilet, and ice on the inside of my windows, even with heaters on all day long. The smell of kerosene lingered on my hands as I constantly refilled the small portable stoves dotted around the rooms, or made the frequent car trip to the local petrol station to fill the half-dozen blue 18-litre polycans we used for refuelling. And woe betide the person who forgot to leave their car handbrake off in winter, and ended up somewhere with a car that wouldn't move. I was fortunate later to live in blocks of flats with large storage tanks for kerosene outside which were automatically topped up by large tankers. As none of the flats I rented were on the ground floor, and there were no lifts, I would have struggled to carry heavy cans of fuel up one or more flights of stairs.

My first Christmas in Wakaba Church

The considerable energy expended in the time-consuming and sometimes hazardous chores of winter turned out to be worth it all, as Christmas brought many opportunities for outreach. I wrote to my prayer partners that I showed slides, and played a cassette tape of the Christmas story on five occasions; I gave four Christmas talks to English classes, preached two Christmas sermons and spoke at two parties for my university students. Pressure on time increasingly forced me to speak in Japanese straight from English notes.

Overtired post-Christmas, I was overwhelmed with memories of the previous Christmas in Singapore. I was so depressed that I did not know what to do with myself. Six months later I was shaken to the core again when I heard that Hikaru was to be married. It was only 18 months since we'd parted, and it would be many years before I was able to share this part of my story with others. Mary had given me a poem on my first birthday in Hokkaido 10 months before. Each time I struggled with what might have been, these words challenged me afresh to live in the present with the God who is 'I am', not 'I was' or 'I will be'.

'I AM'

I was regretting the past
And fearing the future.
Suddenly my Lord was speaking:

'My name is 'I AM'.' He paused.
I waited. He continued
'When you live in the past
With its mistakes and regrets,
It is hard. I am not there,
My name is not 'I WAS'.

When you live in the future
With its problems and fears,
It is hard. I am not there.
My name is not I WILL BE.

When you live in this moment,
It is not hard. I am here.
My name is 'I AM'.

Helen Mallicoat [20]

---

[20] https://www.findagrave.com/memorial/11501005/helen-mallicoat   Accessed 28 February 2021.

11

主と共に歩みて

Songs of the Lord in a foreign land

> By the rivers of Babylon we sat and wept when we
> remembered Zion.
> There on the poplars we hung our harps, for there our
> captors asked us for songs, our tormentors demanded
> songs of joy; they said, 'Sing us one of the songs of Zion!'
> How can we sing the songs of the LORD while in a foreign
> land? (Psalm 137:1–4)

The heartfelt cry of the last verse was my own as I looked
back on my first year in church planting at Wakaba Church. I
introduced my April 1988 prayer letter with these words and
went on to share some of my thoughts. How could our church
planting team sing the songs of the Lord, here in the
community of Hanakawa? It was not a cry of despair and
homesickness as it was for the exiles in Babylon in the sixth
century BC, desperately longing to be back in Jerusalem
(Zion), but the longing to be a more effective communicator
of the gospel; the ache to see Jesus breaking through the
linguistic, cultural and religious barriers to transform lives
forever.

I was spurred on by words from the editorial of the Japan
Christian Quarterly Vol 54 No 1 Winter 1988:

> Japan is too important to be only an afterthought on the agenda . . . There may be no greater challenge for world missions in Japan today. God forbid that we be asleep at this time of God's opportunity . . . Active communicant church members in all Protestant and Roman Catholic Churches in Japan today amount to 0.5% of the population. Sunday worship attendance is half of that, and so only one out of 400 Japanese is in church on an average Sunday. The attendance at Sunday worship in a Japanese Protestant church averages 21 people. The last hundred years *(of mission outreach* – my italics) cannot be called a success story.

In 1988, 20 churches were being planted by OMF workers in Japan. The previous year only 13 people had been baptised overall. Despite concerted efforts in outreach, six churches including Wakaba had seen no baptisms at all. Membership in the 20 plants stood at 272, an average of 13–14 per church.

How did we 'sing the songs of the Lord' in Hanakawa? Here were some of the ways.

Leaflet drops

As December 1987 approached, we mobilised our entire membership of a dozen Christians to hand-deliver special Christmas event invitations to 2,500 homes. We were disappointed when only three newcomers turned up at our main Christmas service. But part of the aim was to get the church known, especially as it was just an ordinary house with a cross on top, tucked away in a back street. So we continued posting through letterboxes month by month in snow or heat—our constant prayer: 'Lord, please inspire people to read these leaflets, and not just ditch them in the bin.'

Several years were to pass before we caught a glimpse of an answer to those prayers. Wolfgang and Dorothea Langhans, our church planting team leaders had moved on, and *Pastor Ueno was leading the church. A mother and her adult daughter turned up to service one day.

'How did you find us?' we asked.

'We have been reading the church leaflets for years, and decided it was time to come along,' they replied.

Subsequently both mum and daughter were baptised. I'd always found it an effort to get out and put my assigned leaflets through letterboxes. Had it all been worth it? The answer was a definite 'yes', even if only two people met Jesus as a result. In addition, Akiko, a young lady responsible for leafletting the roads where this mum and daughter lived, was overjoyed to hear how God had used her and grew in faith.

Outreach through English

In the early days of OMF's work in Japan, church-based language classes were effective in meeting a felt need on the part of many Japanese to explore a world beyond their shores. Twenty-first century Japan is very different—awash with foreigners and secular language schools. Most schools now have at least one English teacher who is a native speaker, and language classes, in churches in cities in particular, do not attract the numbers they once did.

But we made the most of the opportunity still available in the late 1980s, and widely advertised hour-long classes for adults and children. We offered 50 minutes of English followed by 10 minutes in Japanese, introducing a Bible verse or some aspect of Christian faith. To our joy, some who came for English also discovered Christian faith for themselves. As far as I'm aware, none of my own students came to faith. But some studied the Bible for a while; others came to special events, and some remain close personal friends to this day. In one case, there was an unexpected indirect result from this planting of tiny seeds.

'Could you offer a language and cultural immersion experience for foreigners studying Japanese by inviting them to your home?' This was an item on a questionnaire I sent out in May 1993 to 70 former English class contacts. *Mrs

Moriyama was one who responded, and unburdened herself in the course of a phone conversation.

'I am at my wit's end,' she explained. 'My son, *Koichi, stopped going to school two years ago. He's 17 now. We've had professional counselling. I tried a Buddhist sect, and studied with Jehovah's Witnesses for a while. I'm desperate. Is there anything Wakaba Church can do for him?'

I visited the Moriyama family with Pastor Ueno, and Koichi started to come to church once a month to play table tennis, and hang out with the young pastor. After a year of relationship building, he felt secure enough to start attending the Sunday service. He understood little at first, but gradually realised the difference he saw in Christians was the outworking of God's love for them. He was baptised on 5 February 1995 — a journey that had started with his mum's brief contact with the church English class six years before.

'The snacks were great!'

Teaching children was, by any measure, my least favourite occupation! It was pandemonium at the end of each English class as 25 children raced for the small entrance, to scrabble and fight over the shoes they'd kicked off in a heap as they came in. But the noise of departure was music to my ears. My most exhausting class was over for another week!

We may never know if our ministry to countless children ever bore fruit or not. But in later years I came to realise how important reaching children was. I loved to ask Japanese 'How did you become a Christian?' or 'What was your first contact with church?' Frequently the answer would be 'I went to a church kindergarten' or 'I used to go to Sunday School. The snacks were great!'

It takes courage for many Japanese to enter a church unless they are personally invited. They may be afraid of family opposition. Once there, church culture, the language of the Bible and in prayer is alien and incomprehensible. They may have preconceived ideas that Christianity is a foreign religion. Nor can newcomers be anonymous in the mostly tiny churches of Japan. Positive childhood memories of church pave the way for an easier entry to church in later life.

Invited to sing

A lady in one of my English classes approached me. 'I sing in a local ladies' chorus. Would you like to join us?' she asked.

'I'd love to,' I replied.

I'd thoroughly enjoyed singing in my school and university choirs. But I'd also lost the natural friendship community I had as a teacher in Japan. Being single, I found it hard to make friends outside church. I persevered with the choir for a year, but struggled to get to know people; the financial cost was considerable, and the time commitment before a concert was more than I could give. I didn't enjoy the music; the conductor insisted I was a soprano when I'd always sung alto, and there was no way I was going to learn off by heart the words in Japanese of every song! All in all, it was a disappointing experience. I'm convinced that mission takes place most effectively as we build relationships. But in those early years in church planting, I found it difficult to penetrate the close-knit, group-focused Japanese society. Being naturally shy and still insecure in Japanese, the fault also lay to some extent with me.

My limited contact with the chorus did, however, lead to one opportunity. In December 1989 I called at the home of an acquaintance to invite her to a special Christmas event. Several chorus members were having a cup of tea, and they welcomed me to join them. I spotted the chance to get them along to church in a natural way.

'Would you consider singing some special items at our Christmas Day service?' I asked.

In the end eight ladies came. Not one was a Christian, but during rehearsals I answered various questions about

Christianity. They thoroughly enjoyed themselves, heard the message of Christmas and made our Christmas service that little bit extra special.

Special outreach

At Christmas we organised a dinner event in a local restaurant. The aim was to reach people who would not come to a church service, but would be willing to hear a Christmas message and enjoy fun and games in the neutral atmosphere of a restaurant. The first year over 50 came. They heard a Japanese pastor give a great message, and a Christian couple shared the story of their coming to faith. We were overwhelmed by the response the following year when 110 (75 adults) came. Fifteen adults and seven children were contacts from English classes, in contrast to the previous year when no one had shown interest.

We put much time and energy in one-off events like this. Some were 'successful', others extremely discouraging. In April 1988, I braved the curious stares and under-breath comments of scores of young teenagers to hand out 150 leaflets in front of the local junior high school. I also posted 60 invitations to young contacts inviting them to a special Saturday video meeting. Not a single person came! It was easy enough in the late eighties to get crowds of younger children, especially at Christmas with the appeal of presents and food! We welcomed 50 children to the Kids' Christmas in 1987, far more than the regular 15–20 who came to Sunday school. But it was very difficult to reach the 12- to 18-year-olds as I'd discovered in Nishiyamato. A handful attended English classes, but were not easy to teach, as attendance was often at the insistence of parents rather than from personal choice.

Prayer—'an act of evangelisation'

Prayer was a priority as we discussed how to sing the Lord's songs in Hanakawa. Indeed, it was the most important 'how' of all church planting activity. In April 1988, I wrote in a newsletter:

> I am challenged to make prayer a priority. It is not easy because it does not feel very 'productive'. I find the following quote helpful. 'Prayer must not only be a companion of evangelisation, it is essentially an act of evangelisation (James Kihara, quoted by Thomas, International Bulletin, October 1987, p. 169).

It was a great strength to pray together with OMF colleagues — at the weekly missionary prayer meeting and twice-yearly OMF Days of Prayer. I valued the weekly team meetings where prayer was a priority. I was challenged by Wolfgang Langhan's forward thinking as he encouraged us to pray consistently for the future marriages of several Christian working girls. We keenly felt the absence of young men in our fellowship, and we were well aware of the family and societal pressure on young women to marry in their early twenties. Some parents were even reluctant to allow their daughters to be baptised, for fear this decision would leave them on the shelf forever! On the other hand, experience had taught us that when a Christian married a non-Christian they often drifted from Christian faith.

Two of the Christian working girls met young men keen to marry them. Both girls explained they could not marry non-Christians and, in time, both lads believed. A third young lady married a Christian in another church some years later.

Prayer for families

Wolfgang had a burden for non-Christians in the families of our church members. He continually kept this prayer concern before the church and missionary team. I prayed more out of a sense of duty than with real faith, until it dawned on me that we were beginning to see answers to those prayers. In July 1989 Wakaba had 16 members, nine of whom were the sole Christian in their families. *Mrs Aoki, who since childhood had lived in terror of death due to the loss of a grandparent, was the first person to come to faith at Wakaba Church in 1981. Six years later, her parents who lived next door started to come more or less regularly. Sadly Dad, a retired teacher, never made a public confession of faith, and eventually stopped coming. Mum, on the other hand, came to every church event for years, but continued to sit on the fence. Would she ever step out in baptism? She kept us wondering and many praying, until the glorious day came at last, almost 24 years later, on 30 January 2011!

The *Sugiyama family

The Sugiyamas were another example of how faith spread through the family. Like Mrs Aoki's mum, Mrs Sugiyama's story shows that coming to faith for a Japanese can be a very long process, in which God uses a variety of experiences and people along the way. Mrs Sugiyama's first contact with Christianity was through attending a Catholic kindergarten as a child. Although she subsequently went to a Buddhist junior and senior high school in Hakodate, south Hokkaido, this early influence led her years later to choose a Catholic kindergarten for her eldest son and daughter.

The second contact came in 1975 when her third child was in primary school in Fukushima on Japan's main island. *Kaori had a playmate who invited her and older sister *Mariko to Sunday school. A Christian from the church became their piano teacher. This led to the starting of a monthly Bible study in Mrs Sugiyama's home which continued for over four years.

'I enjoyed the studies, but I just couldn't accept the miracles of Jesus,' said Mrs Sugiyama. 'I went to church once, but was thoroughly put off when everyone started speaking all at once in weird prayer languages called "tongues".'

When the family moved again to the northernmost part of the main island, the Christian piano teacher continued to send

Christian magazines, and encourage Mrs Sugiyama to go to church. During the 18 months in Aomori, she did go five or six times, and she began to think there might be a living God after all. The girls no longer went to Sunday school but, seeing her mum worrying about the elder brother's university entrance exams, Kaori announced, 'You don't need to worry. I've told God about the exams so everything will work out fine!'

In 1983, the Sugiyamas moved north yet again—this time to Hanakawa in Hokkaido—but there was no getting away from God here either. It was not long before Mrs Sugiyama met OMF church planter, Tony Schmidt, and bought a ticket for a Christian film being shown at the infant Wakaba Church in Tony and Pat's home. At the close of the film, she filled in a questionnaire expressing further interest, started to attend services and was baptised in 1985—a journey to faith that had taken 40-something years.

Despite her prayers as a teenager for her brother's exams, hairdresser daughter Kaori never showed any spiritual interest while I knew her. However, Mariko and I met regularly for Bible study on a weekday for three years up to 1990. I was never quite sure then where she stood in her relationship to Jesus, but was delighted to hear of her baptism five years later when I was in the UK. Working first in a department store, and later in a care home, meant Mariko rarely had a Sunday off. Church involvement was sporadic, but her two sons continued to attend church right through their teenage years with their grandmother. In this way, our prayers for Christian influence to permeate families were answered.

'One Year to Retirement!'

I splashed these words across the top of my April 1989 prayer letter. Readers might have thought, 'Only two years old in OMF, and you're planning to retire?' No, this was the missionary team at Wakaba preparing to retire from leadership, and hand the running of the church over to a Japanese pastor.

Steps to independence

I recorded the steps taken towards independence so far:

Oct 1980	Church started in the home of OMF workers Tony and Pat Schmidt
Jun 1981	Average attendance at Sunday service of four
April 1982	Church moved to rented accommodation
Jun 1987	House and land purchased
April 1989	Membership of 16 (14 active); average attendance around 20 Japanese.

Our aim was for Japanese leadership and financial independence from OMF in April 1990.

Our four specific goals were:

1. To find God's person for the job
2. To pay off the £12,500 loan on the building as the church would now need to pay a pastor's salary.
3. To increase membership to 25, particularly praying for men—there was only one man with leadership potential.
4. To train church members for Japanese leadership.

Calling a pastor was an awesome responsibility but, by October 1989, the person we felt to be God's choice had accepted the offer. The financial goal was not reached by the time of his arrival in April 1990, but everything was paid off by the end of that year. Numbers also did not increase as much as we prayed for but, with the help of our Japanese advisor pastor from a neighbouring church, the membership was prepared for transition as well as it could have been. In March 1991 there were 20 members, and the pastor and his wife were able to move out of the church to nearby accommodation.

There were many setbacks and discouragements in church planting, but what a privilege it was to see a church, that started with one missionary couple and zero Japanese Christians, grow in 10 years to the point where it was able to transition to Japanese leadership and independence. The next 30 years were by no means plain sailing. But at the end of 2020 it had a membership of 41 and average Sunday attendance of 38 adults. In 2018 the average Sunday attendance across Hokkaido's 361 churches stood at 32.4. These comparative statistics suggest that Wakaba Church continued to live up to its name 'Young Leaf Church', and is still growing fresh green leaves.

Nothing sums up its story better than the words of Psalm 118:23: 'The LORD has done this, and it is marvellous in our eyes!'

12

主と共に歩みて

University teaching

It was noisy and difficult to make ourselves heard. I sat at a table in the university cafeteria with a handful of students who'd responded to an invitation to join me to study the Bible in English during the lunchbreak. It was April 1987 soon after the start of the university year, and my new job was teaching English part-time at Hokusei University. Many in my classes were training to be English teachers. They were keen for more opportunities to converse with a native speaker, even when it meant studying the Bible. Hokusei University was founded by Protestant missionaries; there were regular chapel times, and I had complete freedom to invite students to read the Bible with me. My only regret was that, as a part-time teacher, I had no room on campus to call my own. I was not to know that if I'd had a room, I would have missed what was to be a very significant friendship over many years.

The student was not in any of my four classes. Clutching a tray of food, she came up to the table and, rather rudely I thought, interrupted our Bible study.

Over the surrounding din, she addressed me in good English. 'I haven't seen you around before. Are you a new teacher? What are you doing?'

Inwardly annoyed at the interruption I replied. 'We're studying the Bible.'

'Can I join you?'

'Why yes, of course,' I replied, ashamed of my instinctive negative reaction.

It turned out that she was a fourth-year student and, in a few months' time, would go on a year's exchange to a college in Iowa, USA. Satoko had nominally Christian parents, had been to Sunday school as a child and had considerable knowledge of Christianity. She struggled with the question of whether she could be a Christian and a Japanese at the same time. When we read Romans 5:10, which describes those without faith as enemies of God[21], she exclaimed indignantly, 'I'm not a Christian, but I'm not an enemy of God!' The year in the States could be crucial in her spiritual journey. In July, little knowing that right close to me in Sapporo was someone who could help me much better, I wrote to the OMF US representative geographically closest to Iowa, 'I have a student interested in Christianity who is going to Buena Vista University in Storm Lake City, Iowa, for a year in August. Do you know any churches or individuals you could put her in touch with?'

An amazing God-incidence

A few weeks later, Alan and Elaine Mitchell, an OMF couple, approached me at a meeting in Sapporo. 'We have the letter you sent to the US about your student!'

'How on earth did you get hold of that?' I asked in great surprise as I couldn't imagine any possible connection. It transpired that Elaine's mum lived in Storm Lake City! The

---

[21] 'For if, while we were God's enemies, we were reconciled to him through the death of his Son, how much more, having been reconciled, shall we be saved through his life!' (Romans 5:10).

OMF representative knew this, and so had sent my letter all the way back to Sapporo to the Mitchells.

'I also have a good supporting church in Storm Lake. We can put Satoko in touch,' Elaine explained.

Elaine wrote to the pastor, met Satoko before she left Sapporo and gave her a letter to deliver to the church. Was this all just an amazing coincidence? No, it was a precious God-incidence orchestrated by the God who had lovingly gone ahead to prepare a place for her in Storm Lake where she would be gently nurtured into a personal relationship with Jesus.

Building relationships

'I had a wonderful time on Tuesday. It was my first time to be invited to an "Open House." I heard your story about yourself. I thought God's will, which led you to Japan, was so powerful and mysterious. Your story was very interesting.' These encouraging words were from one of my Hokusei students who attended an 'Open House' at Wakaba Church in September 1987.

I invited 70 students, and was thrilled that 23 accepted the invitation to come on one of two afternoons for fun and games in English, slides of England, tea and cookies and a brief talk. Ten of the 23 came another day to learn how to bake cakes. None of them showed any particular spiritual interest. After telling them how I became a Christian, one commented I'd been very serious as a student — the implication being 'We're not!' My aim was to build relationships, praying that seeds would be sown in some hearts. That year, in December, I hosted two Christmas parties for the same students. They enjoyed themselves so much I couldn't get them to go home! More importantly they heard a clear message about the true meaning of Christmas.

'I feel so empty'

*Hajime, a second-year student, was one of the five who responded to the initial invitation to English Bible study. I arranged to meet up with him for a brief half hour once a week on his own, as he wasn't free at the same time as the others. This was providential as Hajime was spiritually at a very different stage from the rest. He'd been baptised as a teenager in an OMF-related church, but had since drifted right away.

'What took you to church initially?' I asked.

'I was so impressed by Jesus' teaching in the Sermon on the Mount that I wanted to know more,' he said.

Now a deep-seated emptiness and absence of joy had caused him to search again for spiritual reality. I longed to see his life touched and transformed by the peace and joy of Christ's presence. But it did not happen while I was meeting with him.

'When I hear you talk about the lordship of Christ, I feel I will lose my freedom. That's one reason I stopped going to church,' he explained.

I had sporadic contact for some years before losing touch. When he moved to another city to teach, I introduced him to a church there, but legitimate school responsibilities every Sunday would have made it very difficult to attend even had he wanted to.

*Keita

'During the summer vacation I began to think it would be nice to be able to believe,' the student said.

I could hardly believe my ears. Keita had faithfully come to English Bible study for four months before the summer, but insisted he was only interested in English. However, the shocking and totally unexpected death of a close student friend had shaken him to the core. He accepted several

Christian books, and came to church on and off for a couple of years.

Apart from Satoko, I only had passing contact with the students above. God alone knows what they are doing now, and the state of their hearts towards him. But, looking back, I thank God for the many opportunities he gave me in the short space of eight months. By so doing he was also gently reassuring me that I WAS in the right place.

I taught at Hokusei for one academic year before reluctantly deciding to commit to church work full-time. However, I did have the opportunity to teach at another university from 1989–90, and again for one term in 1992 when I filled in for OMF colleagues who were back in their home countries, spending time with family, supporting churches and prayer-partners.

Hokkaido University

In November 1988 I asked my prayer partners to pray about the possibility of a teaching job starting in October 1989. OMF worker Hilda Wigg was an experienced teacher who taught English part-time at Hokkaido University. She and her co-worker invited their students to an extra-curricular English Bible study on campus. Then, as the next step, to come round to their home on a Wednesday night. Over the years, many became Christians. Hilda was due to be away for a year from autumn 1989. Would I take over her job, and keep it open for her while she was away? I was gaining experience in church planting, and feeling more anchored. This university was much nearer than the previous one. I felt it right to say 'yes' but, seven months later, I'd still not heard the result of my application.

Hilda was told, 'We'll make a decision at our meeting on 23 May.' But the 23rd came and went. We heard nothing. Did that mean the verdict was 'no'? A week passed.

Hilda went to enquire. 'Oh, did you want to know the outcome?' said the Japanese professor, as if surprised.

The meeting had been deferred until 8 June. This time Hilda got a phone call straight away. Another blow. The meeting had been held, but no decision reached. Did they have someone else in mind? The next meeting was scheduled for 27 June.

Somewhere in the middle of all this, a copy of the current OMF UK *East Asia Billions* magazine came into my hands. I opened it up to the prayer diary inset, and there staring up at me was my own photo alongside Hilda's, and the request to pray that I would get her job at Hokkaido University. Unbelievably, the date of that prayer request was 26 June, the day before the scheduled meeting. My heart leapt when I saw this perfect timing. There was no way the compiler of the prayer diary could have possibly known that the 27th was a significant date in regards to this request. We ourselves had only known two weeks before. But the Lord knew. I was immensely encouraged to know that many people in the UK would be praying specifically about the appointment, just before the decision was to be made. A small matter perhaps, but to me a touch of assurance from the Lord that the decision made would be the right one, and a reminder once again that when he puts his sheep out, he goes before them.

I got the job.

My last stint as a university teacher was one term from April to July 1993. When offered the job in November 1992, my first instinct was to turn it down. I had my hands full with the Japanese Language Centre and part-time involvement at Wakaba. However, outreach to students was very difficult without a legitimate reason for being on campus. OMF worker, Nancy White, wanted to work with students in her second four-year term in Japan, but was currently in Seattle, US, and not available to teach until October 1993. Would the university agree to a job split between the two of us — myself for the first term and Nancy thereafter? Humanly speaking it was unlikely. They hadn't met Nancy; they might turn her down on the grounds of inadequate qualifications; and there was the disadvantage of a changeover of teacher mid-year. This time we did not have to wait long for an answer. They must have been desperate because, on 14 December, we got confirmation of the job-share. One more instance of God preparing the way and allowing me to fill in for those four months to hold open the door to student ministry for Nancy.

13

主と共に歩みて

Change of direction

Our new Wakaba Church building was dedicated on 12 July 1987. I had retreated wearily upstairs after the last person had gone when there came a knock on the front door. It opened, and a voice called out, *'Gomen Kudasai'* ('May I come in?') Up my narrow stairs came a young lady in her twenties who lived round the corner. Sitting at my desk I could see the back of her house. *Saori had started attending church out of the blue, three or four weeks before but, in the bustle of moving, no one had had time to get to know her.

Her request took me by surprise. 'I'm getting married on 22 November in a downtown hotel. I want a 'Christian' ceremony led by a white foreigner, but the hotel doesn't have anyone available. Can Wakaba Church provide someone?'

The church-planting team gave this request much thought and prayer. As neither bride nor groom were Christians, and their plans were already made, team leader Wolfgang agreed to perform the ceremony in the hotel chapel, while I played the organ.

'Christian only for a moment'

This is how one article summed up the attitude of an increasing number of young Japanese choosing to have a Christian-style wedding in a hotel chapel.[22]

In 1982, 90% of couples had traditional Shinto wedding ceremonies. In 2011 two-thirds chose chapel weddings. This trend had nothing to do with religion, but reflected the appeal of the trappings of a Western style wedding — notably a Western priest and white wedding dress. Hence the saying: Japanese are born Shinto, married Christian, and die Buddhist.

Saori was planning for her wedding long before the fashion for church weddings reached its peak. Nevertheless, the thought was in our minds — would Saori be 'a Christian only for a moment?' Having got her heart's desire, would she stop coming to church? No, having opted for a 'Christian' wedding she had decided she had better find out what Christianity was all about.

'I would love that,' she said eagerly when I invited her to study the Bible with me. As we met weekly from July through to November, I discovered Saori was thirsty for knowledge, and an avid reader who bought seven books on her first trip to the Christian bookshop downtown! We talked in depth about serious matters, but she was also a lot of fun. Her favourite snack with a cup of tea was not a cake or biscuit, but a tomato! She kept me stocked up with home-grown ones from her parents' garden all that summer.

In September, I took Saori to a concert at a neighbouring church. The two gospel singers had been professionals in the secular world before becoming Christians, and had a powerful testimony. Saori was thrilled to win a book written

---

[22] Heading borrowed from an article entitled 'Japanese Church Weddings: Christian Only for a Moment' https://jpninfo.com/21021 Accessed June 23rd 2020.

by one of the singers, and indicated a desire to believe by putting up her hand at the end. I was not sure she fully understood what it meant to follow Jesus, but she was well on the way.

Her fiancé was working in Yokohama near Tokyo. It was not until August that we had a chance to meet him briefly. It seemed the couple had never discussed religion. He showed no spiritual interest, and there was no further opportunity to meet him again before the November wedding. But Saori gave her first tearful testimony when we said farewell to her at church the week before the wedding. Her parents were appreciative, and came to Christmas events that December.

We introduced Saori to a church in Yokohama, and she went on her first Sunday in their new home. She was lonely during the daytime without a job and a husband working long hours. She hoped to make friends at church. By May 1988, she was certain she wanted to be baptised. 'My husband has consented, but I am not going to tell either of our parents until afterwards, as I am afraid they would forbid it. Will you baptise me at Wakaba Church?' she asked.

We agreed on condition that she did baptism preparation with the pastor of her new church and became a member there rather than with us. We borrowed a neighbouring church with a baptistry for the 7th August baptism, the first in nearly two years for Wakaba.

The opportunity to walk with Saori in her spiritual journey, from first contact through to baptism, was a very special privilege and an unusual experience. I met many in later years who showed some degree of spiritual interest. I started Bible study with some, but more often than not their interest dwindled away. We worked hard for meagre results. But within three months of my starting ministry with Wakaba church, God had brought Saori with a prepared heart across my path and, in the remarkably short time of 14 months, she was baptised!

Finding new spiritual wings

After the first Bible study with Saori, I wrote 'I feel as though God is confirming yet again the rightness of me being in church work.' In my journal I quoted a book by Ian Barclay, *He is everything to me: An exposition of Psalm 23*. The quote referred to Deuteronomy 32:11, which speaks of God's care for his people being like that of the eagle that tips its young out of the nest to help them learn to fly, but is underneath to catch them, and carry them if needed.

The author commented, 'Where eagles dare, they learn to fly. So often, the sufferings and adversities of life are the proddings of God. If only we would dare to take the plunge, maybe we would find that we could use our spiritual wings' (Barclay, 1972 p. 53).

God had tipped me out of my nest. I had not chosen to leave it. At times, I felt I was dropping through a gaping void towards a fatal impact with the ground. But God was hovering protectively around me and beneath me, to prevent that freefall from ending in disaster. 'Perhaps I am finding new spiritual wings,' I wrote in my journal.

With such thoughts in my mind, I reluctantly decided not to renew my contract at Hokusei University for a second year. It was a hard decision. I could see the great potential in student ministry, in many ways more fruitful than church planting. But Hokusei university was an hour and a half's drive away. By October, I had concluded that the tension of balancing two diverse ministries was too much. It was right, I felt, to give my time fully to working with the church team as we moved towards independence. I would have to exercise those new spiritual wings with less of a framework for my days and be ready to take more initiative.

In 1990, I was due for a year in the UK reconnecting with family, supporting churches and supporters after four years with OMF. Wakaba would be independent by then. Where was God leading me in my next four-year term?

In the early months of 1989, I struggled considerably with this issue, but eventually surrendered. 'OK, God, I'm willing to continue in church ministry full-time if that is what you want me to do.' I also told Tony, our OMF Hokkaido leader, my decision. At much the same time, I began to help the OMF Japanese Language Centre Superintendent develop language tools for missionaries in the two-year language programme.

I surrendered my will to God's, not knowing that he was about to give me the desire of my heart.[23]

---

[23] 'Take delight in the Lord, and he will give you the desires of your heart' (Psalm 37:4).

A change of direction

A single phone call in April 1989 brought an exciting new prospect before my eyes.

'Miriam, can you come and meet Field Council today or tomorrow?' said Tony, the OMF Hokkaido leader.

The leadership Council for OMF Japan had just started three days of meetings. I was puzzled. 'Whatever did they want to talk to me about? It was too early to make decisions about my next designation.'

At the meeting the next day the Field Director made a startling suggestion: 'We're wondering if you would be interested in taking on the job of supervising the Japanese language school.'

Had I heard correctly? Such a responsible position so soon? Inwardly, my heart leapt with excitement. But, apparently, I showed no sign of this outwardly as they probed into my reaction to the idea.

'You had us puzzled as you didn't seem very keen on the idea!' Tony said later.

Unconsciously I had dampened my enthusiasm for fear of hurt and disappointment, if Council decided in the end that I wasn't the right person for the job.

The job involved school administration, hiring and supervising Japanese staff, finding and setting up homes for new missionaries, orientating them to life in Japan and countless other practical things. I wasn't sure I could cope with all that. Council deliberated for several weeks then came up with the idea of creating a new role for me of 'Language Advisor'. I would work with Melville and Salome Szto from Singapore, who would supervise the school overall and deal with practical matters. I would focus on improving the Japanese language and cultural training, given to both new mission workers and those already out in full-time ministry. I was thrilled to bits. This was a job that fitted me like a glove. Everything I had learnt about teaching English as a Foreign

Language was readily transferable to teaching Japanese as a Foreign Language. I started in January 1990, and continued in this role until spring 2011 — a total of 21 years except for home assignments.

'So God, was THIS the reason you led me into OMF?' I asked. 'I'm very grateful, but couldn't you have done it in a less painful way?'

14

主と共に歩みて

My life as Language Advisor

My new workplace was unique. It was fluid, fascinating, frustrating and fulfilling. The study programme for career missionaries was two years full-time but with one-to-one classes and no term system, there were constant comings and goings. Coping with multiple nationalities, abilities and learning styles was fascinating, but frustrating. Advising adult missionary learners on learning Japanese was far more challenging and significant than facing a class of 50 Japanese teenage girls or a university class of 70 students as I had up to now! I was investing in the futures of these missionaries as church planters or student workers. Good language ability would play a key role in their survival in ministry long term.

Supervising Japanese teaching staff was a nerve-racking experience from beginning to end! The teachers had certain ways of doing things. My attempts to introduce teacher-training sessions along with curriculum changes often met with initial opposition. Used as the teachers were to the language mistakes of beginners, they would not allow me, the Japanese Language Advisor, to get away with blunders — especially in the use of the complicated respect language (honorifics) that was so vital when I asked them to do something for me. Every time I opened my mouth, I felt I was under scrutiny!

What is JLCC?

This was how two co-workers described JLCC (the Japanese Language and Cultural Centre) in October 2008:

At the moment JLCC is: 10 teachers
1 Language Advisor
21 Students
2 LOT (Language and Orientation Training) Coordinators

JLCC is also: 1 Singaporean
1 Mexican
2 Germans
4 Australians
3 Americans
1 Swiss
1 Canadian
10 Japanese
9 Brits
2 New Zealanders

In addition, JLCC is: 35–45 language classes a day
About 160 classes a week
Over 7,500 classes a year

JLCC is: - new workers experiencing countless 'Why they do it that way?' moments
- new workers in the monotonous grind of reviewing yet another list of vocabulary

- new workers feeling about 2 inches tall because they have lost fulfilling jobs and the ability to communicate
- new workers trying to help their children cope, when they themselves are not
- new workers making mistakes & slowly, slowly, gaining confidence in speaking Japanese.

All this is JLCC

It surprises me now to be reminded that there was only one Asian OMF worker in October 2008. In the 1990s we bulged at the seams with Korean OMF workers while, in the millennium, the numbers from other parts of Asia grew substantially. These included second-generation Chinese whose parents had emigrated to Western countries. In 21 years at JLCC, I myself helped run the school alongside colleagues of various nations — Singapore, Indonesia, South Africa, Britain and Germany. Adjustments were needed each time on both sides.

Help!

Dealing with practical emergencies was not part of my job description, but some of my most vivid memories are of crises that arose when students lacked the necessary language skills to cope alone.

The phone would ring, 'I'm at the police station with a taxi driver who ran into my car downtown. I need you to talk to the police!'

My heart sank. This was the kind of situation I dreaded. I gripped the receiver with sweaty hands as I waited for a member of the police to come on the line. Somehow, I stumbled through the required responses to his questions and, to my great relief, did not have to rush downtown to extricate our new worker from the clutches of the police!

Another phone call was just as panicky. 'My kerosene stove is blazing away although I've turned it off. I'm terrified it's going to blow up!'

Fire brigade duly contacted, I leapt on my bicycle (it would be the day I had left my car at home!), and pedalled as hard as I could to the student's home. Thankfully, by the time I arrived windswept and panting, the firemen were there, and the fire had died down of its own accord. But it had been a close call—the metal on the front of the stove was buckled, and the wall nearby too hot to touch.

It wasn't just students who had emergencies. A desperate call came from one of our Japanese staff one day. She was at the nearby department store where she had gone for lunch. Would I pick her up? She was having a panic attack, and couldn't stop shaking. I dropped everything, and rushed over.

'Shall I take you home?' I asked.

'May I go to your flat?' she replied. Gone was my afternoon as I made tea and lent a listening ear.

Tensions and joys

During my years at JLCC, colleagues and I faced a number of crises related to salaries, conditions of employment and the teaching abilities of Japanese staff. It was far from easy being foreign employers in Japanese culture and, at times, conflict robbed me of a night's sleep.

But it was not all tension. It was an unexpected joy to welcome Satoko as a member of our Japanese teaching staff from January 1990 until July 1992. Remember her? The student I met in the cafeteria at Hokusei University in April 1987? She returned to Sapporo from her year abroad in Iowa wanting to be baptised. I introduced her to Sapporo International Church in downtown Sapporo, a new church plant under OMF leadership, with only two members and no young people. It was very different from her experience of church in the US. When the missionary leadership changed, she struggled again to adjust[24]. Nevertheless, I was thrilled to attend her baptism on 5 November 1989, and to meet her parents.

A few months later, a distraught Satoko knocked on my office door. One look at her face told me something was very wrong.

'My Mum's been diagnosed with an incurable disease,' she said tearfully. 'Would you visit her in hospital?'

Shocked at the news, I was concerned for Satoko. 'How would this young Christian woman cope? Would I be able to establish a rapport with Masako whom I had only met once?'

I discovered that both Masako and her husband had been baptised 30 years earlier, but had drifted away from church. In hospital, Masako started to read the Bible again — a chapter a day — and I prayed with her on each visit.

'I feel like Noah must have felt,' said Masako one day. 'Shut up in the dark, cramped conditions of the ark for 150 days, rain constantly falling and waters continuously rising. When is God going to release me from my pain?'

We talked about Noah's faith — how, despite all evidence to the contrary, he believed God, and was rewarded with a safe homecoming.

Masako was never vocal about her beliefs, but she did have an impact on those caring for her.

One nurse told Satoko, 'Patients as ill as your mum usually scream in pain, and say the most awful things. Your mum never did. Her Christian faith must have sustained her.'

---

[24] Japanese who become Christians overseas often find it difficult to find a real 'spiritual home' back in Japan, either because of the differences in church culture, or because there simply isn't a church nearby. Many drift away, but OMF International among many other agencies now works hard to prepare newly Christian 'returnees', both practically and spiritually, for the situations they will find themselves in back home.

A Japanese funeral

Masako died on 22 November 1990. I spent a lot of time at the hospital in the final week thanks to the miracle of special handwritten permits, issued by the senior doctor in charge of the unit where Masako was. These enabled Marianne Murphy, an OMF colleague and myself to

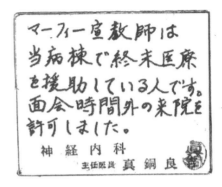

come and go at any time of day or night, regardless of visiting hours. My colleague's permit clearly stated she was a Christian missionary giving support to a terminally ill patient.

The days following Masako's death were exhausting for me, let alone for Satoko and her dad. I arrived home at 3:00 a.m. on 23 November, and the wake was on the evening of 24th followed by the funeral at 10:00 a.m. on the next day, as is the usual custom. Family members struggled not just with their grief, but also with objections from superstitious tenants of the building where the church rented rooms. They were reluctant to permit the coffin to rest in the church overnight.

Satoko had asked me to speak briefly at both services. My script had been long prepared and corrected, but as I stood up to speak, I heard Satoko quietly weeping in the front row. It was all I could do to get through, without breaking down myself.

Satoko invited me to the crematorium after the funeral (a privilege usually reserved only for close family). Lunch, during the long wait as the body was cremated, was a typical boxed *obento* — fish, meat, assorted vegetables, pickles and rice, each tastefully displayed in their individual compartments in the box and eaten with disposable chopsticks. We sat on the tatami floor to eat at low tables in a traditional-style Japanese room, with sliding paper doors onto the corridor where we had tidily left our shoes facing outwards ready for us to slip our feet into later.

At last, we were called back to the room with the oven in it. On a trolley in the centre, rested the recognisable bones of Masako's body among the ashes. I held back as the assistant encouraged the family to use pairs of long chopsticks, and lift the bones up and place them in an urn. He identified the bones as they did so. Satoko urged me to join them. I had found the first experience of doing this quite shocking. There was no running away from the dreadful reality of physical death, and I was sure I never could follow this custom with a member of my own family. By now, however, it was an immense privilege to share in this poignant moment.

Back at the church, it was time for refreshments and sharing memories. Like his wife, Satoko's dad was a baptised, but lapsed, Christian. He assured me he believed. Indeed, the death of his wife brought him right back to the Lord, and he became a faithful, committed member of his daughter's church for many years to come.

How privileged I was in my role at JLCC to minister, not only to my mission family, but also to our Japanese teachers too.

A five-year apprenticeship

An enjoyable part of my job was introducing new missionaries to Japanese life and culture, by organising trips to primary schools, to tea ceremonies, to a calligraphy class and to homes to learn Japanese cooking. I shall never forget an evening with the chef of a sushi restaurant — observing, experimenting and, of course, eating this most famous of Japanese dishes. Smiling Mr Oba in a spotless white chef's uniform, popped out of the kitchen to welcome us, and then promptly set to work preparing the vinegar and other seasonings to mix into the cooked sushi rice. Next, he prepared the raw fish. We were mesmerised at the swift deftness with which he sliced tuna, scallops, squid, octopus and shrimp into bite-size pieces for adorning the balls of vinegared rice.

It all looked so easy—at least until it was our turn to have a go at making the simplest kind of sushi—makizushi or wrapped sushi. These were rolls of sushi rice wrapped in *nori* (crisp, paper-thin pieces of edible, toasted seaweed), with a stick of cucumber in the centre. My feeble efforts at cutting my roll into slices produced six rounds of uneven width far from the aesthetic standards of Japanese cuisine! The cucumber was slightly off centre, and the edges were ragged where I had struggled to cut cleanly through the *nori*. We realised that the mouth-watering sushi, so skilfully and beautifully produced before our wondering eyes, was the result of years of patient training.

I asked 30-year-old Mr Oba the inevitable question. 'How long did it take you to train as a sushi chef?'

'About 10 years. I've been in this job for 15 now, but the first five years I was only allowed to wash dishes and clean up.' (Wow! Some commitment there, I thought.)

'Do you go to market to buy the fish yourself?' asked someone else.

'Yes, at 5:00 a.m. every morning,'

'When does the restaurant close?'

'About 1:00 a.m.'

'Gracious, when do you sleep then?'

'I don't very much!'

Our evening with Mr Oba gave us a glimpse into the world of hard apprenticeships, and the sheer effort that lies behind so much of traditional Japanese culture. I knew I wouldn't be prepared to spend five years washing dishes and cleaning floors before I could even start training to be a chef.

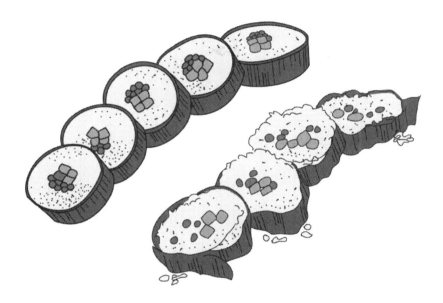

'And yet,' I mused, 'isn't that the very attitude that Jesus looks for in me and my fellow missionaries?' We needed the humility and willingness to stick at mundane tasks, whether it was myself 'wasting' time on making changes in the school timetables, or missionary students plodding away at learning never-ending lists of new words. We all wanted to jump straight into the more glorious and glamorous task for which we had come to Japan — introducing Jesus, our best friend, to Japanese people. We wanted to be bearing fruit for Jesus now! Learning patience and perseverance was not easy, but essential for long-term mission workers in the spiritually resistant climate of Japan.

Of course, it was all worth it. Despite the frustrations of some parts of my job as language advisor, I loved seeing OMF workers grow in both their language ability and in their relationship with God. Their many testimonies moved and encouraged me. I was stretched to the uttermost in my role as

Language Advisor. It was tough and frustrating at times, but I thrived in this job and was fulfilled.

15

主と共に歩みて

The language S.H.I.P.

> I attempted to learn Japanese by reading a book called *Japanese at a Glance* on the plane from San Francisco to Tokyo. This is not the method recommended by experts. The method recommended by experts is to be born as a Japanese baby and raised by a Japanese family in Japan.
>
> Dave Barry, American journalist[25]

The above tongue-in-cheek quote reflects the fact that Japanese ranks with Arabic, Chinese and Korean as one of the four most difficult languages in the world. I knew that only too well, not just from personal experience, but from my years working with different nationalities studying Japanese. Pronunciation was easy for a Westerner, but very challenging for Chinese and Korean speakers. The Koreans, however, were naturals in using the honorific language that tried the patience of Westerners, who simply could not accept the need for these important social niceties.

---

[25] https://www.chicagotribune.com/news/ct-xpm-1992-09-27-9203270940-story.html   Accessed 24 February 2021.

Chinese speakers had a head start with learning the 2,400 characters in daily use. In Japanese many of these can be read in at least two different ways depending on the context, doubling the volume of learning. The simple character for 木 ('tree'), for example, is pronounced *ki* when it stands alone, but *moku* when combined with the character 材, *sai*, as in the word for 'timber' or 木材 *mokuzai*.

With up to 15 strokes in one Kanji character, it was not always easy to figure out stroke order. One frustrated Japanese learner said, 'I wore glasses for the first time when I was 11. Suddenly the world was beautiful, and I could see the details of leaves and twigs on trees. I only wish I had glasses to do the same for learning Kanji, so I could see them clearly at a glance!'

Others described language learning as, 'Trying to drink from a fire hydrant, and being overwhelmed by the sheer volume of water directed at you,' or 'An endless stream of bafflement that makes you feel like a child,' and 'Words are like rubber balls, slippery and bouncy, moving so fast you can only grasp one or two at any one go. By the time you have your dictionary out, another 20 have bounded past!'

New workers with no prior knowledge of Japanese, studied for two years, full-time five days a week, with no term system, and only the four weeks holiday per annum allowed to all OMF workers. It was customary to have three, 50-minute periods a day, one-to-one with a Japanese teacher — two for conversation, and one for reading and writing. We suggested three hours of self-study a day for review and homework.

There was no room for pride in learning a foreign language. You had to be willing to be laughed at, to make mistakes, to be largely dependent on others and to feel as helpless as a new-born baby. You were constantly at a disadvantage through being unable to pick up linguistic and cultural cues well enough to grasp what was going on. You were stripped of your security, status and everything that gave you significance. You often felt emotionally and physically drained.

Remarks like the following were common: 'Can I reduce my class hours? My head is jammed full, and the more I learn the less I remember. I thought things would be better after a holiday, but nothing's changed.'

'I really enjoyed studying the first year, and felt I was making good progress, but suddenly all my enthusiasm and impetus has vanished.'

Such comments were typical of what I called 'the second-year blues'.

During a few months back in the UK in 1999, I used the letters of the word SHIP to describe some of the qualities required in cross-cultural learning.[26] I explained to church groups that crossing cultures was like sailing out of a safe, well-known harbour to an uncertain future on unknown seas, with the threat of inevitable storms.

---

[26] This idea came from an article written in November 1998 by Simon and Megumi Crittle from Australia who were at that time with OMF in Japan.

However, as someone pointed out, 'A ship in a harbour is safe, but that is not what ships are built for.' Likewise, Christians are not called to stay home in comfort.

S: 'Self-discipline' and 'Strategies'

Life was very different from what people had been used to, as the following comments showed:

'In the States, I had my own office in the church, and kept my work and home life separate. Now four of us live in a tiny three-roomed apartment, and the children expect me to play with them when I'm at home. Sometimes I go and sit in my car to pray or study, because there is nowhere else.'

'I have classes all morning, then the children come home from kindergarten, and demand all my attention, while my husband is out for his afternoon classes. It's 9:00 p.m. before the children are settled in bed, and I can give a thought to language study. By the end of the week, I'm too worn out to take anything in.'

'When I was pastoring a church, my days were varied and interesting. Now I do the same thing day after day, and I find it so tedious.'

As Language Advisor, I helped individuals come up with strategies for dealing with the particular problems they faced: how to carve out quality time for study, to ward off boredom or find places to study in peace and quiet. In orientation sessions, they learnt about Japanese culture and religion, but also discussed topics such as setting priorities, managing stress, attitudes and expectations, learner styles, memory techniques, the key role of listening and how to create the social contexts to practise the language they were learning.

H: 'Humility' and 'Humour'

Humility accepts that one's preferred way of doing something is not necessarily the right way or the only way.

This was true for both the students and for me as Language Advisor.

'Everything about Japan was wonderful until I got here,' said *Kat. 'Now I feel angry about everything. Japanese culture doesn't allow you to praise your own child. But if I do as they do and put my child down, isn't that being untruthful?' (Was this an instance where a missionary mum did not need to bend 100% towards adopting Japanese culture?)

'I'm depressed every time I go to church,' said *Judy. 'I don't understand much, but it's the same every week. So formal and rigid, it feels like the church is tied up in chains and there's no freedom or joy.'

I immediately identified with Judy's frustration as I had initially felt it too. Sometimes it took years for Westerners like us to realise that formality and freedom were not mutually exclusive. Indeed, formality could in itself be freeing. Many Japanese felt more comfortable with formality and, in being comfortable, they were also free.

'Why doesn't the pastor invite me for a meal?' said a short-term worker teaching English at a Japanese church. 'Why does he insist on me wearing a skirt to teach?'

To this young lady the absence of an invitation to the pastor's home implied she was not fully welcomed or accepted. If she was more comfortable in trousers why shouldn't she wear them? It was all too easy, if unconscious, for cross-cultural workers to interpret the behaviour of Japanese people through the lens of their home culture. It was important to ask themselves questions. In the young lady's case, examples might have been 'Why might the pastor not invite me to his house? Is this a common way of showing hospitality in Japanese culture? If not, in what other ways do Japanese people express hospitality? Am I conveying a different message to my students when I wear trousers as opposed to a skirt? Does one mode of dress show more respect than the other? Could wearing a skirt make my message about Jesus more acceptable to my students?'

As far as possible, our aim as God's ambassadors in Japan was to follow the example of the apostle Paul, who declared, 'I have become all things to all people so that by all possible means I might save some' (1 Corinthians 9:22).

It was important, especially with mistakes, to be able to laugh at oneself, as did *Arthur who joked, 'I have a signs and wonders ministry. I do the signing, and the Japanese do the wondering!'

One couple invited their Japanese teacher for a meal. In her best Japanese, the wife apologised, 'Dinner won't be ready for 30 years!' Meaning '30 minutes', of course.

*Sun Hee from Korea startled her listeners one day. 'I'm going to have an arranged marriage!' The word she used was *o-miai*. What she meant to say was 'I'm going to visit someone in hospital (*o-mimai*).' The difference one consonant can make!

*Margaret told the story of the lost *booshi* or 'hat':

> My friend gave me a lovely, pink, fluffy hat before leaving home. I really like it — it is unusual, warm, and good for the snow . . . but I'm sure everyone now knows me as the pink fluffy headed foreigner. I had taken it off in a department store, and was carrying it in my hand. Somehow, when I went to pay for my purchase, I realised I had been all round the store and now had no hat. But did I know the word? I didn't know either 'hat' or 'lost'. 'Forgot' I knew, and 'pink' (*pinku* – easy enough) I knew . . . and I had a matching scarf . . . So I embarked on the long project of explaining . . .
>
> Somewhere in this shop . . . I forgot . . . pink thing . . . like this (pointing to scarf), but this sort of thing' (pulling imaginary hat on).' Personified PUZZLEMENT stares back at me, trying to work it out. I try again.
>
> 'You want to buy a hat?' she asks, trying to help, but getting nowhere.

'No . . . '(I repeat the riddle with more emphasis.) Eventually she realises it is a lost item, and hands me to someone else. I start all over again, and the new assistant brings me round the back corridors to the office. On the way I'm beginning to feel SO stupid that I still can't say, 'I've lost my hat.'

Just before we reach the office, she says, 'English is OK.' I really laughed. Why didn't she tell me earlier? And there it was . . . the pink fluffy *booshi* sitting in front of a sober faced security man who probably thought I was as empty-headed as anyone who wears a pink hat should be.

'Even monkeys fall from trees,' says a Japanese proverb. In other words, even experienced people make mistakes. I spoke at Wakaba Church one Sunday from Acts 9. In verse 15, God tells Ananias that he has chosen Saul to carry his name to the nations. Without giving my choice of word a thought, I made my point about the precious responsibility we have, as Christians, to be bearers or carriers of God's Word. I used the word *hakobiya* for 'carrier'.

Afterwards church member and JLCC teacher, Mrs Tamura, came up to me. 'I'm telling you this just in case you preach on this passage at another church, she said. 'The word *hakobiya* is used in Japanese only for drug smugglers! You should use the word *hakobite*.'

Whoops! In this case, I'm sure my audience got the meaning, and maybe even remembered the point better for my mistake! But I wonder how many times I put my foot in it without anyone telling me.

I: 'In Christ' and 'Incarnation'

Isobel Kuhn (1901–57) was a missionary to the Lisu tribe in Yunnan (China) and Northern Thailand, whose books I devoured as a teenager. She was shocked to be told, 'When you get to China, all the scum of your nature will rise to the top.' She wrote 'I was totally unprepared for the revolt of the flesh that was waiting for me on China's shores' (Kuhn, 1959, p. 40). This was true of us too at JLCC. OMF missionaries in language study needed to be sure they were in Japan through God's clear leading, and secure in their identity 'in Christ'. Occasionally there were those who began to doubt, and even returned home. Others grew as they heard God speak to them through his Word.

*Amy struggled with learning Japanese:

> It wasn't just learning the language that was difficult; it was also difficult coping with some of my not so pretty emotions that rose to the surface. I wanted to be good at Japanese, and I struggled with being jealous of others who were better at it than I was! One morning, six months after arriving in Sapporo, this struggle weighed heavily on me. Then I read Hebrews 4:15: 'For we do not have a high priest who is unable to feel sympathy for our weaknesses, but we have one who has been tempted in every way, just as we are — yet he did not sin.' Jesus can sympathise with my weaknesses and struggles — all of them — even jealousy of others' ability with Japanese! That dreadful morning became a turning point.

*Rachel was about to finish language study, and venture into ministry:

> I'm really scared. I won't have compassionate listeners anymore, and I have nightmares about getting up to speak, and forgetting every word of Japanese I have. But God spoke to me through his promise to Moses in Exodus 4:12: 'Now go; I will help you speak and will teach you what to say.' I've written this in large letters on a card above my desk. God will help me when I don't know what verb or tense to use.

*Tom looking back on his two years of language study said:

> Life felt pretty good when I was working as a lawyer and on the leadership team of my church. The hardest thing in

coming to Japan was that our two sons (one and three years old) struggled. My wife and I expected to struggle, but assumed the kids would adapt easily. For two to three months whenever our elder boy saw a Japanese child, he would go up and scream in his face. He stubbornly resisted entering any Japanese environment. I could not get through to him, and so I became angry with God. I had to learn that they are not my kids, but God's. Thankfully the older one is settled now and fluent in Japanese.

Asked what language learning is, you might answer 'an intellectual activity'. But it actually arouses all sorts of emotions, as we have seen. Language learning is, in fact, 'a risky form of incarnation in which one becomes vulnerable, and subject to criticism and correction, and to damage to one's self-image. It's safer, and easier, and much, much more comfortable to remain discarnate.'[27] Only by fixing our eyes on Jesus and his incarnation — his putting aside of his divinity and being born into our world as a human being — could we find the grace to become incarnate in Japanese culture.

> Consider what it meant for the Son of God to come to earth from heaven, to live among sinful people and then to die on a cross. Talk about culture shock! He came from the harmonies of heaven into the discords of earth, from holiness and glory to sinfulness and shame, taking upon himself a body in which he would experience the normal trials of humanity: weariness, hunger, thirst, physical and emotional suffering, and, eventually death. (Wiersbe, 1997, p. 31)

---

[27] Stevick, Earl Wilson. 'Let the words, too, become flesh' p. 14. Originally a paper delivered as a plenary address at a conference in Colorado Springs in October, 1998, it can now be found at https://docplayer.net/44022544-Let-the-words-too-become-flesh-1.html

P: 'Perseverance', 'Patience' and 'Practice'

Language and culture learning requires 'the wisdom of Solomon, the patience of Job and the years of Methuselah,' is a saying often tossed around in mission circles.

Our goal as OMF in Japan was for each member to reach the highest possible standard of Japanese language and cultural ability. But some always struggled with language. Occasionally a teacher would comment perceptively, 'X' will never be a fluent Japanese speaker, but he has the makings of a good mission worker.' Godly character, love for God and love for people could do much to overcome limitations of language as people persevered.

I once heard the story of a Chinese Malaysian educated in English and involved in prison ministry. Usually, his messages were translated into Chinese, but one day the interpreter was not there, and he stumbled through in his own broken Chinese. At the end, he asked the congregation how it had been. One reply was startling, but comforting:

'It is better to hear the Word of God in broken Chinese than to have no Word of God and a broken heart.'

Knowing that in Japan, too, even broken language could heal broken hearts gave me, and many colleagues, the patience to persevere.

16

主と共に歩みて

JLCC on the move

Boom! Whatever was that almighty crashing noise? I rushed out to discover that a mountain of frozen snow had slid off the roof and deposited itself right in front of the language school entrance. A student had just gone through the door. A second later, he could have been badly injured. While hazards like that were part and parcel of daily life in a Hokkaido winter, our rickety building was falling apart at the seams.

The possibility of a new building had been discussed for years. By the spring of 1992, it began to look more than a pipe dream. Far to the south, a dear Christian lady living in Ichikawa city, Chiba prefecture, had gifted a large plot of land with a church and several other buildings on it, to OMF. The total value was an incredible two million pounds sterling and the church, with a congregation of around 40, was a good size for Japan. OMF Japan was about to move its main headquarters from remote Sapporo to this far more convenient location only 20 minutes by express train from Tokyo station. A parcel of the gifted land would be sold to fund the building of a guest home and office block there in Ichikawa and, if there was sufficient money left over, a new language school in Sapporo. We began to dream: No more frozen toilets, draughty classrooms or matchbox-sized offices, and conversations frequently began with 'When we have our new JLCC, we'll have this or do that', as we let our imagination run away with us.

Our landlord had died several months previously, and his son wanted to sell. Could we buy and rebuild on the same site? Melville Szto investigated, but no, we were in a residential area with building restrictions that would not permit the kind of facilities we had in mind.

Things were at a standstill when, in May 1992, Melville went on what was intended to be a simple courtesy visit to the new landlord. The latter dropped a bombshell!

'Unless you buy, I need you out of the building by the end of August. I have to sell urgently in order to pay inheritance tax.'

The move of the main headquarters to the Tokyo area was on for July. This would free up an upstairs apartment and a couple of offices in the Sapporo Headquarters building we called 'the Area Centre'. But there was no way we could fit in six offices, eight classrooms however tiny, a teachers' room, a library and meeting room. Financially, we were in no position to rent or buy elsewhere. And anyway, where would the additional £300,000 for rebuilding come from? We set aside extra time for prayer every Tuesday lunchtime.

The hastily convened 'Move' committee met first on 12 June 1992. The dark, dingy room in the Area Centre matched our gloomy thoughts. Melville opened the meeting, 'I have no idea where to start or even what we should be aiming for. OMF International Headquarters in Singapore has no spare funds so we do not have the option to rebuild on this office site.'

The problems seemed insurmountable, but God had put a former architect from the UK into our OMF family. David Highwood had previously designed the Area Centre, two holiday houses and a school for OMF children in different parts of Hokkaido. David was heading up a church plant several hours drive away, but wrote a letter that miraculously arrived just as our meeting began. As we read, our gloom brightened into purpose and excitement.

> We don't have to completely rebuild. As an interim solution, how about knocking down the side with the garage and replacing it with a classroom block? We can plan for a permanent purpose-built centre in five years' time.

Subsequent calculations showed that the cost of the 'add-on' would be roughly equivalent to five years' rent at our current language centre. OMF owned the Area Centre land and building, and it was rent and mortgage free. As we stayed not just five but almost twelve years in the Area Centre, we ended up saving a huge amount in rent that would have been needed, had we moved elsewhere.

By early July, we had architect's plans, and the go ahead from OMF International Headquarters in Singapore to spend eight million yen (£34,000). But the arrival of the first estimate a few days later was a major blow. The anticipated cost of reconstruction was more than double what we had to spend. Back we went on our knees as we requested more estimates. To our astonishment, Christian architect, Mr Takahashi, offered to waive his fees and came up with an estimate that we could afford. However, time was not on our side. Could we find building contractors willing to take on such a small job, at very short notice? WE couldn't, but God could and did!

This was not our only request for God to do the impossible. The end of August and the deadline for leaving our present building was fast approaching. We pleaded with God, 'Please let the landlord allow us a month's extension to the end of September.' To our great relief the landlord agreed and, on a baking hot August day, in lieu of Melville who was away, I signed an imposing legal document committing us to vacate our rental premises by the end of September. Work on the

Area Centre began on 28 August and, although the interior was not completely finished, we moved to our new premises on 30 September 1992.

The five-year plan unrealised

Five years in JLCC Number Two stretched out to seven, eight, ten and eventually eleven long years. By 2002 our makeshift building showed major signs of wear and tear, and was potentially dangerous. Wooden window frames warped in the extremes of cold and heat, and we struggled to replace them after removing them to clean. Large numbers of new workers in the late 1990s, and changes of OMF personnel, made it difficult to pursue a dedicated search for a permanent home. But this began in earnest with the advent of a new millennium and a new language school director, Dale Viljoen, from South Africa.

I constantly asked my prayer partners to join us in prayer. In May 2002, I wrote:

> We are looking to buy, or build something by this coming winter. Despite much searching we have not found the right place to buy. If we rebuild on our present site, we would have to find temporary accommodation for four months, and our hearts sink at the thought!

Weeks stretched into months, and the plea remained, 'Do pray on!' At the same time, I was asking prayer for a different new 'home', but that is a story for a later chapter.

The 'Red Building'

Talk of 'the Red Building' began to make its way around OMF circles. Not far from our then JLCC and Area Centre, OMF workers Mike and Rowena McGinty had discovered a three-storey office building for sale, with red tiles on its outside walls. It was ideal for our purpose, and a three-minute walk from an underground station giving fast access to the city centre, just 10 minutes' ride away.

There was just one problem — it was way above our budget. But God is the God of the impossible. Months went by, and I was in the UK when the startling news came.

'The Red Building's still not sold yet and, you won't believe it, but the price has almost halved! The company has gone bankrupt and must need funds urgently. We think we should go for it.'

OMF Singapore gave the green light, and Dale made the first down payment on 28 April 2003. Major alterations and renovations took a further year, but a chaotic moving day dawned at last in April 2004 followed by a joy-filled dedication service on Sunday 31 May 2004. The red building was now officially renamed the OMF Hokkaido Centre.

As 100 Japanese brothers and sisters poured into the three-storey building we heard exclamations of amazement from every side. 'It's so beautiful!', 'What a contrast to the old building!', 'I never imagined it would be so big!' Even, 'Can this be OMF? It's so high tech!'

On entering, all eyes were immediately drawn to the stunning illuminated sculpture of a dandelion head in the entrance hall, representing the theme of mission in Japan and beyond.

'Dandelions? But they are just weeds!' might be your instinctive reaction. But just think how prolific they are in seed-bearing and reproduction. Round the corner to the left, was the first flight of stairs. Painted dandelion heads scattering seeds ascended the wall towards a hand-carved relief map of Japan.

Some aspects of my job as Language Advisor were tedious. Hours spent on the daily timetables felt like a dreadful waste of time. My attempts to help and encourage missionary learners sometimes backfired. But as I trotted up and down the stairs in this new JLCC building, the dandelion seeds reminded me that God could take even the most mundane task done for him, and make it fruitful.

'Bear fruit with patience'

The main part of JLCC was on the first floor. As you walked into the bright student lounge your eye was captivated by an unusual design on the wall. Vividly coloured squares represented the many nationalities, church backgrounds, gifts and personalities that OMF members brought to Japan. But with a number of Japanese language teachers added to the mix, there was great potential for friction, particularly in the first two years of language and culture acquisition. This was a time when emotions boiled over, and insecurities surfaced all too easily as newcomers were stripped of their usual sources of support and self-fulfilment. The words beside the rainbow-coloured squares — 'Bear fruit with patience' (Luke 8:15, NKJV) — were pregnant with challenge.

Seven small classrooms spreading out from the lounge continued the theme of 'bearing fruit', each brightly painted in a different hue. Most rooms were designed for one-to-one classes, but a couple catered for larger groups.

Join me in your imagination on the second flight of stairs in the Hokkaido Centre. If you could read Japanese you would gasp in wonder as your eyes took in the characters (called *Kanji)* for 'man or person' (人 *hito*), marching up the wall towards a map of South East Asia. Each character was transparent, and stood out in relief from the wall. Each was filled with a different kind of seeds or bean. Your eyes would alight on the words 'Go yourself, send others'.

The different beans in each 'man' Kanji character reminded us that countless individuals and families are needed to fulfil the call of global mission. At the time of writing, OMF has over a hundred career mission workers in Japan, and tens of short-termers. But 'people' (*hito*) are still constantly needed for all sorts of other ministries — short term, long term, young or not so young, reaching out to Japanese or helping support the missionary team, managers for guest homes, English teachers, office assistants, musicians, photographers and computer geeks, to name just a few. Name a gift or skill, and it can be put to use somewhere!

One *hito* character marching up the Hokkaido Centre wall was filled with soya beans, another with kidney beans, others with pumpkin or sunflower seeds. All different sizes, shapes and colours, but all contributing to the team. 'Go yourself, send others.' This was, and still is, a vision in which any Christian can play a vital part.[28]

Wolfgang Langhans, by then OMF Japan Field Director, issued an unforgettable challenge on that memorable May dedication day:

> If you come back in a year's time, or two years' time, or even ten, and look at the seeds and beans in the 'person/*hito*' characters on the wall, they will be just the same as they are now. Why? Because they have not been taken out and planted. How are YOU getting on with the task of planting the precious seeds of God's Word entrusted to us?

---

[28] For example, through the 'Six Ways To Reach The World — Learn, Pray, God, Send, Welcome and Inspire.' Follow the link: https://omf.org/us/6-ways/ for a five-minute video explaining the Six Ways further.

For the next seven years much of my ministry revolved around the OMF Hokkaido Centre, its beautiful interior design a constant visual reminder of why I was there.

17

主と共に歩みて

Family in the UK

In the days before computers and mobile phones brought instant, 24-hour connectivity round the world, an international phone call was both costly and rare. If unscheduled, it was likely to signal the kind of emergency that anyone with loved ones on the far side of the world dreaded. Mine came in the middle of a committee meeting in a colleague's home, from the Area Centre.

'Miriam, we have just received a call from the OMF UK office. Your dad is in hospital, and your mum wants you to contact her immediately.'

My parents had retired from South East London to Gloucester in 1985. Now it was 1989. My father had fallen off his bicycle on the way to church one September morning, and doctors had diagnosed a stroke. I hastily booked a flight home, arriving in time to celebrate his 82nd birthday in hospital with an oversweet, thickly-iced shop-bought cake, as neither my mother nor I were in a fit state to consider home-baking. Dad struggled to get his words out, and he puzzled his doctors by not responding to treatment as expected. They investigated further only to discover he had an inoperable brain tumour.

The prognosis was six months, although that turned out to be an over-optimistic estimate. Meanwhile steroids had a remarkable effect temporarily, and he was able to come home. I was committed to a one-year teaching contract at Hokkaido University, and I'd already missed the first two weeks of classes. I could stay no longer, but my mother had limited mobility herself, and she depended a great deal on my father. We prayed hard about finding the practical support with cleaning and shopping that she would need until my planned return to the UK for a year in January 1991.

My mother was reluctant to ask for help from social services, so I advertised in the local newspaper, and asked for replies by letter. Wendy Rees sounded ideal. Unknown to me, she was churchwarden at Christ Church, Brunswick Square near Gloucester City Centre.

When I phoned, she took me completely by surprise. 'I know your dad. He was a great help with taking services and preaching when we were without a vicar.' My spirits soared at the prospect of having a trustworthy Christian to support my parents.

'What are you looking for in terms of hours?' Wendy asked.

'A couple of mornings a week,' I said.

She paused a moment before speaking. 'Oh, what a shame. I really need to work every day.'

Disappointed, I phoned the others who'd responded to the advert, and interviewed two or three. No one seemed the right fit. The days slipped by in indecision.

Then Wendy phoned again unexpectedly: 'I haven't been able to get your parents' need out of my mind. As I prayed, I felt God rebuking me. "You've only been thinking about how much money you could get with more work. What about serving me?" I will come twice a week to help.'

I nearly fell down the stairs in a headlong rush to share the news with my mum in the kitchen. I shouted out in my excitement, 'God answers prayer.'

'Of course, he does!' she replied.

Wendy became a close friend of my mum's as well as cleaner, shopper and personal assistant, and she went far beyond her brief in supporting my parents. She was just one of many good friends who, in their love and care for my parents, contributed to cross-cultural mission by enabling me to continue in Japan. I flew back to Sapporo with a heart full of gratitude to God for his generous provision.

'Jehovah Jireh' and 'Jehovah Shammah'

Three months later, in January 1990, the early morning temperature of -15°C in Sapporo proved to be too much for my ancient little car. Its refusal to start meant I was unable to get to church that Sunday morning. In the quiet of my living room, as the freezing cold kept people indoors and mountains of snow muffled the sound of traffic, I was overwhelmed by anxiety for my parents, especially my dad. I knew he was struggling with breathing. How was he getting on? Was my mum coping all right?

It was hard to be so far away and of no practical use to them. I'd been doing a study on the names of God. Two suddenly popped into my mind. Jehovah Jireh—'The Lord will provide' (Genesis 22:14) and Jehovah Shammah—'The Lord is there' (Ezekiel 48:35). The book I was reading explained that 'The Lord is there' could also be translated as 'The Lord is present' or 'The Lord is here'. God whispered to me reassuringly, 'Don't be anxious about your parents. I am there present with them providing all they need. I am also here with you now.' I was at peace again.

In this way, my heart was to a certain extent prepared for my mum's phone call on 22 February 1990, 'Dad's gone.' I did not even know that he'd been hospitalised two days earlier. Once again, I made the long journey back to Gloucester.

'I found this in the bag of belongings that were returned from the hospital. It's addressed to you, but never got posted,' my mum said on my arrival. She handed me a blue aerogramme letter dated 20 February. Dad's handwriting was shaky, and each line sloped off more at a diagonal, the further down the page they went. 'I'm back in the Gloucester Royal, Ward 20 again. Wendy drove Mum and myself by car this morning . . . The last two or three weeks have been pretty grim.'

But did he dwell on himself? No, he devoted a whole paragraph to his distress over the lack of biblical teaching at the church where he was assisting. 'The vicar has decreed that the length of Sunday sermons should be five minutes at 8:00 a.m., 12 at 10:00 a.m. and 12 at 6:30 p.m. But the 10:00 a.m. service is timed to last 70 minutes which equals 58 for ritual and 12 for the ministry of the Word.'

In closing, he assured me that friends were offering help. 'Mum is coping magnificently . . . thanks for all your prayers. Don't worry about me. I am in the Lord's good hands. Just longing for the opportunity to preach again. Much love, Dad.'

When I had time to reflect on Dad's last words, and his longing to his dying breath to share the wonder of God's word wherever he could, I knew the baton had been passed on to me. Dad would preach no longer, but I could. The love and passion for God's Word that shone out of his final words to me was his legacy. I determined to continue that legacy, and take whatever opportunities came my way to share God's Word.

The funeral took place on 1 March 1990, my 37th birthday. My Bible reading that day was Psalm 84. Time and again in future days, I came back to verses 5–7 in particular:

> Blessed are those whose strength is in you, whose hearts are set on pilgrimage. As they pass through the Valley of Baka they make it a place of springs; the autumn rains also cover it with pools. They go from strength to strength, till each appears before God in Zion.

I heard Psalm 84 read on at least two other, for me, very

significant occasions. One was at my farewell at St Philip and St James, Hucclecote, on 22 September 1996 as I returned to Japan after burnout. The other was at my mother's funeral on 1 February 2002. In neither case was I aware this Psalm would be read.

But each time I set my heart afresh to journey with God wherever he led, trusting that he would enable me to 'go from strength to strength' as I relied on him. Bereavement, the breakdown of my own health and set-backs in ministry were some of the dark valleys I would walk through. At times I battled to focus my thoughts on Jesus and to keep walking forward with him. I clung to the promise that as I did so, God would transform the Valley of Weeping (*Baka*) itself, and not just bring me through it. Dryness and desolation, suffering and sorrow would result in abundant refreshment and restoration both for myself and for others.

Home assignment 1991

Less than a year later, I was back in Gloucester for my first 12-month home assignment. Vital elements for this time were to build links with churches, prayer groups and individuals; to spend time with family; to receive spiritual input from conferences and study; and to rest! But, over all this, loomed the question of my mother's future.

I was prepared to stay back in the UK, but Mum was adamant. 'No, I don't want that. God has called you to Japan,' she insisted.

We began to visit residential homes. In most cases, our first impression was more than enough to put us off while one that might have been suitable had a waiting list of 400! We prayed together daily, 'Lord, show us the right place. We can't do this without you.' Then we discovered Guild House. From the moment we walked through the front door, we felt this was the place. Meals were provided, but residents could furnish their own rooms, and maintain a certain degree of independence. The decor was attractive, and the gardens were a delight. Mum's clergy widow pension added to her state pension was enough to cover costs. The manager, who turned out to be a Christian, understood my need to settle Mum before January 1992 and my return to Japan.

'How long is your waiting list?' I asked.

'We don't have one' was the surprising response. 'We will let you know when a room becomes vacant.'

I hated the uncertainty of this. The chances of a room in time looked slim, and our prayer changed. 'Lord, we would love to have a room in Guild House. With you, anything is possible. If it is your will, please open the door.'

It began to open in July. 'We have a room temporarily available in July. Would your mum like to come for a short stay?'

I leapt at the manager's offer as I was due to be away for several weeks. I would not have to worry about Mum having a fall with no one around. Mum was reluctant—it was emotionally hard to accept this first step towards giving up her independence. But, to her surprise, she really enjoyed herself! It was a great treat to be given a bath, and she found it easier to accept help from carers than a daughter. Of course, Guild House had the equipment we did not have at home.

Not long after this came another phone call. 'We have a room available from August. However, you will need to decide quickly if you want it.'

'I don't want to move while you are still here,' said Mum. 'You don't go for another five months yet.'

I could understand her reasoning, but I could see a problem: 'If we don't take the room now, there is no guarantee another will become vacant by the end of December.'

After lengthy discussion and further prayer, we came up with a compromise. We would take the room from August, and spend that month furnishing it. Mum would move in September, but come home regularly to stay while I was still around. Guild House couldn't have been more amenable to our desires, and all parties were satisfied.

Guild House was a wonderful home for my mother for the next 10 years until she left for her longed-for heavenly home. I continued ministry in Japan, assured that she was content and well cared for. Yet again, God had gone before.

18

主と共に歩みて

Burnout

So much is made of the iconic image of Mt. Fuji as a symbol of Japan that, back in 1977, a friend and I decided we must climb it, before I returned to the UK for further studies after my first two years in Japan. Mount Fuji is Japan's highest mountain at 3,776 metres — 2.7 times the size of Ben Nevis, the UK's highest mountain. Severe weather means it is only open to climbers for two months, in July and August.

One website warns of the challenges as follows:

> The ascent to the summit does not pose any major difficulties regarding climbing skills. Only at some points, the terrain is rather steep and rocky. Abundant signs along the trail warn the hikers of other minor problems such as sudden wind gusts and falling rocks. However, the main challenge of the climb is the fact that it is very strenuous, and the air gets notably thinner as you gain altitude.[29]

---

[29] 'Climbing Mount Fuji' https://www.japan-guide.com/e/e6901.html   Accessed 23 January 2020.

This website also recommends walking shoes with good protection for the ankles, and warm clothes for the sub-zero temperatures at the summit.

Back in August 1977, we climbed in blissful and youthful ignorance of these recommendations. After all, the base of Fuji was overwhelmingly hot and sticky, with the usual 35°C plus of summer in Japan. Surely ordinary shoes, a light sweater and anorak would be adequate? We opted for the tricky night-time climb with great expectations of the beautiful sunrise we would see.

Night was closing in as we set off at 6:00 p.m. from the trail's fifth station. (There were 10 stations in total.) Although we started at 2,300 metres up (well above the summit of Ben Nevis), the next four hours were gruelling, as I'd done nothing to train for this arduous challenge! Vast numbers of climbers on the rocky narrow trails meant having to queue at times. Being unable to go at my own pace was draining. Pitch darkness and a clammy mist were pierced only by the light of our torches, making it difficult to negotiate the rocky terrain. How thankful I was to reach a stone hut! We paid for a bunk bed, and stretched out for a while, although hopes of getting any sleep were dashed by constant comings and goings. At

3:30 a.m., we noisily slurped down a warming bowl of noodles. (It's considered impolite NOT to make a noise when eating noodles in Japan.) Then we tackled the final 90-minute climb.

Progress was hard-going and slow. Would we make it in time to see the sunrise? — the reason we'd chosen the arduous night climb. Would the heavy mist swirling around us clear or not? Expectations ran high but, alas, we reached the crater to find it still veiled in thick mist. It was transformed from black to grey to white as day dawned, but without one ray of sunshine. I was so disappointed. Five and a half hours hard toil, only to miss the sunrise. I shivered in my single sweater and light anorak until the sun eventually came out, and warmed me with its rays.

The descent was, if anything, more taxing than the ascent, and took three and a half hours. Thick clouds below us blocked what should have been spectacular views. We slipped and slithered on the volcanic scree, and small lumps of ash constantly found their way into my trainers. Blisters, bruises, scratches, aches and pains — you name it, we had them!

Despite missing the sunrise, I was immensely proud of my achievement. I had the summit stamp on a piece of paper to prove I'd made it to the top. Looking back, I can see how my experience was a metaphor for some painful experiences I was to go through in the mid-1990s.

Burnout

The back of the right side of my head felt as though it was encased in a tight and excruciatingly painful iron band. I did not know it then, back in September 1994, but this dreadful headache was to be a constant companion for a very long time indeed. I'd woken far too early that morning and, with time before the morning service, rode my bike to a local park. Arriving home, I collapsed in exhaustion on my futon on the tatami floor. Whatever was happening to me was terrifying. It was as though my body and emotions had completely packed up on me.

'This is burnout'[30], said OMF Japan Field Nurse and close friend, Mary Alexander.

The warning signs had been there for some time — increasingly disrupted sleep patterns, frequent headaches, irritability, anxiety and the fact that time off failed completely to restore physical and emotional energy. But I'd ignored the signs and continued to push myself to the limits. I arrogantly believed that burnout could never happen to me. Even when the crunch came, I naïvely assumed that a few weeks rest would get me on my feet again. Little did I know that I would be away from my beloved Japan for two years, unable to work, or even to be with people. As health failed to improve, I sank deeper into depression, which continued to a greater or lesser extent for nine years until, mercifully, in 2003 doctors eventually prescribed an anti-depressant that worked wonders.

Glimmers of light in the dark

Back in 1977, I wrote of my Fuji climb as follows:

'We couldn't see anything below us during the daytime but, during the night, there were times when the mist cleared and we had clear views right down to the foot of the mountain.'

---

[30] Here is one definition of burnout. 'Burnout is a state of emotional, physical and mental exhaustion caused by excessive and prolonged stress. It occurs when you feel overwhelmed, emotionally drained and unable to meet constant demands.' https://www.helpguide.org/articles/stress/burnout-prevention-and-recovery.htm   Accessed 23 January 2020.

The occasional glimmers of light that came during my time of burnout and depression, gave me hope that God was still there and that, one day, things might get better.

Two months into burnout I faced the long journey back to UK with increasing dread, despite the great comfort of having my friend, Mary, travel with me. I struggled to concentrate with my excruciating headache, but attempted to read a few sentences each day from Amy Carmichael's devotional book, *Rose from Briar*. Four days before flying, I read:

'See, I am sending an angel ahead of you to guard you along the way, and to bring you to the place I have prepared' (Exodus 23:20). It was a tiny glimmer of light in my darkness, and a reminder of the promise with which my journey to Japan had started — when he puts his sheep out, he goes before them.

The morning of our flight from Tokyo dawned. How would I get through the long journey without cracking up? I was utterly amazed to read:

'The angel came back a second time and touched him and said, "Get up and eat **for the journey is too much for you**"' (my emphasis)!

God's words spoken loud and clear to a depressed and despairing Elijah in 1 Kings 19:7 were also desperately needed heart-food, laced with a touch of humour for a fearful Miriam.

A Japanese flag

The next glimmer of light, in June 1995, was just as remarkable. During the preceding eight months in the UK, I'd learnt much about myself, and discovered helpful books on burnout and depression. Counselling confirmed that I was a very high introvert energised by time alone. It was not selfish to withdraw in order to give out. I learnt that three factors had accentuated my perfectionist tendencies: the model of a Christian minister inherited from my wonderful, but workaholic, father; working alongside some super-capable mission colleagues, and unconsciously trying to be like them; and living long-term in a culture which valued work above all else – and didn't know the meaning of 'rest'. Unconsciously I'd signed up to the idea that the ideal Christian worker is one totally dedicated to the work, at the cost of personal and family life. Many Bible talks I'd heard and given myself on sacrifice and total commitment fostered that belief.

I was learning what had led to my burnout, but health-wise I was descending deeper into depression. My return to Japan was postponed several times, and it was not until I was at last prescribed antidepressants in summer 1995 that sleep began to improve slightly.

In June, I attended a Friday morning service at Harnhill Centre of Christian healing in Gloucestershire. I could not cope with services where I knew people. Halfway through the service the leader said, 'I would like to share the following visual images and Bible verses we felt God gave us as we prayed earlier. Do come up for prayer later if you feel any of these apply to you.'

One of the images, 'a Japanese flag flying', flashed into my consciousness, and I heard no more as the tears began to flow. I went up to the chancel for prayer but, I was so choked up, I could barely get out the words, 'Japanese flag'.

Puzzled, one of the two with me asked, 'Do you have some connection with Japan?'

Somehow, I managed to explain, and she got very excited. She was the very person who'd had the picture of the flag! They prayed lovingly for me, and the lady said, 'I don't know what the flag means, but I do know that God wants to communicate with you. He knew you were coming today!'

Another glimmer of light in the darkness – the personal touch to reassure me that God WAS still there, even when I could not sense him.

For the rest of 1995 I continued to rest, and attend helpful courses and retreats. Towards the end of the year, I began to speak at small OMF gatherings or church groups. OMF leaders were encouraging me to return to Japan in 1996, so my prayer for the New Year was that God would confirm to me that this was right. I signed up to attend a *Wholeness Through Christ* prayer ministry course. The organisers suggested pooling transport with anyone living nearby. I didn't know the people on the list, but I phoned one couple not far away who kindly agreed to pick me up. Halfway to our destination, we stopped for a cuppa on the motorway, and began to share more about ourselves.

Suddenly, Christine exclaimed, 'I thought you looked familiar. You're the lady who came for prayer about the Japanese flag at Harnhill last summer, aren't you? And you won't believe this, but it was my first experience of being on the prayer ministry team. I was so encouraged by how God worked!'

We were doubly blessed to discover how much that episode had meant to each of us. David and Christine were to become precious friends and prayer partners.

New ways of hearing God speak

On 1 January, I'd recorded in my journal my New Year prayer for a confirmation of my return to Japan. How was God going to do that? Maybe, I thought, through one of the two verses that were foundations for my original call to Japan — John 10:4 or Jeremiah 29:10. But that seemed to be asking too much, so I didn't write my thoughts down then. Coincidence, however, was not an adequate explanation when God spoke through Jeremiah 29:10–14 seven times in the months of February and March! The variety of means he used — live talks, a testimony, a recorded sermon, a card through the post, a prayer letter — made it impossible to doubt that he was speaking.

Growing up, I was nurtured in a strongly word-based approach to spiritual life. Bible reading was paramount, and it is still the primary way I sense God speaking to me. But mental exhaustion had stolen from me much of my ability to concentrate. I began to learn that God also speaks in other ways.

The shorn sheep

In June 1996, I was walking beside a river, while attending a Christian conference in Wales. It was sheep-shearing time. My eyes fell on a shorn sheep. This ewe looked pitifully thin, very vulnerable and not at all healthy. But, on either side of this scraggy mother sheep, there were two woolly and bouncy lambs, butting at her flanks, latching on to her teats and sucking away for all they were worth.

I walked on, but the image had burnt itself into my mind. 'Lord, is there something you want to teach me? What does this picture mean?' It was God's gentle, but oh so powerful, message of encouragement: 'Miriam, I know just how vulnerable and weak you feel, but I want you to go back to Japan, because I am going to give you ones and twos to nourish spiritually. You don't need to minister to lots of people. You feel utterly shorn of your abilities, your gifts and your health but, like that shorn mother ewe, you can still feed one or two of my lambs.'

Later that month I called to see some new friends I'd met through *Wholeness Through Christ*. After a time of sharing and prayer, Kenneth said to me, 'When you get home, have a look at Judges 6:14. I don't know what it says but God has given me this reference for you.'

I later opened my Bible and heard God speak powerfully to me — just as he did to Gideon who faced the mammoth task of defeating the enemy Midianites invading Israelite territory. 'Go in the strength you have and save Israel out of Midian's hand. Am I not sending you?'

God was reiterating the lesson of the shorn sheep. 'Miriam, the strength you have is enough. Go in that strength, and forget about not having the strength you think you need. You won't be able to do what you did before, but that's okay.'

Many people prayed for me and affirmed me. 'I'd rather have half a Miriam than none,' said my OMF colleague Hilda Wigg at the Japanese Language and Cultural Centre in Sapporo. I booked my flight to Japan for September 1996, almost two years since the day of my sudden and total physical and emotional collapse.

In 2016 at my last OMF Japan Field Conference before retirement, I shared my burnout experience with around 150 colleagues, and concluded with some of the lessons this bitter trial had taught me: 'Most of you will be far more aware of your personality type than I was before burnout; you have been taught how to care for yourselves amidst the challenges of working in multicultural teams in a foreign culture. You should know yourselves better than I ever did. If you don't, act now, and don't wait to learn the hard way.'

John Calvin said, '. . . true and sound wisdom consists of two parts: the knowledge of God and of ourselves.'[31]

I continued, 'I do believe knowing God and knowing ourselves is the key. Knowing God means accepting the way he has made me. That I am precious to him as I am. That I am not like 'X' or 'Y' missionary. Consciously or unconsciously, we have a tendency to compare ourselves with others. Part of the reason for my burnout was my own tendency to perfectionism. But I also compared myself with others who were far more extrovert than myself — who had a far greater capacity, who were high-energy people, who in biblical terms

---

[31] https://gracequotes.org/author-quote/john-calvin/ Accessed 24 February 2021.

had five talents to my two. Don't use your personality and your gifting as an excuse not to do things you should, but DO know yourself and watch out for warning signs.'

19

主と共に歩みて

Treasures of darkness

It was 31 October 1996, and I'd been back in Hokkaido just three weeks. I was staying at a Japanese Youth Hostel for an OMF regional conference, along with 50 or so OMF colleagues. I was overwhelmed by the mountain of catching up, after two years absence from my job as Language Advisor. The missionary student body had completely changed over the two years, and the international mix was greater than ever with British, Hong Kong Chinese, American Koreans, Australian Koreans, Japanese Americans, Americans and Australians, all with individual language needs, some in families with children. Numbers were the highest I'd yet experienced. Physically, JLCC was bursting at the seams, despite renting an apartment nearby with three extra rooms. Space no longer stretched to an office for myself, and I had to adjust to yet another new co-worker for the first six months. There were also new Japanese teachers to get to know, and I was upset over changes made to the curriculum I'd worked so hard on before burnout. I struggled to let go of the possessiveness I felt towards 'my work'.

'She did what she could'

Desperate to be alone on this conference afternoon, I climbed the steep hill beside the deep caldera lake into the woods above, where I sat on a bench and wept. My OMF family were welcoming and supportive, but the battle was coming to terms with the person I was now — no longer the capable person I'd been before September 1994. Ongoing insomnia, anxiety, depression and the headache that was triggered by the slightest stress, limited my capacity for work for a long time to come. The issues I'd been through in the UK, I had to work through again now I was in Japan. How, in practice, to be a human 'being', and not a human 'doing' as someone helpfully put it.

The Bible passage for communion that evening was Mark 14:1–9. The day of crucifixion is near. Mary anoints Jesus' feet with expensive perfume, only to be harshly rebuked by indignant onlookers for throwing money away. What a slap in the face for Mary. But Jesus acknowledges it as a beautiful act, preparing him for death and burial. What poured balm into my sad heart that night, however, were his next words: 'She did what she could.'

Actually, what Mary did had a massive impact that was to be immortalised in world history. But this is how the Holy Spirit interpreted these words to my heart that evening: 'Miriam, "she did what she could" doesn't mean that she didn't do enough, that she could have done more. You just do what you can, and stop worrying that it is not enough. Others may write it off as not being enough, but it is enough for me, even when it is a lot less than you did before.'

I carefully marked date and place beside this verse in my Bible, and was to remind myself of these words time and again, in years to come.

Coping strategies

People expressed surprise that I'd returned to the same job that had brought about my crisis in mental health. The job of Language Advisor itself, however, fitted me like a glove. What didn't was exposing my introvert self to constant interruptions all day long at the language centre. Restricting the number of days and hours spent at JLCC each week was the first step to survival. Working partly at home, and visiting language students in their homes, gave me more control than being constantly in school.

Even so, my journals reveal that, between spring and winter 1997, I was seriously considering leaving the job, and returning to church ministry. I tried to focus on getting through a week at a time, and not to add to the pressure by wondering how I was going to cope for a four-year term. In the end, all agreed I should only do two and a half years, followed by a six-month UK home assignment. Medication and a review of my job description helped, along with a decline in the numbers of new arrivals to JLCC.

My workload eased, but the constant ebb and flow of new arrivals along with uncertainties over arrival dates, created other stresses. During my 21 years as Language Advisor, the viability of JLCC's existence hung in the balance more than once. In 1999, one of the hardest decisions OMF leadership ever made was to lay off six of our eight full-time Japanese staff. In future years, we took on part-time staff as and when we needed them, although it was not always easy to find suitable candidates who did not need the financial security of permanent contracts.

Treasures of darkness

In April 1997, I came across *Treasures of Darkness* by Jane Grayshon. Former midwife and vicar's wife living with chronic pain, Jane wove her book around God's promise in

Isaiah 45:3: 'I will give you the treasures of darkness' NIVUK 1984).

God, himself is in our darkness, she explained. Exodus 20:21, for example, tells us that Moses met God there. I too began to find treasures in the darkness of depression. Reflecting on a chat with me, one OMF friend encouraged me with a card and the words 'I felt like I saw more of the real Miriam than I've ever seen before.'

I received another card from a colleague I barely knew, in June 1997: 'Now there is a certain quality about you — gentleness, vulnerability — that makes you even more approachable. '

I was utterly amazed by these comments. I had no sense at all of these kind of changes in myself. Any change I felt was negative not positive. But, as months passed, I realised that my vulnerability drew me closer to Japanese Christians who were struggling. I now identified with the anxious, depressed, hurt and physically unwell. I realised that, previously, I'd unconsciously looked down on those with a more limited capacity than me. Japanese Christians expected missionaries to be super-saints. They opened up when they discovered that I, at least, was not.

I grieved that I had to turn down invitations to share a testimony or preach, knowing it would be too stressful. It was nearly a year after returning to Japan before I preached in Japanese for the first time in three years. The audience was my small, but responsive, loving and much-loved Japanese family at Wakaba Church. I'd prayed hard that God would use it to speak to someone, and my nervousness vanished once I started.

A member of the congregation encouraged me when he said afterwards, 'My great niece in Kyoto has leukaemia. I am going to write her a letter straightaway, and tell her all about today's sermon.'

Wakaba Church was pastor-less as our first Japanese pastor had resigned in 1995, and started a new independent church not far away. OMF workers stepped in to give part-time oversight until the induction of the next pastor in April 1998. I was glad to return to a church family that knew me, and appreciated the little I could contribute when energy permitted.

A whistle and the power of God

The phone rang on Christmas Day 1996. Church member and friend, Mrs Tamura, poured out her sad news. Son Akihisa was in hospital with a suspected brain tumour. In his early twenties, he'd been out skiing with student friends, when his arm went strangely numb. On 26 December, Mum, Dad and younger sister, came by on their way home from hospital.

'They confirmed the tumour, and say it is inoperable', they told me. Although they knew Akihisa was not interested in spiritual things, still they asked, 'Please will you tell him about Jesus, and pray with him?'

I did within the next few days, although on subsequent occasions, Akihisa refused my offer of prayer. As his condition deteriorated, however, he became more open and, a year later through his sister's gentle testimony, he put his trust in God. OMF worker Mike McGinty, who'd stepped in to help Wakaba Church for 18 months, told the story of what happened next:

> It was almost midnight on Thursday 26 March 1997, as I joined the Tamura family in their living room with Akihisa sitting in a wheelchair in the middle. The once outgoing and confident college student was nowhere to be seen. It was almost as if a stranger had taken his place. A stranger with expressionless features, a bloated face, legs and arms that sat limply in place, and voice that was all but silenced. Yet despite the signs of physical decay . . . we were all filled with anticipation as other signs of life seemed to be flickering.
>
> Mrs Tamura knelt directly in front of Akihisa, where he could hazily see her through the one eye not yet paralysed, and spoke as only a mother can speak to her child. 'Aki, when you are alone and want to call me, what do you do?' Aki's one good arm fumbled for the whistle tied round his neck, put it to his mouth and feebly blew on it. 'That's great, Aki. But there are many things that I can't do for you that only Jesus can. Do you want him to help you?' Time almost seemed to stand still as Aki nodded his head affirmatively. 'Can you show us how you would ask Jesus for help?' Again, he fumbled for the whistle, and this time blew three definitive blasts, which surely sounded better to our ears than any song a choir of angels could ever produce.

Mike continued, 'Never have I witnessed death and life so vividly contrasted with each other as I did that night, or on the following Sunday evening when a small group of us gathered . . . to witness not only Akihisa's baptism, but the power and mercy of God. Akihisa was especially alert that evening, reaffirming his earlier profession with a distinct "Amen", humming "What a friend we have in Jesus" and joining in communion. It was a celebration of life with friends and family . . . even with death looming on the immediate horizon.'

Akihisa passed into the presence of Jesus on 2 June 1998. I wept, as did so many, but thanked God for the privilege of walking with this family in prayer and presence during the 18 months of his illness. God gave us all many treasures in that particular darkness of disease and death—above all, we saw the mighty power of God at work to save, as churches and prayer partners around the world stood with the Tamura family in prayer for Akihisa.

'I wish I weren't a Christian!'

Another church member, with whom I shared some of the treasures of darkness, was *Ayumi. In September 1997, I visited her in hospital. Eighteen months previously, she'd had an operation for breast cancer, and returned to church after a long absence. Her husband had recently become a Christian, but their three sons aged 19, 17 and 15 had no interest. Now the cancer had spread to her liver and pelvis.

Suddenly Ayumi came out with, 'I wish I wasn't a Christian'.

Somewhat taken aback, I said, 'Can you explain a bit more?'

'Well, Christians have eternal life!'

A puzzled 'Yeees? ' from me.

'I hate the idea of living for ever as the person I am now. I can't stand myself. I'd rather be reborn. And I don't want a Christian funeral.'

Shocked, I wondered how we'd failed to convey to this lady the true meaning of eternal life. Perhaps she'd never had a real encounter with God? She leapt at the opportunity to do Bible study, and so we met regularly until I left Sapporo for six months in the UK in spring 1999. She shared deeply as we got to know each other. We looked up passages about life after death, discussed healing, and why she might consider a Christian funeral. Ayumi grew spiritually. One treasure of darkness was the day, in April 1998, when she said, 'I want to pray aloud today.'

Alleluia! I'd waited patiently for these words for months, careful not to put pressure on her.

In November 1998, the doctors gave Ayumi three months to live. Would I help her plan her funeral? And speak at it? I was honoured to be asked but, in the event, she went to be with the Lord 10 months later, while I was in the UK. I spoke, instead, at a memorial service on the first anniversary of her death.

The lady in the tiger-stripe suit

Vulnerable though I still was, I was seeing the fulfilment of the image of the shorn sheep, feeding two lambs, given me in June 1996. Another needy lamb was a young 23-year-old who, with her mum, turned up out of the blue at a Sunday service in early 1997. *Mio was a bundle of fun. One day she opened her door to me dressed entirely in a yellow and black striped tiger suit, complete with hood, whiskers and tail! But underneath was a hurting, messed up young lady.

She stopped and started with individual Bible study, had a spell in hospital and changed jobs numerous times. But, at last, she was to be baptised on 8 March 1998, along with her mum. However, the week before, something badly upset her at church. 'I'm not going to church anymore,' she declared, and she didn't for a while. Mum struggled too, but eventually went ahead with baptism on her own that Easter.

A couple of months later Mio rang in tears. 'I tried to hang myself,' she said. 'I blacked out, and then found myself on my bedroom floor.'

I dropped everything, and jumped into my car to go and fetch her. Her distraught mum met me on the doorstep, having by now seen the marks of the rope on Mio's neck. 'You don't know the half of what is going on with Mio,' she said.

Perhaps I never did, but Mio shared her heavy burden of guilt over having an abortion, and the struggle with a boyfriend who was hostile to Christian faith, and pressed her to have premarital sex. Her attempted suicide seemed genuine, but accentuated her sense of failure.

She wept, 'I couldn't even make a success of committing suicide.'

I was completely out of my depth, but I got her an appointment with a Christian psychiatrist I knew, and spent many hours with her on the phone and in person. I shared from personal experience when she asked, 'How can I feel God when I am depressed?' She broke off with her boyfriend, and restarted baptism preparation with the pastor.

After her baptism on 11 October 1998, I asked how she felt, and was thrilled at her reply. 'I think I'd been lost for nearly 24 years, but now I've come home.'

Sadly, Mio and her mum left Wakaba Church for another church a year later. I lost touch completely when Mio qualified as a nurse, and moved to Tokyo. But I thanked God for yet another opportunity to walk alongside a hurting individual for a brief while.

Disappointments

Of course, life was not without its disappointments. In January 1998, I'd started a bimonthly Bible study in Ayumi's home as she had friends she wanted to invite. They didn't respond to the invitation, but others did. *Mrs Sato came regularly for a year, and then told someone she didn't believe in God. 'Why on earth, then, had she come?' I asked myself.

*Mrs Hirano was an English contact and former nurse. She went deaf in one ear, and had to give up work. I had no idea if she had any spiritual interest or not, but she seemed to be delighted when I invited her to join us. I recorded in my diary that 'she just seemed to be waiting to be asked'. In June, she went on a week-long trip to Kyushu, Japan's southernmost island.

'I am worried about my son's exams,' she said. 'I prayed hard at every Buddhist temple and Shinto shrine we visited, because I'd learnt about the importance of prayer from you.'

I had taught about prayer, yes, but, oh dear, she'd not grasped that it is WHO we pray to that is key. She continued to attend Bible studies on and off until October 2002. She then phoned to say she wouldn't come anymore without giving a reason.

I could not describe my two and a half years back in Japan after burnout as anything but 'difficult'. Depression still clung to me, and it would be 2003 before I bid it a final farewell, thanks to a change of antidepressant. But, through it all, I learnt precious lessons, and discovered many treasures in the darkness. Not least was the treasure of OMF colleagues who loved and valued me; who accepted me as I was, and patiently worked with me to make life and ministry manageable, and who constantly encouraged and prayed with me.

'I will give you the treasures of darkness.'

20

主と共に歩みて

Another earthly farewell

Burnout was not the only challenge to my call to Japan. There are three major reasons why most Christians serving overseas have to return home permanently—ill health, children's educational needs and concerns for elderly parents. God had enabled me to return to Japan in 1996, despite my slow recovery from burnout. Now I had to face the pain of another person—one that was all the more agonising because I was partly its cause, by nature of my commitment to God's calling to mission.

On 1 April 1999, I began a five-month home assignment in the UK. Church friends met me at London airport, and brought me to the flat they'd rented for me. It had one peculiarity—mirrors hung on every possible wall, and I frightened myself thoroughly thinking I was seeing intruders when I got up to go to the toilet in the night! Curtain rails pulled away from their wall fixings at even my gentlest attempt to draw the curtains, and the rent was higher than the OMF allowance. Prayer supporters kindly made up the difference, and I was thrilled to be only a few minutes' walk from Guild House, the residential home where Mum lived. So, when my friends told me it had been the only suitable, fully furnished flat they'd found in the whole of Gloucester City, I could only say, 'Wow! Isn't God good!'

Three weeks later, my mother had a couple of minor strokes, further reducing the little mobility she still had. The manager of Guild House explained, 'If this had happened a month earlier, your mum would have had to move to a nursing home. As it is, the recent change of status of this home, allowing it to take in high dependency cases, means we can keep her here.'

Again, in the midst of my distress at my mum's situation, I marvelled at God's timing and loving care — enabling me to be nearby when she specially needed me, and for her to stay in the home where she was secure and happy.

'Is this the last time?'

It wasn't all smooth running for the remainder of my home assignment. Before we knew it, it was August, and just weeks before my planned return to Japan for a fourth term with OMF. Every visit to my mum was punctuated by her question, 'Is this the last time?' Frail in body and increasingly frail in mind, the approaching separation loomed over her like a threatening black cloud, magnified by her inability to remember exactly when it would be. My own heart was breaking each time the question came.

Was I doing the right thing in leaving my mum? Should I be staying in the UK as some had suggested?' One Sunday evening in church after a distressing visit, I could not restrain my tears, but wept silently throughout. However, whenever doubts boiled up, I remained confident it was right to return to Japan because of a brief exchange I'd had with my mum one day back in July.

As I sat with her, out of the blue, and unrelated to anything we'd been talking about, she suddenly announced, 'It's a privilege to have a daughter in Japan.'

Taken by surprise, I asked gently, 'Even if it means you have to say "goodbye" to her again soon?'

Too choked up to speak, she just nodded firmly in response, and we said no more on the subject. But, whatever prompted her at that moment, and surely it was the Lord, it was enough to give me a glimpse into her mind. I knew that in her heart of hearts, and despite her personal pain, she was fully supportive of my return to Japan.

When the day came to say the final goodbye, she was completely alert, and bravely took command of the parting. 'Miriam, you'd better go now. Let's not prolong the agony.'

I prayed, hugged her and barely restrained my tears until I was outside the room and had shut the door. Friends and staff told me that once I'd gone, she settled down and was as content as she could be with her limited mobility. My decision had been the right one after all. My greatest comfort was knowing how much she looked forward to heaven. 'How do you want me to pray?' I would ask in weekly phone calls. 'Pray the Lord will take me home, soon,' was her reply.

That prayer was not answered until January 2002. In May 2001, I shared concerns about my mum in an email to prayer partners, Helen and Ian. She was very down each time I rang Gloucester from Sapporo, and was asking when I was next due home.

Back came an email a few days later. 'We've sent £1000 to OMF stipulating that it is for you to use for the airfare when you need to come home.'

Time and time again, I experienced the practical love of friends in ways like this, just when needed. I phoned another prayer partner who visited my mum regularly. 'What do you think? Should I make a short trip to see her?'

Jane Wood counselled me to wait. 'It would upset her routine, and make it ever so hard for her to let you go again.'

In November 2001, some other of my mum's visitors wrote to suggest it was now time to visit. Carers thought Mum was hanging on until she saw me again. I'd just arrived at the OMF headquarters in Singapore to teach the module on language learning during the Orientation Course for new OMF workers; once the course was over, I flew back to Sapporo, spent one night at home and set off again the next day for London via Amsterdam. I gratefully accepted Jane's offer of accommodation as on many other occasions. She lived only a few minutes from Guild House where my mother was. Mum and I had a precious two weeks together with most of the family coming to visit.

Without knowing it, back in Sapporo, I spoke to Mum for the last time on the phone barely four weeks later, on 15 January 2002. I had an arrangement with Guild House every Monday for a carer to be present to hold the phone for her. The following Monday I was shocked to discover that she was too weak to speak, and again I found myself making hasty preparations for the long trip home. Right up to the nerve-racking last minute the travel agent was searching for suitable flights. I was taking part in an OMF workshop along with missionary colleagues on Friday the 25th.

At 4:00 p.m. the agent rang. 'There are no seats on any of the connecting flights for your return via Amsterdam. You'll need to stay a night in Amsterdam. We are waiting for the Amsterdam office to open (Europe was eight hours behind Japan), but we must book at 5:00 p.m. if you are to fly on Sunday the 27th.'

Our workshop was in its final session of prayer for one another. As I shared my dilemma, everyone gathered round me to pray for the tickets, before I headed off to the travel agent. I waited there anxiously for an hour and half, but eventually left with all my tickets in my hand!

My mother entered the presence of her Lord just before 11:00 p.m. on 27 January 2002. My brother, Howard, was with her reading Psalm 31. I'd landed at Bristol airport just an hour before. Having said our earthly goodbyes five weeks earlier,

I had no regrets that I did not make it in time to see her; only great thankfulness for the release she'd longed for.

'Why does God keep me here?'

Mum had often wondered aloud why God was keeping her so long on this earth. She felt so useless. But, if nothing else, she was a testimony to her carers. As I spent time clearing her room at Guild House, staff kept popping in and out to share their memories. I was touched as they spoke of how much they loved her.

*Alice, not a Christian, said, 'I read the little book of Celtic prayers to her over and over again. When I asked if she would like to hear them again, she would nod her head. She had a large print booklet of Bible verses called *Words of Comfort*. I read that to her too.'

My brother Howard had brought a CD of hymns along to play to her. Two days before she died, she was trying to sing along. 'She kept putting her arm up as if reaching up to heaven,' said Alice.

Another told me, 'You couldn't have had a more wonderful mum. When she was in pain and we put her on the hoist, I said, 'What's the worst word you can think of to describe your pain?' I thought it would be good for her to get it out. After some thought she came up with her answer, "Ouch!"'

Friends offered beds for me and family members coming for the funeral. Prayer partners Jane and Martin Leckebusch had just heard of my sudden return to Gloucester. Jane knocked at the door of the house where I was staying, clutching two large bunches of flowers. Four little girls shyly peeped up at me from where they clustered around her feet.

'Do you need a car?' Jane said. 'We have two, and Martin can take the bus to work. If you have a current UK driving licence, we'll put you onto our insurance. You can have it for the next four days.'

This offer of transport was just what I needed to clear Mum's room, and to meet family members arriving for the funeral from all over the UK. Later, however, we needed a larger vehicle to move some furniture. My eldest brother, Lionel, was staying with kind church friends, who learnt of my need. 'Use our camper van,' they said.

Angels in disguise

Lionel and my aunt, Ruth, stayed on after the funeral to help me. Move complete, we returned the camper van and, tired and hungry, we went off in the borrowed car for a late lunch at the local Toby Carvery. On the way back, I was negotiating a busy roundabout on the inside lane of the ring road, when, without warning, the car came to an abrupt halt. Not only was the rain sheeting down and visibility poor, but traffic poured constantly onto the roundabout, and towering lorries splashed us liberally as they trundled past. I got out shakily, but had no idea what to do with an unfamiliar car. I didn't even know if Martin and Jane had breakdown cover.

Ruth, sitting in the back, told me later, 'I was terrified something would run into the back of us!'

Eventually two cars stopped. Someone held up the traffic, while a man in the first car helped Lionel push the car with me steering, across two lanes onto a slip road.

A mum with two teenage boys was in the second car. 'I've got a tow-rope, and can tow you wherever you need to go,' she said.

I was, by this time, at the end of my tether — still jet lagged, sleeping badly and emotionally exhausted. The closing of the curtain on my mum's coffin the previous day, at the crematorium, had had a shocking finality about it that hit me like a physical blow. Earlier, at Guild House, I'd felt a second wave of overwhelming loss as I looked round my mum's room for the last time. It was a week already since she'd left it, and now all physical reminders of her were gone too. The car breakdown felt like the last straw.

As we stood in the pouring rain, my tears mingling with the raindrops beating on my face, Ruth put her arms round me, and explained to the lady that we'd just had Mum's funeral the day before.

'We'll be praying for you,' she responded.

This family were evidently Christians and, to me, angels in disguise! The teenage lads, by this time, had got the bonnet open, and were investigating with Lionel. Their mum said, 'My boys are very good with cars,' and to my astonishment they were. Somehow, they got the engine running.

'We'll drive behind you to your friend's house, just in case you break down again,' they said.

I set off slowly and cautiously, and we made it back safely. God told the people of Israel trekking their arduous way through the Sinai desert to the Promised Land, 'See, I am sending an angel ahead of you to guard you along the way and to bring you to the place I have prepared' (Exodus 23:20).

When I was at my wits' end, stuck on that terrifying roundabout, unbeknown to me God had already sent his angels ahead to guard and guide.

21

主と共に歩みて

New millennium—New opportunities

As the millennium dawned, the world held its breath. Computers were programmed to read two digits and not four, and it was feared that a failure to read '2000' would cause computer glitches around the world. Anxiety over this anticipated 'Millennium Bug' loomed over us, and I still remember the great relief with which I woke in my Sapporo flat that first morning of the millennium. Everything was normal, and we could get on with our lives.

It was not long before an unexpected invitation came my way. Would I consider teaching on the November 2000 OMF Orientation Course for new mission workers in Singapore? I loved the idea of teaching 20–30 hours of lectures on learning a new language. As OMF Japan language advisor this was the sort of thing I had been doing for almost 10 years already. But the programme would be intense. Could I cope with the high level of interaction with many new people? I consulted field nurse and friend, Mary.

She paused for a while, then asked, 'How would you feel if you turned down the invitation?'

'Very disappointed that I couldn't rise to the challenge,' I replied.

We talked through possible coping strategies. One would be to take a short break in Malaysia, before returning to Japan and the busyness of Christmas. After some weeks of indecision, I accepted the invitation, and took another step forward in my recovery from depression and burnout. I could not hide in my comfort zone indefinitely when new ministry opportunities came my way.

But anxiety still mounted as departure day approached. I prayed, 'Lord, please give me a specific word of encouragement.' I had to laugh when I came across Luke 21:14 in my daily reading, and the words 'Make up your mind not to worry beforehand! (NIVUK 1984)' It was a challenge to intentionally turn away from anxiety, to focus on Jesus and concentrate on the job in hand. On day one in Singapore, I shared this Bible verse with the multicultural group of around 20 new mission workers as part of my self-introduction.

On day two, I said, 'Let's recap on what we did yesterday. Did anything strike you particularly?'
Expecting responses related to language learning, I was surprised when Peter, who was heading for Cambodia, piped up, 'The best bit was "make up your mind not to worry", and the next verse which says "I will give you words of wisdom". This is the Lord's promise to me as I face the challenge of learning Khmer!'

God graciously used my testimony to encourage Peter, although I hoped he had also benefited from the main content of the session!

Being interpreted into English!

While in Singapore I had the unusual experience of speaking in Japanese, and being translated into English. How Chuang Chua from Singapore and his Japanese wife Kaori were church planting in Sapporo.

They heard I was going to Singapore. 'One of our supporting churches, Changi Bethany Fellowship has an outreach to Japanese ladies,' said How Chuang. 'Could we offer you as a speaker for their Christmas event? And perhaps you could give the organisers advice on effective evangelism for Japanese?'

I spoke to a large group of 37 young mums with a host of small children. Most were Japanese, but I met some other nationalities married to Japanese. I spent a morning with the Singaporean and American organisers.

'What an amazing opportunity you have here in Singapore,' I told them. 'It would be very unlikely for so many to come to an evangelistic event in Japan.' They asked many questions, and I responded with some practical suggestions.

'Japan is a collective culture. The harmony of the group is all-important, and members will defer to seniority. Rank amongst the ladies may be determined by the status that their husbands hold in their companies. The strong awareness of the pecking order in group relationships means that it can be very difficult for Japanese ladies to express their true opinions. Japanese education also tends to focus on rote-learning of facts rather than developing opinions about those facts.'

I encouraged the organisers of this outreach to Japanese to spend time, whenever possible, with individual Japanese mums developing personal friendships as well as group activities

Back in Singapore a year later, I was delighted to find two Japanese Christians had joined the committee. This time, I spoke to 60 at the Christmas event, of whom two-thirds were Japanese. Some even remembered me from the year before. Others were newcomers, and they were attracted more by the opportunity to socialise than anything else. It was bedlam with 20 babies and toddlers but, forewarned by my experience the previous year, I battled on!

Several Japanese ladies were now studying the Bible in English with a committee member, helped by one of the Japanese Christians. This 'Changi Bethany Church' outreach was just one example of the great opportunities there are to reach Japanese living overseas, who are often much more open than those who have never left their own country.

It's not safe!

This second trip to Singapore in 2001 came just weeks after 9/11, and the horrific terrorist attacks in the USA. Japanese friends protested, 'It's not safe. You should cancel your flight plans!'

That was something I was certainly not going to do, as a trip of a lifetime lay ahead. In November I boarded an almost empty plane on my way to teach in Singapore. For the first time ever, I could have opted to sit in any one of the 10 seats in my row! But first, an exciting side-trip!

Singapore, the year before, had been refreshing in many ways. I had revelled in God's leading as each new worker shared stories of their journeys into mission. I was inspired at daily prayer times, which focused on ministries all over South East Asia. A visit to my godmother Betty Young, in Kuala Lumpur on the way back to Japan, was the crowning joy. Betty had spent her life in overseas ministry in Malaysia, where she married her husband Peter, also from the UK. But her first years overseas were in Sichuan, Western China, where she worked alongside my parents.

Recently one of my brothers had made his way to Guang'an in north-west Sichuan to see his childhood home. 'Perhaps we could visit too,' said Betty, as she reminisced about the difficult years before and after the Communist takeover.

I was mesmerised by her tales about my parents. In the coming months, my plans began to take shape. On the way to Singapore for my second Orientation Course, I stopped off in Kuala Lumpur to meet up with Betty. Then, along with her Chinese friend and interpreter Catherine, we set off by plane, via Hong Kong, to Chongqing, the capital of Sichuan.

'I will build my church'[32]

Betty and my parents had left Guang'an in June 1951 with heavy hearts. Not only did they fear they might never get out of China alive, but they were also deeply concerned for the Chinese Christians left behind. How would the church fare under atheistic Communism? No one knew for years until, at last, news began to trickle out in the 1990s. Like my brother, some children of former mission workers found their way to Guang'an. They provided an address for the church, which was evidently thriving.

We had written to the Guang'an church in advance, but had heard nothing back. We set off not knowing if our letter had reached its destination, or what to expect on arrival. We took off from Chongqing at great speed in a rickety, 16-seater bus, and endured several hours of bumping over potholes. Our bus wove in and out of our lane to the great peril of oncoming traffic. Betty said she felt sure our destination was heaven and not Guang'an! When we got there, Betty was overwhelmed to see the changes 50 years had brought — cars, blocks of coloured flats, and dual carriageways with greenery down the centre. New buildings were shooting up wherever we looked, constructed by workers who shouldered massive girders without the aid of cranes or any other machinery.

A once unknown city had been transformed into a tourist destination for Chinese. Busloads were converging on the nearby birthplace of Deng Xiao Ping who, as President of China, had opened his country to trade and reform in the 1990s.

One thing hadn't changed, however. The church was meeting on its old site, in a yet to be rebuilt part of the city, and we were expected!

---

[32] Jesus' words to Peter in Matthew 16:18: 'On this rock I will build my church, and the gates of Hades will not overcome it.'

What a joy it was to meet the only two people still alive that Betty knew. One was Pastor Pan, now 86, who had come to Guang'an aged 20 at my father's invitation. The other was the very frail widow of my parents' cook.

We passed down a narrow alley with stalls lining the sides. Pastor Pan's flat and the church were on different floors up a dark staircase. Conditions were basic. There was no glass in the windows, no heating and, with November daytime highs of only 11ºC, the older folk were huddled in multiple layers of clothing. Cooking was done on a single gas ring, while the toilet was best avoided.

After Sunday worship in a full church that seated 400, one lady threw her arms around me. She was 16 when Betty and my family left, having started attending church when she was eight. 'Your father taught me to sing,' she said, jumping up and down with excitement when she discovered who I was.

In an all too short four days, we eagerly absorbed what information we could about the church. Catherine was in great demand as an interpreter. Back in 2001, there seemed to be few restrictions. The church was a 'Three-Self' church recognised by the government: Self-Governing, Self-Propagating, and Self-Supporting. With its four daughter churches, it had 1,000 members and another 500 awaiting baptism. We saw the plot of land on the city outskirts where the Guang'an church planned to build a three-storey building in time for their 100th anniversary in 2004.

Sadly, we were not able to keep in touch subsequently. But we had seen, with our very own eyes, that God had never stopped building his church, and we had been assured that he would continue to do so, whether conditions were favourable or not.

On our last day in Guang'an, eight of us gathered in Pastor Pan's sparsely furnished flat for a farewell service. We read two Psalms, prayed and sang, 'God be with us till we meet again.' Actually, as the only one with no Chinese language, I hummed along while they sang, but I doubt I could have sung anyway, for the tears that choked me.

Fifty years previously Pan and the missionaries had not been able to say goodbye in person, but Pan told Betty, 'After you left for Chongqing by boat, my wife—now returned to heaven—and I, went to your house, and we sang together "God be with us till we meet again." We never imagined that meeting would come on earth.'

I was not the only one in tears. It was a wrench to say goodbye as we assured them of our prayers.

'I feel like giving up'

It was an immense privilege to see God at work in China and Singapore, and this helped me keep going in ministry in Japan where it was rare to see real spiritual hunger. 2001–2002 were tough years for me, not least in evangelism. I was involved long-term with several individuals who, for a while, showed interest in Bible study or coming to church. These were 'lambs' that God had put in my path to nurture but who, if I was not very careful, drained me emotionally. Discerning how much time to give them was never easy.

*Mrs Maruyama was a prickly character who was totally distraught when her 25-year-old disabled daughter died.

'I was an unwanted child,' she said. 'Three elder sisters were born before the war and then, after the war, my fourth eldest sister, myself and my brother were born. My parents wanted a boy not me.'

Sons were all-important to Japanese families in those days. Childhood rejection led Mrs Maruyama to devote her entire energy to her disabled daughter, although she had two younger children. It was no wonder her grief was overwhelming. At the close of the Buddhist funeral, she threw herself at the coffin, desperately calling out her daughter's name, over and over again.

*Mrs Kanda living next door, was on social security, estranged from her family and burdened with physical and emotional ailments. She ended up in hospital on one occasion, having drunk poison in an attempted suicide. Once she woke me in the middle of the night banging on my door, so drunk she didn't know what she was doing. She needed an operation, but had no friends to sign the document giving permission. Would I do it? Being a foreigner, I wondered if I was allowed to. But yes, I was authorised, and I accompanied her right to the theatre door. She came to church regularly for a while, and asked me to teach her the Bible.

In hospital one day, Mrs Kanda was in great pain, and couldn't move. I prayed for her. She said, 'The pain's gone,' and she walked with me to the lift when I left. God did some amazing things in answer to prayer for each of these vulnerable ladies. But the 'downs' won out over the 'ups' of their lives and, in time, they all apparently lost interest in learning more of Jesus. In October 2001, I wrote to a friend, 'I feel like giving up!'

A new church designation

It was time for me to move on from Wakaba Church as a six-month return to the UK approached. Where would my church home be from autumn 2003 on?

'I think you'd better go to a Japanese-led church,' said Wolfgang, our new OMF Hokkaido Director. 'Currently there doesn't seem to be a church plant that is an ideal fit. Why don't you visit a few churches, and see where you might feel at home? Your main ministry is with JLCC, so I am happy for you to make the choice.'

Wolfgang knew me well from our three years together in Wakaba Church, and I happily concurred with his suggestion. It was a great opportunity to learn more about churches originally planted by OMF, but that were now independent, and part of the Japan Evangelical Churches Association

(JECA). Pastors wanted to know the reason for my visits, of course. As soon as they heard I might be available, they were only too eager to tell me how they could make use of a cross-cultural worker, without pausing to ask about my experience, or what I thought I might contribute. Nowhere felt right until, about six weeks before leaving for the UK, I got an invitation to speak at a ladies' meeting at Hokuei (Northern Glory) Church.

Hokuei Church, with over a hundred members, was one of the largest churches in Sapporo, and the second church in Hokkaido to be planted by OMF. Its history stretched back to the 1950s. It didn't occur to me to consider this thriving church. I wanted to give what little time I had available from my JLCC ministry to a small, perhaps pastor-less church that needed preaching help. But the welcome at the ladies' meeting and a subsequent Sunday service warmed my heart.

Then Wolfgang phoned. 'Pastor Matsumoto has written a letter to OMF asking if we can send a mission worker to Hokuei. He doesn't know you are planning to move, but would you be interested?'

I knew Pastor Matsumoto a little, as Wakaba Church was a close neighbour, and he had stepped in as advisor pastor when we were leaderless. He had invited me to preach on more than one occasion, but I had said 'no', as I had not yet had the courage to stand up in front of such a large congregation.

I visited Pastor and Mrs Hanna Matsumoto in their home. I only remember one sentence from our discussion: 'We'd like a mission worker who'll stand alongside us in prayer.'

Fifteen years later, Pastor Matsumoto had no recollection whatsoever of saying this, but I never forgot it. These were the kind of people I wanted to work with—a couple who valued, above all else, my prayer support as a co-worker. I was pleased that they had not leapt to suggest what I might do in the church. It was most astonishing, but by the time I had driven the brief 20 minutes home, my mind was pretty well made up. I wanted to go to Hokuei.

There was no stunning guidance or confirming word of Scripture for me—just a sense that Hokuei was the right place. It turned out to be just that, as from autumn 2003, I had a wonderful 14 years of ministry with Hokuei Church and the Matsumotos.

22

主と共に歩みて

A dream come true

One constant of life overseas was the time and energy spent in praying for and looking for buildings—homes for OMF members, rented properties for new church starts or permanent facilities for established churches. Landlords in Japan were often reluctant to rent to foreigners, especially ones engaged in religious activities. Time and again, we got on our knees and prayed 'Lord, please lead us to the right place.' Time and again, hopes were dashed, and faith severely tested, but we experienced many miracles of which our 1992 and 2004 JLCC buildings were but two examples.

We also had to trust God to provide suitable accommodation for home assignments in our passport countries. This was not easy for families with children in particular. Do you choose a location near parents or close to a supporting church? What if you have several supporting churches? Or what if you need to find a good school or schools for your children? As a single person, I had fewer needs for home assignments, but I still found contemplating a return 'home' to be stressful. In March 1997, I was already praying for somewhere to stay in Gloucester in spring 1999!

I had lived temporarily in four different houses in Gloucester during home assignment in 1995–1996. I ran into problems letting my parents' house from afar, and made the decision to sell. I would rent next time, I thought, and buy when the time came to settle permanently in the UK. However, in 1999, I discovered that renting short-term was expensive, and furnished flats were few and far between. My 1999 rented flat in Gloucester had no washing machine or up-to-date telephone socket. As I have previously mentioned, the owner's obsession with mirrors had done nothing to contribute to my peace of mind!

God had wonderfully provided this flat close to my mum in her care home, but I began to realise that renting was not the best option in the future. With the help of Graham Lea, the leader of the Gloucester OMF prayer group, my parents' house was finally sold, and I was confident I could buy a flat with the proceeds. My brothers had generously consented to my parents' request to leave the house in Gloucester to me, and not to all five of their children equally.

I dreamt of a place in the UK to call my own amidst the constant change of life across cultures. A place that would help me to anticipate home assignment with joy, and not as a necessary but intrusive disruption to the flow of life and work in Japan. A place that would help me feel I really was going 'home' to the UK, where life was now less familiar than in Japan.

Friends to the rescue

On my farewell visit to my mum in December 2001, I was staying with Jane Wood. 'I've asked a few of your friends round on Monday evening,' she said. Among them was Antoinette Bowesman.

'On my next home assignment, I'm thinking of looking for a flat,' I told her.

Back in Japan, the 'dream' got pushed to the back of my mind, until March 2002 when an unexpected email arrived from Antoinette. 'I've started to look at flats for you!' I wasn't sure I was ready for this, but I wrote back with some initial thoughts.

> I don't think that I would actually want to buy anything before seeing it physically, so it is too early to look, but it would be wonderful if I had possibilities to look at when I get back to the UK next April. At the moment the last thing I want to do is to get up and go anywhere.

After four overseas trips in five months, I was longing for life to get back to normal! I felt stressed just at the thought of another upheaval for home assignment even though it lay more than a year ahead. But it was an encouragement to know that Antoinette had taken my needs to heart.

Emails went back and forth, as Antoinette investigated possibilities. Things were not as simple as I had imagined. Being so rarely in the UK, I wanted to have family and friends to stay when I was home. My minimal requirements were a two-bedroomed flat on the first floor or above, in case the flat was empty for periods of time; it would have to be in a relatively safe area that was attractive to potential tenants, in good condition in case I didn't have money for repairs and so on. It was a tall order, but having had previous bad experience with break-ins, constant repairs, tenants who stopped paying rent and difficulty in selling my parents' house, I held out for my ideal.

The rise in house prices alarmed me. Suitable flats selling at £54,000 in 1999 were now over £80,000. 'Prices this year could rise a further 10%', I heard. 'It takes 6–10 weeks to completion, even after you decide to buy.' Buying during a six-month stay in the UK began to look impossible, in view of all the other things I needed to do.

I phoned Graham Lea from Japan. 'I know this is a lot to ask, but would you be willing to work with Antoinette?'

I then approached Mary — not Mary, my OMF colleague in Japan — but a retired doctor friend in the Midlands. Her wisdom and personal knowledge of me balanced the abounding enthusiasm of Antoinette, and the caution backed by practical experience of Graham. If all three were able to agree on a suitable property, I would consider it seriously.

It's got your name on it!

In May 2002, my search for a flat appeared as a prayer request in the weekly notice sheet of one of my supporting churches in Gloucester. This was St Philip and St James, Hucclecote, Gloucester. I had begun attending services here in January 1996 and, in September 1996, it joined Brunswick Baptist in Gloucester City Centre as one of my supporting churches. Graham and Janet were among those at St Philip and St James who read the notice. Not long after, they were walking down a narrow lane in Derbyshire near the home of Janet's dad, when a car drew up beside them. Sheila, the driver, was an old friend and had recognised them.

'How's your mum in Gloucester?' Janet asked in the course of the conversation.

'She's been in a nursing home for a whole year,' said Sheila. 'My sister and I are wondering what to do with her empty flat in Gloucester.'

'I know someone who would be very interested. She's a missionary in Japan!' Janet said, excitedly.

Some days later Sheila's sister, Helen, who lived in Gloucester, turned up at Antoinette's door, and things began to move. 'I know Graham,' she said, 'I used to go to the OMF prayer group years ago.'

The trio of friends agreed the flat was ideal in every way. It was in good condition, in a leafy area just a few minutes' walk from St Philip and St James church. Amenities such as shops, library, police station, surgery, chemist, take-aways and even a funeral directors were just a few minutes away. I would have my own private patch of garden, a shed, garage, plenty of other parking space and a loft. It hadn't occurred to me to add the last to my list of requirements, but now I would no longer need to store belongings in a friend's house.

On the phone to Japan, Mary told me, 'It's got your name on it. And you won't believe this, but there's even a patch of rhubarb!' She knew how much I loved rhubarb, which is rarely available in Japan.

Internal decorations and carpets were attractive, and it was likely I could buy some of the furniture from Sheila and Helen. On 10 August 2002, Antoinette wrote, 'It seems that this flat has been waiting for you. There have been so many God-incidences it must be yours.'

I eagerly awaited some digital photos, but rejoiced in the incredible way God was leading. Then, on 7 January 2003, came news of a possible hiccup. Graham wrote, 'Helen's mum died just prior to Christmas. I have received a letter from my solicitor advising that the sale is on hold as Helen's mum's estate will now have to go through probate. It may not be complete by the time you arrive in the UK. We have our OMF prayer meeting in 30 minutes, and our prayers start then.'

At that point, the thought that I might not be able to move in straightaway was almost more than I could bear. But, somehow, probate was granted in three weeks!

The flat cost far more than the proceeds of the sale of my parents' four-bedroom house. Would I have enough money for a fridge, washing machine, and beds that met safety regulations for letting? Either I could do without, or God would supply what I needed. How he did, though, took me completely by surprise. In December 2002, my brother Howard wrote, 'There's a little money coming to you from Mum's estate. Where do you want it sent?'

Then, in April 2003, came the exciting news that the final inheritance of an aunt, who died in 1995, was complete. God, yet again, had gone before. He provided more than enough to buy essential items, and to prepare the flat for letting in September 2003.

I arrived on the doorstep of my new home at midday on 1 April 2003, straight from Heathrow Airport. Graham handed me the key. It was the crunch moment. What if I didn't like this flat I had only seen in photos? Graham, in particular, had worked unceasingly on my behalf, dealing with all the legal details of the sale, and organising utilities. Others from the Gloucester OMF prayer group had put down boards and lagging in the loft, and stocked the fridge and cupboards. I would have to hide my reaction if I was disappointed.

I needn't have worried. It surpassed all my expectations.

A tall order

'I gulped when I read your requirements for a flat,' said Graham, as I explored each room. 'I had no idea how we were to meet this tall order.'

But God had more than met my essential needs. I had my own front door rather than the communal entrance and stairs I had imagined. From the back bedrooms, I could just glimpse the Cotswold hills in two directions. During my first weeks, I watched the cherry tree at the bottom of the garden blossom spectacularly, while the bare trees, back and front, transformed themselves into restful shades of green. It was marvellously quiet. Even the smaller bedroom was large enough for two beds, and the bigger one combined as both study and bedroom.

Worn out from the long flight, I lay down on my bed after my friends had left. Only an earthquake could get me up now, I thought — until I saw, framed in the bedroom window, a spectacular double rainbow with extraordinarily vivid colours. I leapt up and raced for my camera. Later, I feasted on a beautiful pink sunset from the other side of the flat. Both rainbow and sunset set the seal on my home — God's reassurance, 'I chose this for you.'

How I thank God for those who helped me during my missionary career—in countless practical ways, big and small, as well as in prayer. In retirement, it would be my turn to take up the baton of support for someone overseas. But for now, I was heading back to Japan.

23

主と共に歩みて

Hard rocks to springs

'Have you got a re-entry permit?' said the Narita airport official. 'You can join the line for Japanese nationals.'

It was October 2003. I felt odd to be the only Westerner in the short queue for passport control after landing at Tokyo airport. But I was strangely warmed by this acceptance from the country I loved, and excited to be back in Japan after six months away.

In my next two four-year terms of ministry, from 2003 to 2012, I discovered a welcome for the Lord in the hearts of several Japanese people I met. I did not need to write 'I feel like giving up!' as I'd done in 2001. With a change of medication, I'd also emerged from nine years of depression. I still had to watch I didn't overdo things but, for several years, JLCC was not over busy, and I settled seamlessly into life at Hokuei Church. Alongside monthly preaching, I led a group in church following the Sunday service for newcomers interested in exploring more about the Christian faith. In the 14 years I was in charge, there was nearly always one, and sometimes several, in this group, many of whom became Christians. In contrast to Wakaba Church (which was a quarter the size of Hokuei), people just turned up. We did not need to seek people out, although the church was active in outreach.

In 2007, the words and images of Psalm 114 verses 7 & 8 burned themselves into my mind. 'Tremble, earth, at the presence of the LORD . . . who turned the rock into a pool, the hard rock into springs of water.'

These verses recall the incident in Numbers chapter 20, where the Israelites moan about the tough circumstances of desert life, not least the lack of water to drink. God tells despairing Moses to take his staff, and 'speak to that rock before their eyes and it will pour out its water' (v.8).

The rock did just that. The water that gushed out of a hard rock in a barren desert some 3,000 years ago, symbolised for me the hearts I saw being transformed by God's grace into springs of living water, which in turn flowed out in blessing to others around them.

A white cross on a blue cover

There was a rock of fear in the heart of *Mrs Harada who turned up at Hokuei Church in the autumn of 2004. In the dim, distant past, she'd studied with Jehovah's Witnesses, but was terrified by their talk of judgement. Terrified also of her husband, she refused to tell us her address. 'I let him think I am going shopping or to work,' she said.

She wanted a Bible, so I took her downtown to the Christian bookshop. 'This is the version we use at church,' I said, pointing out a Bible in a light blue paper cover with an embossed white cross on it.

She took one look and said, 'Are there any others?' I was puzzled, but didn't comment until she eventually confessed that she was afraid of the white cross in the centre of the front cover. The solution was simple — use the Bible with the cover removed!

I met Mrs Harada regularly with the aim of introducing her to the basics of Christian faith. But she constantly interrupted me and went off at a tangent! Her problems were many — every few weeks she would be in tears at church, or on the phone saying, 'I have to divorce my husband. I can't stand it any longer.' Grown-up daughters living at home had emotional problems. Church attendance and spiritual interest was stop-start for many a long month.

But over the next two years, God's Word began to penetrate the rock of fear in Mrs Harada's heart. She began to show more interest in actually discovering what the Bible said than wanting someone to listen to her. Assurance that God loved her gradually replaced her fearfulness. Her baptism at Christmas 2006 was a great day, but I did not foresee then the other lives God would touch through her in years to come. The first one was her youngest daughter *Nanako.

Two years had passed since Mrs Harada's baptism, and it was now autumn 2008. Mrs Harada came up one day in great excitement. 'My daughter, Nanako, is watching *Lifeline* every Sunday morning!'

Lifeline was a once a week 30-minute evangelistic programme on TV. It broadcast at 5:00 a.m., so I was amazed that a 23-year-old would be up and watching so early. Nanako started coming to church. She was very quiet and shy, so I waited a few weeks before inviting Mum and daughter one afternoon for a cup of tea. I asked Nanako why she'd started coming to church.

'Well,' she said, 'I was watching *Lifeline TV* and, at the end of each programme, Pastor Sekine always invites people to go to church, so I thought I would.'

'So how did you come to start watching *Lifeline*?' I asked.

'I have to get up for my early shift at Mister Donuts which starts at 7:00 a.m. The only other programme on TV at 5:00 a.m. is TV shopping, which I dislike intensely, so I got into the way of watching *Lifeline.*'

I started an individual Bible study on Sundays before church with Nanako. Most of the time I had no idea what she really thought! But nine months later, in September 2009, she too was baptised. Arriving at church on the day of Nanako's baptism, I saw Mrs Harada parking her bicycle. 'You're early,' I said.

It turned out that Nanako, a bundle of nerves, had left at home the story of her journey to faith that she was to read at the service! In a panic she'd phoned her mum to bring it for her. Reading in front of a crowd of over a 100 was a big ordeal for Nanako, but she got through despite some tears.

'Although I felt God's presence and started going to church, I just could not understand sin at first,' she read. 'I was quite clear in my own mind that I had done nothing wrong but, as I studied the Bible, I gradually began to see my sinful nature as it really is, and to understand the meaning of the cross.'

God had dissolved that rock of incomprehension so common to Japanese, and had given Nanako spiritual understanding. What might God yet do in the lives of the remaining family members?

Terrified of going to hell

*Mrs Tanaka turned up at church for the first time on a snowy morning in January 2010, and was ushered into the empty seat beside me. She startled me with her first words at the end of the service. 'I came to church because I'm terrified of going to hell!'

She went on to tell of her experience of hovering between life and death for three days after a heart attack. Doctors had told her family there was little hope of recovery. There and then we opened the Bible to John 3:16, and I explained the hope of eternal life. For the rest of the year, we met regularly for Bible study, after church and also sometimes during the week. Real understanding came slowly, but how we rejoiced at her baptism that Christmas!

'When she first came she seemed so gloomy, but look at her radiant face now,' said the church ladies.

Mrs Tanaka was not healed of physical pain, but grew in the sure hope of healing one day in heaven, if not on earth. I was privileged to come alongside her in the final stages of her journey to faith, while being very aware that God had started chipping away at the hard rock of her heart years before. Her Christian brother and sister had faithfully prayed for her, and shared their personal experience of Jesus with her. Twenty years prior to her first visit to our church, a nursing colleague gave her a Bible. Mrs Tanaka was not interested, and put it away on a shelf to accumulate dust. Now that Bible was dust-free, and Mrs Tanaka carried it to church every Sunday. How important it is to persist in sowing seeds, even when hearts appear as indifferent as hard, solid rocks.

An accessory or a life-changing belief?

*Mr Yagi, a 72-year-old gentleman, turned up out of the blue one Sunday in February 2011. He attended church fairly regularly until December when I suggested he join church member Mr Chiba and me in an introductory Bible study.

'My dog is seriously ill!' he said. 'I had to take him to the emergency vet. My daughter was so worried she got the plane up from Tokyo to see him! I can't make any plans until things settle with the dog!'

I confess I thought the dog was an excuse and that Mr Yagi wasn't really interested in Bible study. But no, come January 2012, the dog was better, and he was happy to meet weekly. It wasn't easy—Mr Yagi was diabetic, and this affected his ability to read the Bible or a Bible study text. He had a great deal to say for himself, and it was not easy to bring him back on track. He had a mind like a sieve, and he would remember little of what we'd studied previously. Unfortunately, he did remember what his Christian grandmother had taught him as a child: 'It is fine to worship the ancestors or at a temple or shrine, as long as you are praying to Jesus in your heart.'

Mr Yagi couldn't accept that inner belief and outward practice must match up with each other. In spring 2012, he spent two months in hospital as his doctor tried to get his diabetes under control. When Mr Chiba and I visited, his Bible was prominently displayed on his bedside table. However, alongside it was also a large, purple, good luck charm made of cloth and bought from the local Shinto shrine. He was sad that his prolonged stay in hospital would prevent him from helping organise the local shrine's annual festival!

'Christian faith is like an accessory to him,' said Mr Chiba despairingly. 'It's like an adornment to dress, rather than a life-changing belief.'

We worked through the basics of faith and the meaning of baptism with Mr Yagi before I left for the UK in July 2012. I would be away 15 months.

'I'll wait to get baptised until you return,' said Mr Yagi. This sounded to me like an excuse not to commit, but to my delight he was baptised on 23 December 2013, long before I returned to Sapporo.

In his testimony to the 100 or so at the service, he said, 'When I trusted that God would accept me just as I am, suddenly everything around me seemed brighter, and I felt at peace in my heart.'

His was another rocky heart that was transformed by the power of God. Several years later, Mr Yagi's wife came to faith too.

> Tremble, earth, at the presence of the LORD . . . who turned the rock into a pool, the hard rock into springs of water. (Psalm 114:7–8)

24

主と共に歩みて

Farewell to JLCC

Much as I loved preaching and evangelism, my main ministry up to spring 2011 continued to be in my role as OMF Language Advisor. This job, however, began to evolve in new directions. By spring 2004, we were in our beautiful 'new' OMF Hokkaido centre, with plenty of room to expand, but only four missionaries in full-time language study.

'Miriam, we must keep JLCC viable,' said Wolfgang Langhans (now Japan Field Director), one day. 'Can you come up with some creative ideas as to how we could serve the wider foreign mission community in Japan?'

Beyond OMF

Since 1990, I'd been writing articles on language and culture for *Japan Harvest,* a quarterly magazine published by JEMA (The Japan Evangelical Missionary Association). The JEMA chair invited me to head up a new JEMA Language and Culture Commission in 2004. I flew to Tokyo four times a year, made contacts with a variety of mission leaders, and became aware that many mission groups or individual churches were sending people to Japan without adequate finances, clear policies or structures for learning Japanese.

My first job was to advertise study materials produced at JLCC on our website. Some, such as vocabulary lists for Bible books, could be downloaded free. Others we provided at a small cost. Particularly popular were courses that taught the patterns and vocabulary for praying, leading Bible studies, sharing a testimony and giving a talk in Japanese. For several years, I represented the JEMA Language Commission at Church Planting Institutes for pastors and missionaries at the foot of Mount Fuji, and began to attend yearly Language Coach Workshops in North Thailand. The latter were of immense help as I met people from far and wide, engaged in the same task of helping learners gain cultural and language skills in cross-cultural mission. No longer did I feel alone in my specialist ministry.

Workshops in Thailand appealed for reasons beyond professional ones. When I entered the lobby of the hotel in Chiangmai for my first workshop, I couldn't believe my eyes. The vast spaces and soaring ceilings took my breath away. My eyes feasted on luxuriant displays of heavily scented tropical flowers resting on the backs of gold elephants. My entire flat in Japan of three small rooms would have fitted into the room that became home for the next five days, while the sparkling blue waters of the hotel swimming pool called to me in a cooling voice. The cost of this luxury was minimal compared to Japan, but I still felt slightly ill at ease, until assured by our workshop organisers that this was the way things were in Northern Thailand and we were not indulging in unnecessary luxury.

On subsequent visits I thoroughly enjoyed the space, and made the most of visiting some of the sights — giant pandas in Chiangmai zoo, handicraft centres and trips to some of the tribal villages of North Thailand, where I caught glimpses of the occasional cross on simple wooden buildings. Of course, Thailand had its problems. One March workshop took place under skies badly polluted by raging forest fires in the mountains during a drought. Schools cancelled all outdoor activities. A couple of my fellow workshop participants were asthmatic. They were adversely affected just by polluted particles that crept into the hotel rooms through the air-conditioning system.

A Japanese OMF couple from Hokkaido were working with the Mien people who are scattered through several countries in the Mekong river region. Daniel and Tamami were often away from their base in Chiangmai but, on one occasion, I went with Tamami to a meeting of Mien Christian young people. I didn't understand either the Thai or Mien language, but I loved watching them sing their hearts out using a newly produced Mien hymn book. I also attended the Japanese church in Chiangmai on more than one occasion. On my second visit, Pastor Nojiri met me at the door and said, 'I want you to share a testimony in the service. We have people who are not yet Christians, and young students who are, but are wondering what God has in store for them. I want you to tell us how you became a Christian, and how God called you to Japan. You have 10 minutes!' A few minutes later I stood up to speak having had no opportunity to prepare, but trusting God to use what I said in some way.

I must have mentioned that I was visiting from Sapporo. As soon as the service finished a short lady approached. 'I'm from Sapporo too,' she said.

'How amazing,' I said, 'which part?' In a city of nearly two million people she could have been up to an hour's journey away! But no, *Mrs Hayashi lived 10 minutes down the road by car!

Mrs Hayashi spent up to three months a year volunteering with a children's charity in Chiangmai. She said, 'I'm not a Christian, and I only come to church once a month for the singing. How amazing we should be here at the same time.'

For her a coincidence but, for me, an exciting God-incidence. Until our meeting in 2005 she'd never been inside a church in Japan. Subsequently she came occasionally to services at Hokuei Church, mostly at my invitation, but sometimes on her own initiative. One such occasion was the Sunday after 3.11 — the triple tragedy of earthquake, tsunami and nuclear accident on 11 March 2011. 'I needed to pray,' she said.

Another day she turned up greatly distressed. After the service, amidst the hustle and bustle of people getting their refreshments, or heading for the door, Pastor Matsumoto and I stood and listened, as she told us her daughter had been diagnosed with cancer. She welcomed Pastor Matsumoto's offer of prayer as the tears cascaded down her cheeks.

'Can I have a Christian funeral,' she said on another occasion, 'even if I am not a Christian?'

I said, 'Why don't we study the Bible together, and explore more about why you might want to have a Christian funeral?'

But she wasn't ready for that commitment. She was attracted by Christianity, but also wary. She'd been principal of a school for physically disabled children. At first hand she'd seen the detrimental effects of attempts by some Japanese religious sects to convince parents that their child's disability was a result of something bad they'd done. Parents were sometimes pressurised to pay large sums of money in the hope of reversing the bad luck they'd brought down on their families.

Annual visits to Chiangmai continued for several years. I was enriched by the high-quality content of the workshops, and enjoyed the break from the fast pace of life in Japan. I was privileged to glimpse more of God's work in other parts of Asia, and experienced at first hand the amazing way God drew someone like Mrs Hayashi into my path.

Back home in Sapporo, there was even more to do as a result of all I learnt. Together with the Japanese teaching staff at JLCC, I trained as an examiner of Japanese oral proficiency, and offered oral evaluations to other missions. Christians from a variety of missions, as well as foreign teachers of English, came to study at JLCC for anything from a week to several months. A small mission group invited me to their conference in Shiga Prefecture, near the ancient capital of Kyoto, to speak to both mission workers and their Japanese language helpers.

Why am I doing this to myself?

In 2006 and 2008, the JEMA Language and Culture commission organised two-night/three-day Japanese language retreats in Honshu. They involved an enormous amount of preparation, but were highly successful. One participant from the US had been working in Japan for 10 years with the Southern Baptists. She wrote:

> Have you ever done anything you thought was really crazy, like 'why am I doing this to myself' kind of crazy? When I signed up to attend the JEMA Japanese language retreat, this was the thought that lingered in the back of my mind. I love living here, but squeezing in time to study and improving my language among all other responsibilities doesn't always happen. I felt I'd hit a plateau language-wise, and wanted to start the journey upward to improving my Japanese. I must admit that l expected only to come home with a headache from thinking too hard!

> But I almost forgot what lay ahead of me after the first night of games, played in Japanese, of course. It was fun! As we guessed at the meaning of certain characters, tried to play 'Taboo' in Japanese, ate together and had times of prayers and worship, I found the time flew by. I was even excited about having Japanese roommates, because I couldn't turn the Japanese language off. The volunteers who came were eager to talk with me, get to know me, and help me with questions I had about Japanese. We joined in group times of studying the history of Christianity in Japan, proper ways of getting yourself out of uncomfortable situations using Japanese (boy, did I need that one!!) and being

culturally sensitive, while sharing the gospel with Japanese. I found myself still thinking in Japanese as I returned to my family. Attending this retreat has 'warmed up the engine', and I'm newly motivated to improve.

I'd never anticipated a ministry beyond OMF in Japan. It involved much travel and hard work, but feedback like this showed it was well worthwhile. Often, what people needed most were resources and confidence that they could learn Japanese. I was able to help them with both.

Sadly, I had to drop out of all JEMA involvement at the end of 2008 as, back in Sapporo, we were overwhelmed with an influx of new arrivals studying Japanese at JLCC. In fact, the language centre remained bursting at the seams until well after 2011. I was at JLCC three days a week (I worked from home the others), but they were long days filled with constant interruptions. Not only did we have to search for more Japanese teaching staff but, amongst the new OMF arrivals, there were more and more who, for various reasons, did not easily fit the mould. How, for example, do you help someone with severe dyslexia to learn Japanese? The students were on a steep learning curve, but so was I!

Goodbye JLCC

One teacher's severe health issues ate up time and energy over a period of months. Other teachers were discontented and angry about conditions of employment. We did our utmost, with the help of Japanese colleagues, to bring our school in line with legal requirements. But, on one occasion, I was the recipient of an unexpected angry outburst over pay that left me shaking physically for several minutes. Another teacher, in a fit of rage, accused OMF of running a set-up that ought to be on the blacklist of Japanese language schools!

I was due for home assignment in 2012 and, after that, to work full-time with Hokuei Church for the remaining four years to retirement. OMF colleague, Alaric Dunsmore-Rouse, was already lined up to succeed me as language advisor but, by autumn 2009, I was over-stretched, and had serious doubts as to whether I could keep going until 2012.

Wonderfully, I never sank back into depression, but I did fear I was heading a second time for burnout as insomnia, headaches and persistent tiredness returned. I wrote to Wolfgang requesting he and our Field leadership team consider me finishing at JLCC a year early. Thankfully, they were sympathetic, and Alaric was willing to change his plans. I was very apologetic.

'I feel dreadful at messing you around, but I'm so grateful,' I told him.

The change of date involved Alaric leaving his present ministry, and taking home assignment in the UK a year earlier than planned.

'Don't worry, Miriam,' he told me. 'Actually, I feel this is of the Lord. It's good for me to return to the UK a year early, for reasons that have only just become apparent.'

Those words lifted a weight from my shoulders. The Lord had yet again gone before in ordering both our circumstances. In my last months at JLCC, I cut out all but the absolute essentials in my schedule and, by God's grace, somehow made it through to March 2011. I handed over to Alaric, content to have achieved all I'd set out to do. After 21 years, it was more than time for someone else to take over — someone better equipped to cope with the new generation of workers pouring in.

'Aren't you going on home assignment now you've left JLCC?' was a frequent question from OMF colleagues. But I needed at least a year to recuperate, and the best place to do that was in Japan where I was most at home. I stayed on in my rented flat near JLCC, and wondered how I would cope with the bereavement I assumed was inevitable. Amazingly, there was none!

A crisis of confidence

I'd been looking forward for some years to moving into full-time church ministry again, and the timing was now right. But I was so exhausted that I faced a crisis of confidence in my ability to continue serving the Lord in Japan until 2017. It wasn't that I wanted to leave Japan. Indeed, I couldn't bear the thought of leaving; but neither could I bear the thought of packing up for a year's home assignment, moving to the now 'foreign' culture of my passport country and then back to Japan. Were I to stay in the UK, what would I do? What chance was there of finding a paid job at the age of 60?

Although they did not put it in so many words, the reaction of close OMF friends was, 'Miriam, don't be silly. You love Japan. You're an experienced cross-cultural worker. What on earth are you thinking of? Of course, you'll come back after home assignment.'

I was isolated in my fear that I was no longer able to cope with the change that cross-cultural life inevitably brings.

Please God, weaken the Japanese yen!

The Lehman shock of 2008 put many of us under financial strain.[33] The yen was 'safe' compared with other currencies and, as it strengthened, up to 20% was wiped off the value of financial support gifts from the UK. In April my support level fell to 69% of my budget. My situation in May improved due to unexpected gifts. But, in October, the monthly email newsletter from OMF UK dropped into my inbox with news that drove me to my knees again. Humanly speaking the financial forecast for 2011 was extremely alarming. I read:

> If our existing cost base remains much the same, and we do not urgently address the issue of members' support levels, the result will be a potential deficit of £993k. Such a deficit will . . . mean that OMF UK will have to cease operating.

To remain in Japan, I needed 90% of my budget to come through support gifts, designated to me personally. The blessing of having my own flat in Gloucester became even

---

[33] On 15 September 2008 Lehman Brothers, the giant US investment bank, 'went bust' leading to a global financial crisis.

more apparent, as I started sending some of the monthly rent income to OMF for my support. But the next email from OMF UK on 22 October 2010 was stark. My support level was 70% of my budget.

> Your support level will have to see an increase in 2011. Will you pray for a rise of 20% of your Total Support Figure and pray towards 100%?

'Please God, you can steady the exchange rates,' I prayed. 'Please, please, weaken the Japanese yen!'

Could insufficient support be God's way of telling me it was time to leave Japan permanently? There were, however, indications to the contrary. The following email from prayer partners was just one example of unexpected gifts:

> We gave an extra £150 recently. We booked for an OMF conference, but had to cancel last minute as I was not well enough to go. We were surprised to get a refund, and felt we could not just put it back in the bank, so sent it for your support!

Pastor Matsumoto at Hokuei Church was aware of the financial challenges facing OMF. One August Sunday in 2011, I missed our monthly elders' meeting as I was preaching elsewhere.

'We took some decisions I need to tell you about,' the pastor said, when I saw him next. One was an amazing token of love from my Japanese brothers and sisters that touched me to the heart.

'We have set up a way for church members to give to your support anonymously. It will be transferred to your bank account each month.' I wanted to refuse but, no, that wasn't allowed. Pastor Matsumoto was unusually direct and firm. 'People want to give, you have to accept!'

The amounts given over the next 11 months were significant. Even better, they were in Japanese yen, and lost none of their value through exchange rates. I was embarrassed to receive gifts from Japanese Christians when so many Christian ministries in Japan were struggling. On an unforgettable day, 11 March 2011, Japan had experienced the triple tragedy of earthquake, tsunami and nuclear accident, with the loss of around 18,000 lives. Japanese Christians were giving generously to relief work, but other ministries suffered. Despite this, church friends were giving to me! It was both humbling and encouraging.

God seemed to be saying, 'See, Miriam, Japanese Christians love you, want you here, and I want you here too.'

There were, however, still issues I had to work through in relation to the future.

25

主と共に歩みて

Not yet time to leave

'What is your life message in a sentence or two? What has God put in you to share with the Japanese church, the distillation of all that he has taught you? What is the legacy you want to leave in Japan?' These were some of the challenging questions put to me by Tony Horsfall in summer 2011.

At the end of 2010, I'd read his book *Mentoring for Spiritual Growth*. A former mission partner in Malaysia and cross-cultural mission trainer, Tony now ran 'Charis Training' with the aim of helping pastors and mission workers experience the grace of God in a deeper way. On 31 December, I made a note. Could I ask Tony to 'mentor' me as I tried to work through my fears about coping with further change? I needed someone outside OMF, but experienced in cross-cultural mission. Six months later, I found the energy to email him, and was delighted with his positive response. Into the late autumn of 2011 through emails and a couple of Skype calls, I began to sort things out in my mind and on paper, as new ministry opportunities began to open up.

A 60th birthday celebration

The Pacific Broadcasting Association (PBA) was a Japanese organisation, using media to introduce Japanese to Jesus. In 26 geographical areas, groups of churches sponsored *Lifeline TV* and *Light of the World Radio* programmes produced by PBA on local channels. I'd seen first-hand how God used *Lifeline TV* to attract one woman in her twenties, and draw her to himself. There were many similar stories.

I'd joined the Hokkaido board in 2004, and was firmly convinced that TV and radio were effective means of sharing the good news of Jesus in a country where few would know a Christian personally. I was acutely aware of the heavy financial burden shouldered by groups of local churches. During my years with the board, the Hokkaido Broadcasting Company moved *Lifeline TV* from 6:30 a.m. on a Sunday back to 6:00 a.m. and then finally to 5:00 a.m. No way could 100 supporting churches with an average membership of 38 afford the costs of buying later programme slots.

In September 2010, I received a phone call from board chair and pastor, Rev. Hirabayashi. Unknown to me, this was to have considerable impact on my future ministry: 'Would you consider going as the Hokkaido representative to a three-day evangelism seminar in Tokyo to celebrate the 60th anniversary of the Pacific Broadcasting Association?'

Me? Wouldn't a Japanese pastor be better? How can I take three or four days out of my hectic JLCC schedule? Will OMF give me the permission to go? Won't I feel like a fish out of water—the only foreigner amidst Japanese from all over the country, whom I've never met before?

Despite my initial doubts, I was so glad I did not say 'no', and thus miss what turned out to be the highlight of 2010. I bonded immediately with my fellow participants through our mutual passion to share the gift of God's love by whatever means possible. I was not only spiritually refreshed, but deeply challenged by the faith in a great God shown by my

Japanese brothers and sisters against many odds. I realised that Christian TV and radio still had a vital role to play in a digital age and, while not knowing how, I was freshly motivated to contribute in any way I could.

A ministry of advocacy

Leaving JLCC six months later in April 2011 made me a relatively free agent, unlike the other board members, all busy pastors who could not be away from their churches on Sundays. The board welcomed my suggestion to offer myself to churches throughout the island, to share what God was doing through *Lifeline* and *Light of the World*. I stepped into a fascinating new ministry across Hokkaido in a variety of church groups.

Imagine a large island the size of Austria. Or multiply the size of the Netherlands or Switzerland by two. This is Hokkaido with a population of five million. It occupies 22% of the total land mass of Japan, but hosts only 4% of its population. Half the latter live in or around the principal city of Sapporo. The most famous inhabitants of Hokkaido's stunning mountain ranges are the brown bears! Active volcanoes soar to a height of 2,300 metres (7,516 feet) in central Hokkaido, inaccessible for much of the year with up to 11 metres or 36 feet of snow — just imagine six tall people standing on each other's shoulders, and you get an idea of the depth. Lower slopes are famous for their powder snow and, in recent years, have attracted skiers from all over the world.

These mountains wooed me in the summer with their hiking trails and beautiful lakes. I revelled in the rare alpine flowers. Occasionally I caught a rare glimpse of a Siberian rubythroat (similar to a European robin), or of a Siberian chipmunk with five distinctive black stripes across its tiny brown body. I never ceased to be amazed at the hidden power below the ground that here and there forced columns of boiling steam out through cracks in the ground.

But it was not these wonders of God's creation that I spoke about as I visited Japanese churches across Hokkaido on behalf of the Hokkaido Gospel Broadcast Ministry. I astonished many Japanese Christians with the statistics I shared. They were mostly unaware that 62% of towns and villages and two cities in Hokkaido had no church. I'd twice driven seven hours north, up the coast from Sapporo to the city of Wakkanai at the northernmost tip of Hokkaido. It was a slow journey in a small car, and on often narrow two-lane roads that wound through every tiny fishing village and small town en route. From Wakkanai, I'd crossed to the islands of Reshiri and Rebun, from where you can see Russian territory on a fine day. I could not forget that there was not a single church on that seven-hour drive north, nor on either island.

I encouraged Japanese Christians to use *Lifeline* and *Light of the World* as tools in personal evangelism — to advertise the programmes, to invite someone to watch with them, or to give them a *Lifeline* DVD or a small book of radio messages. I collected and shared the stories of people I met, whose first contact had been through *Lifeline* or *Light of the World*.

I was receiving as well as giving, in my travels to churches. In August, an elderly lady at one church said, 'I want to thank you for coming to Japan,' and went on to tell me that she'd become a Christian through an OMF worker, 50 years before. By November, I'd met four more Japanese who spoke warmly of their debt to OMF workers. God had to be hinting strongly that there was still work for me to do in Japan.

Do what you, and only you, can do

I charted the pros and cons of returning to Japan for a final four-year term after home assignment. The only negative was the stress of the moves back and forth. I wrote to Tony on 28 September, 'I am still physically and emotionally in recovery mode, but am developing a strong sense that God is saying "I want you here for that final term."'

Tony had earlier reminded me, 'What is important is not the amount you can give, but the quality. Your experience is invaluable, and you have something unique to contribute that money can't buy. At this stage of life, investing in others will be key.'

I told him, 'A number of unsolicited comments from mission colleagues and Japanese over past weeks have encouraged me to believe you are right, and I do still have something valuable to contribute.'

I explained how God had spoken to me through the story of Naaman in 2 Kings 5:1–26. A Syrian general is healed of leprosy; at the command of the prophet Elisha, he bathed seven times in the river Jordan in enemy Israel. I was struck by the role played by the young servant girl of Naaman's wife. She is an unsung hero whose name we do not even know, a slave in a foreign land with no status, mentioned only once in the Bible. She probably would have had no right to speak to her master directly and, as his captive, could very easily have wished him evil rather than good. But no, her heart was tender towards this man of wealth and status, damaged by a deadly disease.

She spoke to her mistress, 'If only my master would see the prophet who is in Samaria! He would cure him of his leprosy.' (v.3)

Did she have doubts when she spoke up? She could have thought, 'What good will it do to tell my mistress about Elisha? No one will listen to me.' If she did have doubts, they did not stop her speaking out. Little did she know that her suggestion would be followed up, that the kings of two nations would get involved in the story and, ultimately, Naaman would be healed. All this occurred through the witness of one young, unknown, captive alien. She did what she could in a foreign country — just one testimony to her mistress, and what an impact it had! She shared knowledge that only she could share.

The message was clear: 'Do what you, and only you, can do.' It was the same message I'd heard years before through God's words to Gideon (Judges 6:14) — 'Go in the strength you have', and in Jesus' evaluation of Mary who anointed his feet — 'She did what she could' (Mark 14:8). It was the same message conveyed by the picture of the scraggy shorn mother ewe feeding two growing lambs.

By the end of 2011, the decision was made and confirmed by OMF leadership. After home assignment in the UK, I would continue to work with Hokuei Church and with the Hokkaido Gospel Broadcast for a further four years. A poem by Edward Everett Hale (1822–1909) expressed my determination:

I am only one,
But still I am one.
I cannot do everything,
But I can still do something;
And because I cannot do everything,
I will not refuse to do the something that I can do.[34]

---

[34]https://www.brainyquote.com/quotes/edward_everett_hale_393297 Accessed 1 January 2021.

Transition is a thief[35]

My decision did not mean that all was now plain sailing. I had two major transitions yet to go through — 'home' to the UK in summer 2012, and back to Japan in 2013. This involved packing up entirely twice, and setting up home from scratch twice, all within a few months. Despite preparing myself in every way I could, adjusting to life in the UK was extremely difficult. I was overwhelmed by the myriad decisions I had to make — about gas, electricity, broadband, phones, buying and insuring a car and house insurance, to name just a few. In Japan, there were far fewer choices. Ignorance meant I did not always make the best choice financially. In four years' absence, much had changed in society, in my home church, in my family and in OMF UK which had recently gone through major restructuring.

The following quote gives another insight into why transition can be so tough:

'When you have been separated from other people, it is effectively for twice as long as the calendar says.'

Eddie Arthur, experienced Bible translator and mission researcher with Wycliffe Bible Translators goes on in a blog post to explain: 'We'd be in Africa for three and a half to four years, during which time we lived through all sorts of stuff, we learnt stuff and our kids got older. When we returned home to the UK, we had three and a half to four years of stuff to share with our friends. The thing is, although they hadn't swanned off across the globe, they too had built up a load of experiences and their kids had grown older too. We had two

---

[35] Apt words in a quote by Jerry Jones at:
https://www.alifeoverseas.com/laughing-in-the-face-of-transition/ Accessed 23 August 2019. 'Transition is a thief. It temporarily robs you of the comfort and confidence that you enjoyed back when you were settled.'

lots of experience, growth and stuff to catch up on. We were effectively seven to eight years apart in life events.'[36]

It was a joy on home assignments to pick up with some where we had left off four years before. With others it was less easy and sometimes not possible at all.

'Don't cling!'

In 2013 the price of beginning to feel settled in the UK, after a number of months, was a growing reluctance to face the inevitable upheaval yet again. I just wished God could pick me up and drop me straight back into a new flat in Sapporo.

One day in April, I was driving home from a visit to a brother and sister-in-law in Dorset. I should have headed for the motorway, but I forgot to check my paper map for the overall route. I was relying instead on my satnav, which took me across country. No doubt it was the most direct route as the crow flies, but it was certainly not the quickest.

When I'd finished mentally kicking myself, I decided to make the most of my mistake, and stop off in Wells, Somerset to visit the cathedral. I was in the round stone chapter house, absorbed in paintings of the 12 Stations of the Cross. I was paying no attention to the small group of people rehearsing a dramatic reading behind me when suddenly two words caught my attention, 'Don't cling!'

The scene was Mary weeping in the garden outside the empty tomb, from John 20. Mary mistakes the risen Lord Jesus for the gardener, and asks, 'Sir, if you've removed Him, tell me where you've put Him, and I will take Him away' (v.15 HCSB).

Jesus simply says, 'Mary'. Immediately she recognises his voice.

---

[36] https://www.kouya.net/?p=12602 Accessed 5 April 2021

How overjoyed she must have been to find that her beloved friend and master was alive. She probably grabbed hold of him, touched him to make sure he was real. She wouldn't have wanted to let him go; she'd found the one she thought was dead and gone forever. But Jesus gently detaches himself from her as he says, 'Don't cling' (verse 17, HCSB).

Tears came to my eyes as I sensed Jesus saying, 'Miriam, don't cling to your life here in the UK.'

Later, when I read the passage in John 20, I discovered that Jesus gave two more commands to Mary: to 'Go' and to 'Tell' the disciples that he was returning to God the Father.

Mary did exactly that, and I was to do the same — to let go of my life in England, and get on with the task of 'going' and 'telling'. My reluctance miraculously vanished, to be replaced by anticipation of my final term in Japan.

26

主と共に歩みて

The true destination of transition

'Naming your grief'

'Leaving and arriving well'

'Coming home'

'Creating place'

'Am I still me? Identity in transition'

'How we get rootedness wrong'

'Unpacking the boxes'

'Resilience in life and ministry'

'The re-entry transition'

'The question of legacy'

A folder labelled 'Transition' on my laptop overflows with articles carrying titles like those above, as I read everything I could find on finishing well in overseas ministry. Between 2014 and 2017, I intentionally said goodbye to many friends, not just in Sapporo, but elsewhere in Japan. I said farewell to my favourite places and welcomed family from the UK and Singapore.

'The mythical aunt in Japan'

Staying with a niece on one home assignment, I was amused to hear her say, 'Growing up I knew nothing about you—just that I had a mythical aunt somewhere in Japan!'

Japan as a travel destination could not realistically be on the radar of my four elder brothers, while they were busy with jobs and bringing up young families. You can imagine my surprise and delight when niece Ilona came to teach English in Japan for a year, following her graduation from university. It was wonderful to host my family in Sapporo for the first time in 2002—not just Ilona, but her mum and dad, Godfrey and Stella, when they visited that summer. They uncomplainingly slept on the floor with their futons crammed into my tiny study at right angles to each other. They did a great presentation about England to the Parents and Teachers Association at a Japanese school, and Stella sang beautifully to Godfrey's piano accompaniment. But my most vivid memory is of a rainy day in the mountains of Niseko. Unable to enjoy the spectacular views, we opted for an *onsen* (volcanic hot spring bath). After sampling the indoor pools, Stella and I ventured outside in our birthday suits, and clambered into a tub labelled with a list of minerals that would supposedly do wonders for our aches and pains. 'Oh,' we shouted out as our feet touched the decidedly gritty sediment at the bottom, and the waters muddied around us. Several elderly Japanese *obaasan* (grandmothers), soaking in neighbouring tubs, didn't even attempt to hide their amusement at these two weird foreigners.

The bamboo fenced courtyard rang to the sound of giggles as we joined their merry conversation, and the usual barriers between strangers instantly vanished. My brother enjoyed his first *onsen*, somewhat less I suspect, alone in the men's bath.

That was the last family visit until 2015 when it suddenly dawned on my other three siblings, Lionel, Murray and Howard along with other family members that, if they were to visit me in Japan, they'd better get on with it before it was too late! The memories of time spent with family in those last three years are precious. After many years living far apart, it meant a great deal to be able to share a little of my life in Japan. Relaxing, sightseeing and having fun together drew us closer—an important step in preparation for my re-entry to the UK.

'Amen, Lord'

At times, I have chosen 'a verse for the year' as a focus for prayer and personal spiritual life. In January 2017, I was reading the book of Jeremiah alongside a commentary by the nineteenth-century preacher, F.B. Meyer—*Jeremiah, Priest and Prophet*.

I came to the first five verses of chapter 11.[37] Here God gives prophet Jeremiah a mission anyone else would have run

---

[37] This is the word that came to Jeremiah from the LORD : 'Listen to the terms of this covenant and tell them to the people of Judah and to those who live in Jerusalem. Tell them that this is what the LORD,

away from! 'Tell the people of Jerusalem and Judah they will be cursed if they don't obey me!'

No wonder Jeremiah has a reputation for lament! Fulfilling his mission was extremely painful and personally costly, but he replied in simple acceptance, 'Amen, Lord' (v.5).

I knew immediately this was my verse for 2017 as I faced leaving Japan. Just two simple words, 'Amen, Lord.' Willing acceptance of the inevitable and painful farewells; and 'Amen' to embracing a new stage of life. Initially I applied this short prayer only to retirement. Little did I know that, several times in the next few months, I would need to say 'Amen' to God's plans when my own were disrupted in unanticipated ways. Within weeks, I was unexpectedly on the way to the UK to say goodbye to my brother, Murray, terminally ill with cancer at the age of 69. I then lived for several months with uncertainty regarding decisions I had no control over, but which would impact me heavily. I texted a dear OMF colleague one night. 'Are the children in bed? Are you up for a chat? I need to let off steam!'

Kesia listened, prayed for me and commented, 'Miriam, don't forget your verse for the year! It's not working out as YOU planned, but God has a purpose in it.'

I prayed again, 'I don't like it, but Amen Lord.'

An almost missed opportunity

Saying 'Amen, Lord' was a lesson I had to keep learning (and still do!). I was in Osaka just weeks before my final departure

---

the God of Israel, says: "Cursed is the one who does not obey the terms of this covenant – the terms I commanded your ancestors when I brought them out of Egypt, out of the iron-smelting furnace." I said, "Obey me and do everything I command you, and you will be my people, and I will be your God. Then I will fulfil the oath I swore to your ancestors, to give them a land flowing with milk and honey" – the land you possess today.'

from Japan, and had walked round the outside of Poole Gakuin, the first school I taught at, on arriving in Japan 42 years earlier.

All I wanted was to sit down in the café, and quietly process the complex emotions aroused by this visit and my approaching retirement. I was a bit put out when the waitress asked me to move to a smaller table. Then a very Japanese 'Haroo' ('Hello') penetrated my ears. A plumpish lady sitting close to me at the next table said, 'Japanese?'

Assuming she meant 'Do you speak Japanese' I responded in the affirmative, which set off a torrent of words from her. Our conversation was more of a monologue as I could barely get a word in edgeways. Inwardly, I began to lose patience as this garrulous lady charged from one topic to another. I certainly wasn't saying 'Amen' to whatever God might want to do through this encounter.

However, when she discovered that I was a Christian missionary, she mentioned going to Sunday school as a child. Her dad was a fully signed up member of a Zen Buddhist temple, but told her she ought to know something about Christianity too!

As I prayed silently for wisdom, she suddenly said, 'I am looking for answers. I would like to become a Christian, but I am not free to choose my own religion. My husband's older brother married a member of the Soka Gakkai religion, and so all his family became members of Soka Gakkai.[38] This brother refuses to take care of the family grave and to look after his ancestors, so my husband has to play that role. His parents are in their nineties, and his dad is in hospital with cancer. I worry about my husband and the family responsibilities we

---

[38] Soka Gakkai – a 'new' Japanese religion founded in 1930 and based on Nichiren Buddhism.

have to take on. I could only become a Christian after my in-laws have passed on.'

She showed me the book she was reading — the stories of three people facing terminal cancer. 'I want to know how to die well,' she said. 'I don't remember much from Sunday school. What does Christianity say?'

I shared some Bible texts with her from my smartphone. To my amazement, she copied them there and then into a notebook, and made notes of what I said. I encouraged her to find a church. We exchanged names and took photos. Only God knows if her questions about life and death were compelling enough to propel her into serious seeking. For many months after, I prayed she would find Jesus' saving grace.

But I also learnt an important lesson. Just that morning, I'd written to several people that my last 'ministry' opportunity in Japan was coming up the following Sunday at a pastor friend's church. I'd asked the Lord to bring newcomers, and that one person might take a clear step forward. I was thinking how wonderful it would be to have such a seal on my ministry in Japan. It never occurred to me that I would have a divine encounter that very day. I nearly let that chance slip, through reluctance to forego my own comfort, and to say 'Amen' to a conversation that seemed to be going nowhere.

The old-fashioned language of F.B. Meyer spoke volumes to me.

> It is not possible at first to say "Amen" in tones of triumph and ecstasy. Nay, the word is often choked with sobs that cannot be stifled, and soaked with tears that cannot be repressed . . . Of what avail is it to utter with the lip a word against which the whole heart stands up in revolt? Is it not, it may be asked, an impiety, a hypocrisy, to say with the mouth a word that is so alien to the sentiments of the heart? In reply, let all such remember that in the garden our blessed Lord was content to put his will upon the side of God . . . Say it though heart and flesh fail; say it amid a storm

of tumultuous feeling and a rain of tears; . . . and you will find that if the will doth acquiesce, the heart comes ultimately to choose; and as days pass, some incident, some turn in the road, some concurrence of unforeseen circumstances, will suddenly flash the conviction on the mind and reason that God's way was right, the wisest and the best (Meyer, 2011, location 578-593).

An English lady and Japan

Wonderfully, God graciously answered my prayer for my last formal preaching engagement too — the prayer that someone new or on the fringe of the church would take a step towards faith. Following two morning services the church invited friends and relatives for an afternoon of fun called 'An English Lady and Japan'. I shared stories from my early days in Japan like the 'bye-bye, my stop' experience. The swirling masses of people and the multiple platforms at the main Japan Rail station in Osaka always overwhelmed me. Trains came and went almost non-stop. One day, confident I had the right platform, and had correctly deciphered the final destination, I boarded a train for home. However, I had no idea that the Japanese words on the side of the carriage read 'express'. I barely had time to recognise my stop as we tore through it at top speed. Carried willy-nilly somewhere I did not want to go, my only thought was, 'How on earth am I going to find my way back?'

Stories like this paved the way for explaining why God had led me to Japan. I interspersed my talk with slides of Gloucester and the Cotswolds. I told them the story of Beatrix Potter's *Tailor of Gloucester*, and introduced a video of the nursery song *Doctor Foster went to Gloucester*. My 80-strong audience had great fun as they rose in spirit, if not in perfect unison or pronunciation, to the challenge of chanting the rhyme with me.

> Doctor Foster went to Gloucester
> In a shower of rain
> He stepped in a puddle,
> Right up to his middle,
> And never went there again.

A chorus of 'oohs' and 'aahs' rose as I showed photos of sheep on the Cotswold hills. Sheep are a rarity in Japan. The highlight for Japanese visitors to Gloucester is often not the cathedral or *The Tailor of Gloucester House*, but the fields of sheep, especially when they glimpse the ones with black heads or feet!

Showing these scenes led naturally to my main point. Jesus calls himself the Good Shepherd who knows and calls his sheep (us) by name. He is the shepherd who is always there to guide and protect us when we allow him. He goes to the extremes of laying down his life for his beloved sheep, and taking it up again in his cross and resurrection. (John 10: 11, 14-15).[39]

One lady was at church for the first time that afternoon, and responded to the invitation to get to know this shepherd God. Soon she was studying the Bible weekly with the pastor's wife, and was baptised that Christmas. It was the first and only time I'm aware of that someone took the first step of faith through a talk I'd given.

'Yes, Lord' is a prayer

Not long after reading F.B. Meyer, I watched a sermon on YouTube called '"*Yes, Lord*" *is a prayer*'. This reinforced the

---

[39] 'I am the good shepherd. The good shepherd lays down his life for the sheep . . . 'I am the good shepherd; I know my sheep and my sheep know me—just as the Father knows me and I know the Father—and I lay down my life for the sheep.

lesson I was learning about saying, 'Amen, Lord.'[40] It was not always an easy lesson. In the New Year, I started to sort out, give away possessions and pack boxes to ship home. I coped best doing it bit by bit. But in August, came a day when it was difficult to stop crying. It was the day friends took my keyboard away. For some reason, this particular possession symbolised the life to which I was saying goodbye.

Transition is a means to an end

It was easy to focus on the transition process itself. I was all too well aware of the countdown to departure.

'Help, only three weeks to go! Will I get everything done?'
'I just need to get through Sunday'.
'It will be a lot easier when "x" is over'.

Thinking this way did get me through. It helped me focus on one thing at a time. But, says William Bridges, there is a wider picture in transition. It should be a means to an end. 'Transformation is the true destination of transition' (Bridges 2001, p. 126).

Benjamin Vrbicek, a pastor in Pennsylvania, pointed me to the kind of transformation I should be working towards:

> Christians should use transitions not as opportunities to reinvent ourselves, but to re-identify with who we are in Christ. Transitions are a time to reaffirm that the defining reality of my life is not in my marital status, nor where I live, not in my children, income, vocation, looks, education or popularity.[41]

I was very much defined by my role in Japan—for a sense of fulfilment. I was accepted, loved and prayed for by my

[40] https://www.youtube.com/watch?v=mG5m93Hzi4k — Carter Conlon, Times Square Church, New York City, 15 January 2017. Accessed 28 February 2021.
[41] https://www.desiringgod.org/articles/am-i-still-me Accessed 28 February 2021.

Japanese church. They were like family. A prayer partner I'd first met in 1991 wrote, 'Miriam equals Japan. I can't think of you without thinking of Japan.' I could hardly think of myself without thinking 'Japan'!

I was about to lose the role of *sensei* (teacher) in the church. I would have to earn respect in a new ministry situation in the UK, to find my feet as a 'retiree'. My future role in church would be different from what it had been on home assignments. My experience of loss would be deep.

I rewrote Benjamin Vrbicek's words and applied them to myself.

> Transitions are a time to reaffirm that the defining reality of my life is not in my ability in Japanese language; in being affirmed and accepted by the Japanese church; in having a job I love — teaching the Bible; in being put on a pedestal as a *sensei* in Japan or as a mission partner back home; it is not in my ability to lead Japanese people to Christ or to preach a good sermon; my identity is not in being comfortable. Transition is a time to reaffirm that the defining reality of my life is that Jesus Christ loves me and gave himself for me.

Vrbicek went on,

> It is no longer I who live, but Christ who lives in me. And the life I now live in the body I live by faith in the Son of God, who loved me and gave himself for me' (Galatians 2:20).

> Paul is saying that in the life he 'now lives' — that is just before, or during or just after all of life's transitions — he is resolved to live in the knowledge that God loves him. This is where he anchors his identity — identifying and re-identifying here again and again).

I had to do that too.

27

主と共に歩みて

Intentional discipling

My final term of service in Japan stretched out before me like a vast blank page. What would God write on it? In August 2013, I set aside two days for a personal retreat, and asked God to help me set ministry goals.

Catching up on some reading, I came across comments by an OMF colleague which were to shape the next four years. Richard Schlitt, International Director of Evangelization, wrote in our July 2013 International Centre newsletter:

> I believe all of us should, first of all, be growing as disciples. Secondly, we should be involved in intentional discipleship of others, taking people from wherever they are on their personal journey, and helping them to know God, know Jesus, follow faithfully and make him known.

These sentiments, of course, were not new to me, but what he went on to say gave me a vital framework in which to see my interaction with people. It went like this:

> Think of people being on a scale of ten in terms of their relationship with God. If they are Christians, they are on a plus scale. If not Christians, on a minus. It doesn't matter whether someone is minus ten or plus three in their relationship with God. Our aim, in every encounter, is to

urge that person a little further up the scale. In the case of non-Christians, that might simply be chipping away at a bit of prejudice by giving them a positive experience of church.

Partnering with God in moving people up the scale

I determined to spend quality time with individuals with some degree of spiritual interest. I'd heard this message before! Minister to the ones and twos. Feed the lambs. But I found it easier to sit at my desk than be with people. People de-energised me, and I disliked superficial chat, though I was well aware a certain amount was essential in relationship-building. The following quote from John Piper was both disturbing in its demands and thought-provoking. When I acquired my first smartphone, and started using a prayer app, I set this quote to pop up daily and so keep the challenge before me.[42]

> There are no meaningless moments in Christian community. Every conversation and every interaction counts for eternity. We are either weakening people's affections for God, or strengthening them.[43]

Back in Japan now with a clear framework for ministry, I turned down requests to do things that did not fit my goals, without feeling guilty.

An antidote to discouragement

*Mrs Nagata showed interest in studying the Bible on and off for about a year before losing interest. But I never forgot our first study.

---

[42] This app, PrayerMate, revolutionised my prayer life, and I highly recommend it.

[43] https://www.facebook.com/DesiringGod/posts/john-piper-there-are-no-meaningless-moments-in-christian-community-every-convers/10155884495289240/

'I want to buy a Bible,' she said to my delight. 'I had no idea it was written by people who actually existed! I thought it was a jumble of myths like our Japanese stories.'

Spiritually, there was no happy end-result to my time with Mrs Nagata, but I was comforted that she'd made at least one significant step up the minus scale by discovering the Bible as history.

Seeing my ministry in terms of moving individuals up a scale towards Jesus was a great antidote to discouragement over meagre results. Over the next four years, I did Bible studies with 17 non-Christians in all sorts of contexts. High hopes for some like *Mrs Kato, a retired teacher, ended in bitter disappointment.

I'd known Mrs Kato for 27 years, and she was now 82. She happily came to church most Christmases, but never showed any deeper interest until the summer of 2014, when it became clear that her husband was approaching the end of his earthly life. I was overjoyed at her unexpected request. 'Please take me to church,' she said.

She struggled with the strangeness of church and 30-minute sermons. Then her husband died, and I wondered if I would see her at a Sunday service again. But by December, she was back.

'I'll go to church on Sundays until I understand the Bible,' she said, as she got out of my car on Christmas Eve. This made my shock all the greater when, just a few weeks later, she told me on the phone, 'I'm not coming anymore.'

Whatever had happened? It turned out that a Buddhist priest was visiting her home monthly on the date of her husband's death to burn incense, and offer prayers before the *butsudan* or home Buddhist altar. Mrs Kato, like most Japanese, had no commitment to Buddhism. She was simply following cultural norms. She didn't know this priest and, if the experience of other Japanese friends was anything to go by, wouldn't have understood a word of the prayers he chanted. However, she was under some obligation to the priest's son.

'I can't ask the priest not to come,' she said, 'but at the same time, it isn't right for me to be involved in both Buddhism and Christianity.'

Embarrassed, she cut off all contact, dismissing 27 years of friendship. That hurt. I had to remind myself that I'd seen her move a little along the spiritual scale. The rest was in God's hands.

Wonderfully, out of the 17 individuals who showed spiritual interest in that final term between 2013 and 2017, seven came to faith, moving from the minus scale in relationship to God right over to the plus. This was thrilling!

'We couldn't open the door'

Remember Mrs Harada, who was too scared to buy the Bible with a blue paper cover and a white cross, firmly embossed on the front? And her daughter Nanako who started attending church after weeks of watching *Lifeline TV* at 5:00 a.m. on a Sunday morning?

God was not finished with this family. Two years had passed since Nanako's baptism, and it was the summer of 2011. She ran excitedly into church saying, 'My sisters are coming today!'

Her twin sisters, by now in their thirties, had been reading their mum's and sister's Bibles at home. After the service, they shrank into a corner hoping to escape notice, but I plucked up courage to invite them to meet for Bible study on a weekday. Eventually they responded with a 'yes' via their mum.

A year later, *Chieko reminisced, 'When we came to the church for the first Bible study, I couldn't figure out how to open the door.' (It slid to the side, rather than opening in or out.) 'You came and opened it from the inside. I felt as though I couldn't get into the church unless someone opened the door for me.' This was a good analogy for the helping hand needed to open the door of their spiritual understanding.

Chieko commented after study number two, 'If I had been reading the Bible on my own, I never would have realised that the father in the parable of the prodigal son (Luke 15:11-31) is a picture of God's incredible love.'

I met with Chieko and *Emiko, on and off, for six years including a year's absence in the UK. Even after all that time, I was not always 100% confident that I could distinguish between these identical twins! Nor was I sure that these very retiring 'stay-at-homes' would ever have the courage to be baptised, but I challenged them to step out in faith before I retired. When they bravely did so, it was the best present I could have received on my very last Sunday at Hokuei Church, on 8 October 2017. The double baptism was a beautiful ending to my ministry in Japan. I looked back with joy on 13 years walking alongside this family, with four members coming to faith.

The impact of a Christmas invitation

In December 2015, a lady phoned the church, 'I read the leaflet about Christmas services you put through my door,' she said. 'I want to come, but I can't walk far. Can someone come and visit me?'

That was how I met *Mieko. The house was a shock. There were things everywhere. I almost choked on the thick cigarette smoke — I could see it as well as smell it — and it was hard to be gracious with the two tiny poodles who gave me a decidedly wet and boisterous welcome! But Mieko was clearly seeking. She waved at a pot plant, and told me, 'Just look at the beauty around — there must be a Creator God.' Sixty years old, she'd been baptised into the Mormons, and had had close contact with Jehovah's Witnesses. But she somehow sensed that truth lay in neither.

I got to know Mieko well over the next 15 months — a troubled and demanding lady who'd suffered much abuse in life from both parents and her first husband. She'd not seen her four adult children since the eldest was 12, when her husband kicked her out of the home. She had a host of physical complaints and symptoms of bipolar disorder. Sometimes she couldn't get out of bed for a week, and at times she was suicidal.

I prayed some desperate prayers, 'Lord, help me to love Mieko when I don't want to, and give me the wisdom and energy to relate wisely to her.'

Through the physical and emotional ups and downs of 2016, Mieko grew in her understanding and trust in Jesus. She began to pray aloud. During her better spells, she came to church, and I visited or invited her to my flat for a brief Bible study. She loved going out to eat, and introduced me to her favourite noodle shop and Nepali curry restaurant — the latter was far too hot for me!

'I really want to understand the gospel,' she said, 'but I find it so hard to concentrate.'

She asked to go through the basics a number of times with a colourful booklet she found helpful. She learnt the words of Deuteronomy 31:8, which had been put to music, and we often sang together in Japanese, 'The LORD himself goes before you and will be with you; he will never leave you nor forsake you. Do not be afraid; do not be discouraged.'

Just before Christmas 2016, she begged me to call round for a few minutes. She sat me down on the sofa, went behind the sliding door into the bedroom off the living room, and came out with a large parcel. 'Open it,' she said. 'It's your Christmas present.'

Astonished, I did so, and discovered a cuddly cream-coloured teddy bear inside! Mieko had bought its twin in brown for herself! I was touched. I was, therefore, all the more shocked when three weeks later she took offence, and stopped responding to my messages.

'I'm not going to church anymore,' she declared adamantly to church members.

I continued to send texts, and prayed without much hope. Against all odds, I eventually got a text response. 'Please phone me!'

On the phone she explained, 'I was at the hospital yesterday, and told my psychiatrist about you and the church. He said, "You need the church and this foreigner. They can help you. Don't cut them off!" So I want to meet you for Bible study again.'

In the light of what was to happen two months later, it was nothing short of a miracle that God used this doctor to restore our relationship. Sunday 12 March 2017 was a day I shall never forget. Mieko rang at 8:00 a.m. Preparing to preach, I nearly didn't answer when I realised who it was. Fortunately I did, to hear Mieko say, 'I won't go to church today, I don't feel well.'

I prayed with her, and promised to ring when I got home in the afternoon. I had no idea this would be the last time we spoke.

At 4:30 p.m. she did not pick up the phone. I was not surprised to get a return call a couple of hours later, but the content was a great shock. It was Mieko's husband to say that she had died in his arms at 3:00 p.m. from a fit. I was so thankful that I'd prayed with her on the phone that morning; and thankful too that the week before she'd said, 'Tell me about heaven', and we'd read together the first five verses of Revelation 21.

> Then I saw a new heaven and a new earth, for the first heaven and the first earth had passed away, and there was no longer any sea. I saw the Holy City, the new Jerusalem, coming down out of heaven from God, prepared as a bride beautifully dressed for her husband. And I heard a loud voice from the throne saying, 'Look! God's dwelling place is now among the people, and he will dwell with them. They will be his people, and God himself will be with them and be their God. He will wipe every tear from their eyes. There will be no more death or mourning or crying or pain, for the old order of things has passed away.'

Mieko's husband said, 'I'll let you know when the details of the funeral are arranged.' Monday morning, he phoned to say the wake was on Tuesday evening, and the funeral Wednesday morning. Would I choose some hymns, and fax them to the funeral parlour?

Greatly encouraged, I did so and thought, 'That's the end of my contribution.'

At 2:00 p.m. on Tuesday afternoon, just five hours before the wake was due to start, I was an hour's drive from home visiting a friend when Mieko's husband rang again. Would I speak at the wake? I hurriedly made my excuses to my friend, jumped into my car and made for home as fast as I could. I had two hours to produce a talk, and change into my black suit. I phoned the church and an OMF colleague to ask them to pray, then sat down in front of my laptop to prepare for one of the biggest challenges of my career in mission. I don't cope well under time pressure, and I had no idea whether I would be speaking at a Buddhist funeral with a Buddhist priest, or what kind of response I would get. It was a case of 'God, you are really going to have to help me here. I'm totally out of my depth.' Amazingly the ideas flowed, and in two hours I had a 20-minute talk in Japanese I was happy to share.

The wake and funeral had all the trappings of a Buddhist funeral with incense and offerings but, to my intense relief, I was not sharing a platform with a Buddhist priest. There was no chanting of incomprehensible prayers, and the only religious input was mine. My knees shook as I stood up to speak to 50 or 60 black-suited mourners, mostly men from the husband's work connections. I shared memories of Mieko, and something of her journey to faith. It was a joy to read the verses from Revelation 21 that I'd read with Mieko the week before, and to share my confidence that she was in a place where all her tears were now wiped away, a place free from pain and full of joy. With three church ladies, I sang the song Mieko loved so much:

> The LORD himself goes before you and will be with you; he will never leave you nor forsake you. Do not be afraid; do not be discouraged. (Deuteronomy 31:8)

Mieko's husband was not a Christian—he admitted to having all sorts of queries about religion—and it was not a Christian funeral, but he said, 'I think this is the funeral she would have wanted—hymns playing and you speaking.'

After the wake, the funeral director apologised to me for the mixture of Buddhism and Christianity! But I was immensely grateful for the opportunity to speak, and for the tangible sense of God's grace carrying me through.

The next day I attended the actual funeral—just 10 people around the coffin and many tears. It was especially poignant as my brother Murray had died from cancer just the week before in the UK. I was grieving, as much for him as for Mieko. Mieko's story was just one of many. The opportunities of those last four years were numerous, amazing and unexpected. In 2013, prayer partners told me they sensed this would be my most fruitful term yet, and so it turned out to be.

My heart was breaking as I boarded the plane to leave Japan on 13 December 2017, a day later than planned. Twenty-four hours before my scheduled flight on the 12th, I woke up to an email from British Airways instructing me to contact their Tokyo office. Snow in the UK had closed down Heathrow airport, and my flight was cancelled. What an anticlimax! I'd geared myself up both practically and emotionally for leaving Japan. Now I felt as though someone had stuck a pin into my fully blown-up and prepared balloon, leaving me collapsed and limp. After some hours of uncertainty, the BA office in Tokyo confirmed that they'd rebooked me for the 13th. But I needed a bed for one more night, and our OMF guest home near Tokyo was full. At the last minute I found a hotel room at Narita airport. Having been given a thorough farewell in Hokkaido over two months before, just a small group of colleagues from our OMF Japan Headquarters office prayed with me before I set off for the local train station and the express train to the airport.

My 90-minute journey to the airport and overnight stay was solitary, but not lonely. In the end, I was grateful for the extra hours of quiet reflection. In the midst of the heartbreak I was at peace, and had a strong sense of fulfilment and completion. My work in Japan was done, and I had no regrets.

28

主と共に歩みて

But it's NOT home!

Re-entry with a bump

Four nights later, back in my flat in Gloucester UK, a disturbed body clock forced me into weary wakefulness at one in the morning. Perfect timing, as it turned out, to pray for the 10:15 a.m. service just about to begin at Hokuei Church in Sapporo. And what a special service that was with the baptism of five young men I knew well. I'd requested a DVD of the service by post because I had no internet connection in my flat yet, and I was sure that no friends would wish me to invade their house for a couple of hours at one o'clock in the morning to watch remotely! But when the sleep that my jet-lagged body longed for evaded me, I was only too glad to share with my Japanese church family in thought and prayer for the next couple of hours.

Fast forward to 10:30 a.m., and my first Sunday service at St Philip and St James, Hucclecote. I turned the heavy ring handle on the wooden porch door to a chorus of 'Welcome home, Miriam' and 'Are you home for good now?' I'm ashamed to say my response to my UK church family was less than gracious, even with the excuse of little sleep, and acute grief at not being able to share in person this significant Sunday with my Japanese church.

'It doesn't FEEL like home,' I said, while inside I was crying out 'It ISN'T home!'

Back in my still bare flat, I sensed God's gentle rebuke. I knew perfectly well it was the right time for me to return to the UK. Not to embrace this transition wholeheartedly was to question God's will and leading for this new season of life. I would miss Japan acutely for a long time to come but, there and then, I made a conscious decision to start talking about 'being home' instead of 'being back'.

I set out, in that simple change of word, to embrace all that being home meant, without internal kicking and screaming. I said 'Sorry, Lord,' and started to thank him as best I could for all the many blessings I was already experiencing by being home in the UK.

'Bold and stout-hearted'

'I'm going to share from Psalm 138,' said the speaker.

I was in Kent for an OMF workshop, involving a Monday to Friday debrief and re-orientation for workers on home assignment and retirees. As Rosemary read, verse 3 leapt off the page of my Bible and straight into my heart. 'When I called, you answered me; you made me bold and stout-hearted' (NIVUK, 1984).

I felt the complete opposite — vulnerable and tearful; panicky and stressed out with the process of setting up home. My sleep did not improve until September when I made an appointment with the doctor, and went back on a small dose of antidepressants. It would take another year or more to feel settled. But for now, six weeks into re-entry, I was comforted that this stage would not last for ever. As I kept calling on the Lord, finding my identity in his love for me, he would answer; anxiety would lessen and I would grow in resilience and stout-heartedness.

Six nights at the beautiful Penhurst Retreat Centre near Battle in Sussex was God's next gift to me in transition. We woke one morning to a magical world cocooned in snow. The staff couldn't get to work but, fortunately, the freezer was well-stocked with prepared meals! Two retreats ran back-to-back—'New Directions' for Christian workers returning to the UK after ministry overseas, and 'Running the Race' for full-time Christian workers facing retirement. Halfway through the first retreat, I seriously doubted the wisdom of booking for the second with a new group of people to get to know. But I was so glad I did, as I gained many helpful insights.

One was how to distinguish between self-pity and self-compassion. How could I avoid being sorry for myself and making others feel sorry for me, and at the same time look after myself? Our speaker put it this way: 'Think of how you would recommend a friend to take care of herself. Then give yourself permission to do the same or similar. This is self-compassion.'

Another insight related to closing the door on the past: 'Most people either live in the past or in the future. Closing the door on the past doesn't mean forgetting the past, but making sure that it is not dominating the present. Don't continue to evaluate everything now in terms of the past.'

I had an overwhelming urge to let everyone I met know that I'd spent a lifetime in Japan. I don't know whether this was a form of showing off, but I felt people would not know the 'real' me if they did not know this about my past. This was one way my past dominated my present. Comparisons were another: 'It was so much easier to do "xyz" back in Japan.'

Melissa Chaplin is a trained life-coach experienced in working with cross-cultural issues. She describes the awkwardness of re-entry in her book *Returning Well: Your Guide to Thriving Back "Home" After Serving Cross-Culturally.*

> Returning to your primary culture can be like wearing someone else's shoes: even though they're your size, your feet don't fill the grooves like they are supposed to, and the awkward sensations seem constant. Your feet ache for the day when the shoes truly feel like they are your own. (Chaplin, 2015, p. 96)

I desperately needed to talk about Japan, so opportunities to speak in churches and small groups were like ice-cold drinks on a hot day. Being listened to was therapy for my heart and soul.

The cost of returning 'home'

One day, a small group at church was discussing the cost of being a Christian. Someone asked about my experience. What had been the cost of going to Japan in short-term cross-cultural mission as a young 22-year-old? Of joining OMF 32 years ago? Of spending my entire working life in a foreign culture?

Instinctively I replied, 'It was a tremendous privilege. It was simply a case of following Jesus one step at a time. I certainly had no idea a short-term commitment for two years would turn into forty-two.'

Life in Japan was not always easy, but was the cost to me in following Jesus greater than that of a Christian who stayed in their home country? An unanswerable question, as one individual's calling and sacrifice cannot be compared with that of another.

On reflection I wondered if the greatest cost in a life-time of journeying with Jesus hadn't been the wrench of leaving Japan, the country I loved, and retiring to the UK. It was a far greater transition than going to Japan in the first instance, and I no longer had the resilience of a 22-year-old! I came across a blog post for expats with an intriguing title: 'Repatriating Normally: Ten Things That Make Coming Home Feel

Weird.'[44] I strongly identified with three of these — 'feeling incompetent', 'feeling homesick at home' and 'mourning'.

Incompetent and homesick

I reached the checkout on my first supermarket shop on one return to the UK. As the cashier totted up the total on her machine, I packed my bags and brought out my cheque-book and pen to sign in payment. The cashier looked at me rather strangely. Had chequebooks changed, while I'd been away, I wondered? I hadn't used mine for four years but, surely, my cheques were still valid?

'You have a cheque card?' asked the cashier.

A questioning 'Ye-es?' from me. This was the card I'd previously used when shopping to validate the signature on my cheque.

---

[44] http://www.thecultureblend.com/repatriating-normally-10-things-that-make-coming-home-feel-weird/
Accessed 4 April 2020.

'What planet have you come from? If you have a cheque card, you don't need to write a cheque. Just stick your card in the machine here and enter your pin number.'

I imagined the impatient customers lined up behind me thinking 'what a crazy woman!' Cheeks reddening in embarrassment, I meekly obeyed the cashier's instructions, and escaped as fast as I could with my tail between my legs. How dearly I wanted to explain that I'd been away for four years; not on another planet, but on the other side of the world in a culture which, as yet, knew nothing of cheques and cards.

On a later visit 'home' to the UK, I spent my first night at the home of a friend who kindly met me at Heathrow Airport. Discussing how to buy a rail ticket for my onward journey the next day, my friend asked, 'Is your debit card contactless?' Never having heard the word 'contactless' before, I had no idea whether it was or not. The possibility that for smaller payments it was no longer necessary to put your card into a card machine had never entered my mind. Changes that were barely imperceptible to others living permanently in UK society caught me off-balance, made me feel incompetent and added to the ache for the familiar.

Mourning

I'd been home in the UK seven months when I read 'Ten Things That Make Coming Home Weird'. The overwhelming sense of floundering in an unfamiliar culture had largely diminished, but the mourning had not.

> Clearly repatriation and death are not the same. That said, mourning is an absolutely legitimate part of this transition. It is healthy and natural. The defining characteristic of grief is that it is a process. Mourning is not the same as venting. You don't just get it out of your system one day, and then 'poof' it's gone.

The grief was acute at times — for physical places and things, but most of all for people. I missed the close relationships and deep prayerfulness of the OMF Japan family. I constantly wondered how those I'd walked with on their faith journey were getting on. Some I heard about, others I didn't. In either case, I had to commit them into the Lord's hands in prayer, and remind myself that his work could go on without me!

Up to 70% of cross-cultural workers experience some significant degree of depression after re-entry to their home country. Not surprising then that I fell into that category.

Ongoing emotional tiredness made it hard for me to reach out to others. There was new leadership in the church. Some familiar faces were gone, and others were new to me. As soon as I heard them, I noted down on my phone both the names of those new to me, and those whose names I should have been able to recall, but couldn't! Clearly, while in Japan, my brain had dumped information about Gloucester I didn't need. A few days after arriving home, I met Margaret from church on the bus.

'I need to make an urgent internet call to my Japanese insurance company to finalise my car insurance here, but I can't do it before 11:00 p.m. I don't like to ask anyone if I can use their internet that late!' I said.

When she kindly offered me her internet I said sheepishly, 'I know you are just round the corner from me, and I can picture your house inside and out, but the memory of how to get to you has completely gone!' We patched up my memory by walking from the bus stop together to Margaret's house before I went on home.

I was immensely grateful to people who invited me for coffee or meals, who offered practical help with home and garden, who gave advice or sensed when I was struggling and gave me a hug. It was important to join a fellowship group to get to know people. Until a more permanent role in church became clear, I joined service rotas for welcomers and readers — doing simple things that didn't drain my energy, but helped me to feel I belonged. Above all, this season of painful adjustment was eased by the prayers of countless friends.

What and When?

A big challenge was to know what to take on and when. Suggestions and invitations came from many directions. 'Give me a year,' was my usual reply. I needed time to settle, and to discover what God was now calling me to do. I loved to teach the Bible and, in preparation for retirement, I'd trained as a reader or lay minister in the Church of England between 2008 and 2013.[45] I was licensed to St Philip and St James, Hucclecote, Gloucester in 2013.

'We're very much looking forward to having you on board when you are ready,' said Mark Close, our new vicar.

This warm welcome encouraged me greatly, and I looked forward to preaching and leading services once I was more settled. Back in February on retreat, I asked, 'I have lots of potential ministry opportunities, but how will I know when I'm ready for ongoing commitments?'

'When you can do two things in a day and not feel shattered the next,' said an experienced psychiatrist and counsellor. Her answer proved to be a helpful tool in monitoring energy levels and planning schedules.

I found another quote from Chaplin (2015, p. 23) helpful. 'If cultures were like friends, then one key to transitioning well is realizing that sometimes the best way to get reacquainted with an old friend, is a lot like getting to know a new friend.'

---

[45] The normal training was three years study one night a week with church placements and some study weekends locally. However, the diocese made special arrangements for me to submit assignments from Japan during the first four years, and finish up with one year in Gloucester during home assignment.

By the end of 2018, I'd come a long way in getting to know 'the old friend' as 'a new friend'. On 24 December, I drove from Gloucester to Anglesey to spend Christmas with family, as I'd done 10 days after landing in the UK, a year previously. As I followed the same route, inevitably my thoughts went back. I suddenly realised how far I'd come in re-settling. No longer did I feel I was teetering on the edge of a cliff. I was settling into a flat which was taking on my personal stamp after years of letting, I was enjoying singing in a choir and taking flute lessons, I'd made new friends, I'd given 35 presentations on Japan, I was beginning to pick up ministry at St Philip and St James and could see the way forward regarding other ministry involvement.

What could I say but, 'Thank you, Lord, for going ahead of me in this year of re-entry, just as you have done at every stage of my life so far.'

29

主と共に歩みて

Fit me in somewhere

Fit me in somewhere
in this giant jigsaw, God,
somewhere in this work of art
you're working,
select a space my shape can fill
and with a puzzle maker's skill
let my contours find their fit without contortion.

Teach me which patch I am, God,
in the cosmic quilt you're quilting.
Show me where my square of selfhood is of use.
Let the colourful complexities
of the pattern that is me
find their purpose in the placement that you choose.

Show me my position, God,
in this group photograph.
Stand me where you want me to stand.
Put me next to whom you will.
Make me stand, for good or ill,
precisely in the place your plan demands.

Tell me what I am, God,

in this body you are building:
a tongue to taste,
a nerve to serve,
an ear to hear.

Give me grace
to not be, gracefully,
the parts I am not called to be
and to play with elegance
the roles I'm given.

Fit me in somewhere
in this giant jigsaw, God,
somewhere in this work of art you're working.
Weave your wondrous tapestry
until the twisted, tangled threads of me,
surrendered to your artistry,
form an image that is beautiful to see.

(Kelly, 2007, pp. 41–42)

This poem perfectly expressed my prayer in retirement. I officially became a retired member of OMF six months after arriving home in the UK. I had a rude awakening to this reality when my OMF email account suddenly stopped working on 13 June 2018, despite repeated attempts to input my password as requested. I contacted OMF IT support and woke up the next morning to a response. 'Your account expired due to your retirement and needs to be reinstated!'

It felt like a slap in the face. 'You no longer belong to the family!'

But, of course, it was the fault of a system that automatically logged the change in my circumstances, and acted accordingly. 'Please change the settings so that future retirees don't get the same nasty shock' was my plea to IT support.

Mission presenter and mentor

Despite this momentary hiccup, I was still very much part of the OMF family. But I was now attached, for practical purposes, as a retiree to OMF UK, who welcomed me into two volunteer roles. One was on the Wales and West OMF Area Ministry Team. This team works in pairs to carry out ministry debriefs at supporting churches with OMF workers on home assignment, and helps process new candidates.

The second role was as mission presenter and mentor on the West Midlands Bridge Asia team. The aim of this group is to inspire churches and individuals. In other words, to encourage people into active participation in one of the six ways of mission — Learn, Pray, Send, Welcome, Inspire and Go. As mission presenter, I actively looked for opportunities to speak to various types of church groups or at main services. Fascination with Japanese *anime* (or 'animation') meant we were seeing a large number of young people interested in serving in Japan.[46] I did orientation with those from the West and Wales region considering or committed to going to Japan with Serve Asia, OMF's short-term mission programme. We offered prayer support, while the Serve Asia workers were overseas, and debriefs on return. Some were keen to continue meeting for a few months to discuss how they might apply lessons learnt to their lives back home. I loved working with the Area Ministry and the Bridge Asia teams, and the privilege of engaging with short-termers.

---

[46] *'Anime* (ア ニ メ) is a word derived from 'animation', and is used by Japanese people to refer to any animated drawings, no matter their country of origin. In English, it is mostly used to refer specifically to Japanese animation: https://gogonihon.com/en/blog/a-small-glimpse-into-history-of-japanese-anime/ Accessed 28 October 2020.

I had some idea before leaving Japan that opportunities like this to assist OMF UK would come my way. But I was taken by surprise when the door to Japanese ministry opened wide.

Japanese diaspora[47]

In early February 2018, while in Kent, I bumped into Selvan who headed up a small mission called *Japan Christian Link*. A month later, we met up at the home of a Japanese Christian in Sevenoaks, Kent, for a Bible study in Japanese. How I wished I had the opportunity like Selvan's, to join regularly in a Japanese Bible study group.

'Will you get involved in ministry to Japanese once you're settled?' Selvan asked.

'If only I could — but I don't know any Japanese in my area,' I replied.

'How far are you from Worcester?'

'Not sure. Why?'

'There's a church there with an outreach to Japanese. They might well appreciate your help.'

My antennae were now waving wildly. I looked up Google maps, and discovered that Woodgreen Evangelical was very close to an M5 exit. On the motorway, I could be there in 45 minutes from home. Selvan put me in touch with the assistant pastor and, in June 2018, I went to visit. After observing the Tuesday morning English class, I sat down with Andy in his office.

'It was amazing to meet eight young Japanese ladies this morning,' I said. 'And with several babies and toddlers. How did this come about?'

---

[47] Originally, the term was used in reference to the Jewish diaspora, but more recently it has been used for any people group living outside their homelands.

Andy explained, 'Some years ago, out of the blue, two Japanese turned up with their children at our Mums and Toddlers group. We discovered there are about 20 families whose husbands work at Mazak, a Japanese manufacturing company half a mile from church. We struggled with the language barrier, so we began an English conversation class every Tuesday, just for them. The church has become a place where they meet each other socially, and some come two or three times a week in term-time. There is a considerable turnover of people as most have three- or five-year assignments. This can be frustrating, but new families are soon drawn in.' I began to wish I lived in Worcester and not in Gloucester!

Andy beamed as he recalled the next development: 'We realised that back in Japan, where the Christian population is less than 1%, these mums are unlikely to meet Christians. We were missing the natural opportunity of sharing the good news, if we did not offer them the chance to study the Bible, as well as English.'

Back in Japan, these Japanese ladies would have been at work, and their children in school or at a nursery. Here in the UK, they were not permitted to work. They had time on their hands.

Andy continued the story, and I sensed he'd just thought of another opportunity. 'We started a Bible study on Monday mornings using "Life Explored" and "Christianity Explored" study materials as we have bilingual booklets and videos dubbed in Japanese. We've had up to five come, but it's hard work. We've no idea how much they understand. Can you help us? The church will pay your petrol costs.'

I would have said 'Yes,' even without that kind offer. So from autumn 2018, every Monday morning in term time saw me heading north on the motorway to Worcester.

A visit to Gloucester Cathedral

'Why do churches use candles at Christmas time?' asked Yuka.

I'd brought five Japanese ladies from Worcester to see the fabulous knitted nativity scene in Gloucester Cathedral. Nearby, stood a larger-than-life poster panel, depicting a single candle flame piercing the darkness around. I pointed to the words of Jesus prominently displayed alongside the poster, and briefly explained their meaning. 'I am the light of the world. Whoever follows me will never walk in darkness, but will have the light of life' (John 8:12).

Behind us, an animated conversation in Japanese was going on about the Advent Prayer Tree. I was struck by the parallels between this prayer tree and the prayers written on wooden tablets hung on similar structures at Buddhist temples and Shinto shrines in Japan. 'Oh dear, I hope they don't decide that all religions are the same,' I thought.

As I turned, one lady said, 'We were just commenting how different the prayers here are. In Japan, we would write prayers for ourselves, but these prayers are all for others. Why is that?'

I explained that Christmas is all about giving, because Jesus was the first and greatest Christmas present there ever was. God gave his one and only Son Jesus. 'This is how much God loved the world: He gave his Son, his one and only Son. And this is why: so that no one need be destroyed; by believing in him, anyone can have a whole and lasting life' (John 3:16, MSG).

It wasn't the time or place for a detailed explanation of what Jesus came to do. But I did explain that, when we experience the wonder of God's gift of life for ourselves, we are inspired to give gifts ourselves. We give the gift of ourselves, of our time and energy to others, when we pray for them — when we ask God to bring hope and healing into their lives.

Medical matters

*Yaeko was one of the ladies intrigued by the Advent prayer tree. She was nearing the end of her first pregnancy and, a couple of weeks before, she'd asked me to accompany her to Worcester hospital for an ultrasound, and a meeting with the hospital consultant. With long waits at each stage, we had five hours to get to know each other! I'd never been present at an ultrasound scan before, and was thrilled by the miracle of life I saw on the screen, even as I struggled to interpret the unfamiliar medical terminology.

It was more thrilling still to go deeper in conversation with Yaeko than we could on a Monday. Unprompted Yaeko said, 'I would never have thought about the meaning of life, or whether there is life after death, if I hadn't come to church. I have never experienced anyone close to me dying. Christianity is fascinating.'

I was soon well acquainted with two surgeries, a midwifery centre and two hospitals in Worcester and Birmingham, as different ladies needed help with interpreting. My knowledge of Japanese medical terms grew in leaps and bounds too!

Time with individuals was often as valuable as the Bible studies themselves when, despite bilingual materials and some Japanese input, they struggled with English. Their cultural background did not encourage them to express their opinions, even if they'd had the language to do so. As church member Sharron and I led on alternate Mondays, we had little idea what was going on in their heads. I hesitated to use too much Japanese during the studies, as some came because we studied in English. Despite these frustrations, we trusted God to be at work, and to open up minds and hearts to new ways of thinking, as he had done with Yaeko.

A church mobilised for cross-cultural mission

In Japan, it was particularly difficult for OMF workers to build relationships with men because of their notoriously long working hours. Even in the UK, they worked more hours than their British counterparts. However, Woodgreen Evangelical Church came up with creative ideas to invite whole Japanese families to special events on a Saturday. Several dads came to watch Japan play Samoa in the 2019 Rugby World Cup on a big screen in the church. Over food and fun, the husbands interacted with British Christians, and they heard a brief evangelistic talk by a church member that was translated into Japanese. Many of the ladies had no British friends, and children struggled when they began at school with no English.

'My daughter is alone in the playground every day,' said *Mami.

Her little girl had just started in reception, and there were no other Japanese children in that school that year.

'Do you know any Christian families with children in that school who could befriend the family?' I asked Sharron. Wonderfully there was one. The two families became friends, and the little girl began to settle.

*Fumie said, 'I've brought several summer kimonos or *yukata* with me from Japan. I wonder if I will ever get the chance to wear them?'

I resorted to Sharron again. 'Could we organise a cultural event with church people, where Fumie could dress them up in kimonos?'

Sharron was involved with 'Oasis', a church ladies' group. On Thursday mornings they met for Bible study twice a month, and socialised on alternate weeks. They agreed to turn one of the socials into a joint event with the Japanese ladies. Oasis members looked stunning in *yukata,* and it was wonderful to see Christian women making an effort to bridge the language barrier with the activities we prepared. Some ongoing relationships developed, and both sides were keen to have more joint events.

This illustrated an important aspect of my role at Woodgreen — encouraging church members to share their friendship and faith with individual Japanese, helping Christians in cross-cultural mission on their doorsteps. I also provided resources to church members on culture and Christian concepts that Japanese people often find difficult to grasp.

'Sin', for example, is translated *tsumi* in the Japanese Bible but, in Japanese society, the word only means a crime against the law. The words of 1 Corinthians 13:4–8a are familiar to many Japanese as they are often read at the fashionable Western-style chapel weddings.

> Love is patient, love is kind. It does not envy, it does not boast, it is not proud. It does not dishonour others, it is not self-seeking, it is not easily angered, it keeps no record of wrongs. Love does not delight in evil but rejoices with the truth. It always protects, always trusts, always hopes, always perseveres. Love never fails.

I would read this definition of love with Japanese friends on the journey of faith, and then substitute my own name for 'love.' 'Miriam is patient, she is kind. She does not boast, she is not proud . . . she is not self-seeking . . . ' I explained that my life certainly didn't match up to this definition of love however good a person I might seem to be, and this falling short of God's perfect standard was what we meant by the biblical word *tsumi*.

Before leaving Japan I'd not imagined having regular contact with Japanese people in the UK during retirement, but God's sovereignty knows no geographical bounds! Through a 'chance' meeting in Kent, God opened the door for me, living in Gloucester city, to connect with a Japanese community in Worcester that I did not even know existed. Furthermore, it was a community that was already closely linked to a church, actively reaching out to them.

What could be more amazing than that? And what similar opportunities of sharing God's love across cultures might there be from our doorsteps or in our workplaces?

In Gerald Kelly's words, God had prepared a space my shape could fill and, with a puzzle maker's skill, he let my contours find their fit without contortion.

30

主と共に歩みて

Be utterly amazed

'Help, there's no hole!'

I was about to officiate in my capacity as lay minister in my first burial of ashes. I was in a neighbouring parish and off my home ground, so I'd asked the lady in the church office to show me the correct grave the previous day. This was the right spot, but the ground remained untouched, and the ceremony was due to start in 15 minutes. Panicked, I rushed off in search of the gravedigger. Fortunately, I found him hard at work not far away.

'Excuse me, but I need you to dig a hole for ashes quickly,' I said.

'Are you talking about the "X" family's grave?' he replied. 'This is it! Look, it's the right name on the stone, and here are the pink flowers I was told to look out for.'

I had great difficulty persuading him that he was digging the wrong grave. He was not mistaken, either about the flowers, or about the top name on the gravestone, although the flowers were faded plastic, and not the deep crimson of the fresh carnations on the other grave. I showed him the list I was clutching.

'Look, here is a list of the seven names on the stone and slabs below. Six names are different.'

Convinced at last he rushed off to the right grave. To my relief, a persistent drizzle kept the three family members in their cars in the car park with the ashes until the last minute, and we were just ready when they arrived!

As a lay minister in the Church of England, I was licensed to officiate at funerals, but it was 21 months after returning to the UK before I found the courage to do so. Three Saturday training sessions in spring 2019 introduced me to the excellent diocesan vision for funeral ministry, and provided me with practical resources, particularly for non-churched people. I didn't need to be convinced of the vital significance of offering support to bereaved families. I shadowed my vicar and others, but wasn't sure I was up to doing the same as them myself. In August 2019, I came across a quote by Elisabeth Elliot: 'If we wait until we are sure we'll do a thing purely and perfectly, we'll never accomplish the will of God on earth.'[48]

'Okay, God, I get it. You're telling me it's time to take the plunge.'

I accepted the next funeral at which I was free to officiate. As I met distraught family members on the steps of the crematorium, it dawned on me that this was not about me and how I felt, but about being there for them, and bringing the presence of God into their grief. My nervousness vanished and I got on with it. Soon after, family members responded to the invitation to our annual memorial service.

Over refreshments they said, 'We want to come to the carol service next month,' and they did.

---

[48] https://twitter.com/MissionalQuotes/status/1227200626410557445 Accessed 1 March 2021.

The encouragement of this ongoing contact confirmed the rightness of stepping out into this new ministry.

Inevitably, I made mistakes. Mourners could choose to have the curtains closed or left open at the end of the funeral service. I recommended to the daughter of one deceased gentleman, that she should choose closing the curtains as a step towards emotional closure. The funeral safely over, I went home in a glow of satisfaction, only to realise in bed later that night that I'd forgotten to press the button, and had left the curtains open! I hoped she hadn't noticed, and I wrote the words 'Close curtain' in red on future scripts, until the button press became an automatic response. On another occasion, the daughter of the deceased interrupted me in full flow, to remind me that she was supposed to read a poem!

A few short months after officiating at my first funeral, the Covid-19 pandemic turned the world upside down. By mid-March 2020, the UK was in complete lockdown for several months. Church buildings closed and services moved online. Those clergy and readers in the Gloucester Diocese over 70, or with underlying health issues, were no longer able to officiate at funerals. For me, the door to other ministries had shut temporarily, but this door was wide open. God had pushed me out of my comfort zone just in time to serve in the strangest of circumstances—seeking to bring comfort to bereaved families who were not able to gather together to mourn a loved one, to share memories or to hug and comfort one other as they would have done in normal circumstances.

Ordination

Along with the nudge to get going with funerals, it became apparent that God was 'putting me out' in yet another direction, with the promise to 'go before'.

'Why didn't you get ordained?' Mark, my vicar, had asked back in January 2018 when we met for our first proper chat.

'It seems to me you have been doing the work of an ordained minister in Japan.'

And I had, but taking the extra step from reader ministry to ordination in the UK had not been a practical possibility with my prior call to overseas mission. Now, I assumed that my age and the need for further training would disqualify me. I had more than enough on my plate with making a permanent home for myself in the UK, and finding a niche in my lay minister role.

The niggling feeling I should be doing something about ordination persisted, however, and so I regularly began to ask the Lord to show me if this was from him or not. By summer 2019, I felt ready to find out more and, with Mark's encouragement, approached Revd. Pauline Godfrey whose role in Gloucester Diocese was to explore vocation with individuals. To my surprise, there was a possibility of being ordained as an Ordained Local Minister (OLM) in my own church, even at my age. I discovered an online video in which Pauline shared about her own journey to ordination. [49] Someone gave her helpful advice — 'just take the next step'. I kept taking the next step too and, in May 2020, I got the green light from the local Bishop's Advisory Panel for ordination in 2021.

God's leading, or rather propelling, was again unmistakeable, and I was thrilled. That did not mean that all was plain sailing. I had a strong desire at times to shrink away from this and the other 'new' callings of retirement. After all, wasn't I entitled to sit back and enjoy this stage of my life? I picked up *Dirty Glory*, a book by Pete Greig, founder of the 24/7 prayer movement,[50] and found a clear nudge from God in the following words (2016, p. 124, location 1989):

> It's easy to pioneer when you're too young to know what it will cost you, when you feel immortal and invincible and the whole of life is an adventure waiting to begin. But

---

[49] https://youtu.be/Gvr6I1H8vOc
or https://www.gloucester.anglican.org/2017/ourlifestory/
Both accessed on 3 October 2020.
[50] For more information on Greig see https://www.24-7prayer.com/team/14/greig accessed on 3 November 2020.
24/7 was a global movement whose goal is to 'revive the Church and rewire the culture' through non-stop prayer night and day. (https://www.24-7prayer.com/ accessed on 3 November 2020). It began in 1999, when a simple, student-led prayer vigil suddenly went viral. Today, 24-7 Prayer is an international, inter-denominational movement of prayer, mission and justice; a non-stop prayer meeting that has continued for every minute of this century so far, in over half the countries on Earth.

pioneering a second time is hard. Abraham was one of the few who never settled down – even in his old age he lived like a stranger in a foreign country. (Hebrews 11:9)

Don't settle in Harran

As Greig points out, Abraham was almost diverted from his calling to leave Ur of the Chaldees in southern Iraq, and head for the promised land of Canaan when, for some reason we are not told, he and his father made a stop in Harran still 600 miles from their destination – and not just a stop but a 'settling'.[51]

> Terah took his son Abram, his grandson Lot son of Haran and his daughter-in-law Sarai, the wife of his son Abram, and together they set out from Ur of the Chaldeans to go to Canaan. But when they came to Harran, they settled there. (Genesis 11: 31)[52]

Was Terah ill perhaps? He certainly died in Harran. Thankfully, Abraham responded to God's call, and set out again after his father's death, or Christian history would have been very different. But the phrase 'they settled there', implying that they stayed for some considerable time, disturbed me. To remain in Harran – to refuse to move out of my comfort zone in response to God's nudging – was dangerous. 'Lord, may I never settle permanently in Harran when you want me on the road,' I prayed.

I don't know where following God will take me in years to come, but John 10:4 remains as true now as it was 46 years ago. Time and again, the God who thrust me out, sometimes far beyond my comfort zone, went ahead of me bringing me

---

[51] Harran was probably situated in modern day Turkey.

[52] God only later gave Abram his new name 'Abraham', symbolising his new identity as the father of many nations (Genesis 17:5).

into greater blessing and fulfilment. This is the God whom I thank for my past, and to whom I entrust my present and my future.

> When you keep surrendering your life, your plans and preferences, again and again, to the Lordship of Jesus, saying 'yes' to whatever he says, you look around one day blinking in amazement at the ways he has deployed you, the places he has taken you, the person he is enabling you to become. (Greig, 2016, p. 308)

Look . . . and be utterly amazed.
For I am going to do something in your days
that you would not believe,
even if you were told.

(Habakkuk 1:5)

The God who goes before – Bible references

The Bible is full of references to God or his angel going before (or ahead of) his people. Here are just a few references from the Anglicised New International Version (NIV), 2011.

God in the pillar of cloud: Exodus 13:21

> By day the LORD went ahead of them in a pillar of cloud to guide them on their way and by night in a pillar of fire to give them light, so that they could travel by day or night.

God speaking to Moses: Exodus 32:34

> Now go, lead the people to the place I spoke of, and my angel will go before you.

Moses to God referring to the Egyptians: Numbers 14:14

> And they will tell the inhabitants of this land about it. They have already heard that you, O LORD, are with these people and that you, O LORD, have been seen face to face, that your cloud stays over them, and that you go before them in a pillar of cloud by day and a pillar of fire by night.

God stops Balaam: Numbers 22:26

> Then the angel of the LORD moved on ahead and stood in a narrow place where there was no room to turn, either to the right or to the left.

Moses to the people of Israel: Deuteronomy 1:29–33

> Then I said to you, 'Do not be terrified; do not be afraid of them. The LORD your God, who is going before you, will fight for you, as he did for you in Egypt, before your very eyes, and in the wilderness. There you saw how the LORD your God carried you, as a father carries his son, all the way you went until you reached this place.'

In spite of this, you did not trust in the LORD your God, who went ahead of you on your journey, in fire by night and in a cloud by day, to search out places for you to camp and to show you the way you should go.

Moses to the people of Israel as they are about to cross the Jordan: Deuteronomy 9:3

But be assured today that the LORD your God is the one who goes across ahead of you like a devouring fire. He will destroy them; he will subdue them before you. And you will drive them out and annihilate them quickly, as the LORD has promised you.

Moses to Joshua: Deuteronomy 31:8

The LORD himself goes before you and will be with you; he will never leave you nor forsake you. Do not be afraid; do not be discouraged.

Deborah to Barak: Judges 4:14–15

Then Deborah said to Barak, 'Go! This is the day the LORD has given Sisera into your hands. Has not the LORD gone ahead of you?' So Barak went down Mount Tabor, followed by ten thousand men. At Barak's advance, the LORD routed Sisera and all his chariots and army by the sword, and Sisera abandoned his chariot and fled on foot.

God to David: 1 Chronicles 14:13–16

Once more the Philistines raided the valley; so David enquired of God again, and God answered him, 'Do not go directly after them, but circle round them and attack them in front of the poplar trees. As soon as you hear the sound of marching in the tops of the poplar trees, move out to battle, because that will mean God has gone out in front of you to strike the Philistine army.' So David did as God commanded him, and they struck down the Philistine army, all the way from Gibeon to Gezer.

David when under pressure: Psalm 59:10

> God will go before me and will let me gloat over those who slander me.

God to Cyrus of Persia: Isaiah 45:2

> I will go before you and will level the mountains; I will break down gates of bronze and cut through bars of iron.

God to his people: Isaiah 52:12

> But you will not leave in haste or go in flight; for the LORD will go before you, the God of Israel will be your rear guard.

God to his people: Zechariah 12:8

> On that day the LORD will shield those who live in Jerusalem, so that the feeblest among them will be like David, and the house of David will be like God, like the angel of the LORD going before them.

Deliverance promised: Micah 2:13

> The One who breaks open the way will go up before them; they will break through the gate and go out. Their King will pass through before them, the LORD at their head.

Jesus about himself as the Good Shepherd: John 10:4

> When he has brought out all his own, he goes on ahead of them, and his sheep follow him because they know his voice.

Some questions for reflection

Thank you for reading this far! Do take a few moments to reflect with the following questions; first, on your own spiritual journey (questions 1–4), and second, on how you yourself might follow the call of God afresh in global mission.

1. What amazing things has God done in your life so far, even in the most difficult of circumstances? Take a moment to thank God now.
2. Are there times in your own life when you have experienced that sense of God preparing the way ahead for you, perhaps only when you have looked back? How does the idea that he is 'the God who goes before' encourage you in this present moment?
3. Have you sensed God's gentle urging to take a step forward with him? Maybe a first step into faith or a further step into fresh adventures with him? Are you prepared to take that step trusting that God is with you?
4. Consider the impact of God's Word on your spiritual life. Has God spoken in ways that have shaped your own journey with him? How can we hear his voice more clearly?

++++++

5. For those bringing up young families or in contact with young people, are there ways you might encourage an interest in other cultures and global mission? What was the impact of Miriam's childhood experiences in her path to cross-cultural mission?

6. The writer's cross-cultural ministry would not have been possible without the countless individuals and churches who supported her in a multitude of ways. Sometimes the assistance was a one-off or given indirectly; for example, through care of her parents. List as many examples from the book as you can of people who were involved in Miriam's mission to Japan without them ever making a physical move.

7. Are there ways you could be more involved in mission as a result of reading this book? Perhaps in some of the ways mentioned in question 6? The *About OMF International* page may help get you started.

About OMF International

Miriam served with OMF International, which was founded by James Hudson Taylor in 1865 as the China Inland Mission. We serve the Church and share the good news of Jesus Christ in all its fullness with countries across East Asia. And we're for all Christians who want to be relevant in mission. We're a forward-thinking gospel-focused movement that pursues every avenue to reach East Asians for Jesus. In a changing world, we need to find the most effective means possible.

Today this looks like around 1,400 workers from 40 countries serving across East Asia. Their ministries vary from church planting to medical work, from sport to theological education, each of them seeking to serve the Church and share the good news of Jesus Christ in all its fullness.

Find out more about OMF and work in East Asia by exploring our free resources at omf.org. There you can also find contact details for your nearest OMF office.

Follow us on social media by searching for 'OMF International' on Facebook, Twitter or Instagram.

Discover more about our work in Japan by visiting https://omf.org/japan.

Bibliography

Barclay, Ian. *He is everything to me: An exposition of Psalm 23.* London: Falcon Books, Church Pastoral Aid Society, 1972.

Bridges, William. *The Way of Transition: Embracing Life's Most Difficult Moments.* Massachusetts: Da Capo Press (an imprint of Hachette books), 2001.

Carmichael, Amy. *Rose from Briar.* Fort Washington, Pa, USA: Christian Literature Crusade, 1973.

Chaplin, Melissa. *Returning Well: Your Guide to Thriving Back "Home" After Serving Cross-Culturally.* Sioux Falls, USA: Newton Publishers, 2015.

Elliot, Elisabeth. *Passion and Purity.* Grand Rapids, Michigan: Revell (a division of Baker Publishing), 2013.

Grayshon, Jane. *Treasures of darkness – Facing the problem of personal suffering.* London: Hodder & Stoughton, 1996.

Greig, Pete. *Dirty Glory.* London: Hodder and Stoughton, 2016

Horsfall, Tony. *Mentoring for Spiritual Growth.* Abingdon, Oxford: BRF (The Bible Reading Fellowship), 2008.

Kelly, Gerard. *Spoken Worship.* Grand Rapids, Michigan: Zondervan, 2007.

Kihara, James, quoted by Thomas, Norman E., in 'Evangelization and Church Growth: The Case of Africa,' *International Bulletin of Mission Research*, Vol. 11, No.4 October 1987, p. 169. Available at http://www.internationalbulletin.org/issues/1987-04/1987-04-165-thomas.pdf (Downloaded 1 January 2021).

Kuhn, Isobel. *In the Arena.* Newington Green, London: China Inland Mission (now OMF International), 1959.

Lewis, C.S. *The   Lion,   the   Witch   and   the   Wardrobe.* London: HarperCollins UK, 2009.

Meyer, F.B. *Jeremiah, Priest and Prophet.* North Carolina: Heritage Bible Fellowship, 2011.
Available at https://www.amazon.co.uk/Jeremiah-Priest-Prophet-F-Meyer-ebook/dp/B0052AC5PG.   (Downloaded   15 December 2016).

Peterson, Eugene. *A Long Obedience in the Same Direction.* Downers Grove, Illinois: Inter-Varsity Press, 1980.

Saunders,   Oswald   J. *Cameos   of   Comfort — Encouragement   from Corinthians.* Singapore: OMF Books, 1984.

Wiersbe, Warren W. *The Cross of Jesus — What his words from Calvary mean for us.* Michigan, U.S.A.: Baker Books, 1997.
Available at https://amazon.co.uk/Cross-Jesus-What-Words-Calvary-ebook (Downloaded 28 February 2021).

Glossary of Japanese words

Anime アニメ A word derived from 'animation' and used by Japanese people to refer to any animated drawings, no matter their country of origin. In English, it generally refers specifically to Japanese animation.

Benjo 便所 Toilet (a word only used by males, now fairly rare).

Booshi 帽子 Hat, cap.

Butsudan 仏壇 Home Buddhist altar.

Ganbaru がんばる To do your best, to try hard, to keep going.

Gomen kudasai ごめん下さい May I come in?

Hakobiya 運び屋 Drug-smuggler.

Hakobite 運び手 Bearer, carrier.

Hito 人 Person.

Ippoo tsukoo 一方通行 One-way street.

Ise ebi 伊勢海老 Spiny Japanese lobster. (They are called *Ise* lobsters after the town of Ise and its famous bay in Mie prefecture but are also fished elsewhere in Japan).

Juku 塾 Cramming school.

Katto desu ka? カットですか？ Would you like a (hair) cut?

Kanji 漢字 Kanji, one of the three scripts used in the Japanese language, are Chinese characters, which were first introduced to Japan in the fifth century via Korea. Kanji are ideograms, i.e. each character has its own meaning and corresponds to a word. By combining characters, more words can be created. For example, the combination of 'electricity' with 'car' means 'train'. There are tens of thousands of characters, of which 2,000 to 3,000 are required to understand newspapers. A set of 2136 characters has been officially declared as the 'kanji for everyday use'.

Ki 木 Tree.

Kochira koso こちらこそ A phrase used in response to a greeting like 'thank you' or 'nice to meet you' meaning 'thank you too' or 'it's nice to meet you too'.

Kuu 食う To eat (male language only).

Meshi o kuu 飯を食う To have, eat a meal (males only).

Mokuzai 木材 Timber.

Nippon Sei Ko Kai (NSKK) 日本聖公会 The Anglican Episcopal Church in Japan.

Nori のり Crisp, paper-thin pieces of edible toasted seaweed.

Obaasan おばあさん Grandmother(s) (literally); older woman or women.

Obento お弁当 A cold box lunch of vegetables, pickles, fish and/or meat with white rice.

Omedeto gozaimasu おめでとう ございます Congratulations.

Omiai お見合い An arranged meeting between two people to explore the possibility of marriage.

Omimai お見舞い A visit to a sick person.

Onsen 温泉 Volcanic hot spring bath.

Oshikko おしっこ (I need) a wee.

Pinku ンク Pink.

Sensei 先生 Teacher.

Senshu arigato gozaimashita 先週ありがとうございました

(Literally: last week, thank you). Thank you for your help, time (or whatever it was the person being thanked had done) last week.

Shokuji o toru 食事をとる To have, or eat a meal (used by both men and women).

Shampoo desu ka? シャンプーですか？ Would you like a shampoo?

Shiwasu 師走 The ancient Japanese calendar name for December. The first character means 'monk' or 'teacher' and the second 'to run'. Even calm and serene Buddhist monks rush around in the busy run-up to the main holiday of the year which starts on January 1st.

Tatami 畳 Traditional Japanese-style floor mats made from woven soft rush straw called *igusa* straw.

Tearai, Otearai (polite) 手洗い、お手洗い Toilet (women will commonly add the polite prefix 'o').

Toire, otoire (polite) トイレ、おトイレ Toilet (with the optional polite 'o' mostly used by women).

Tsumi 罪 Sin (biblical usage); crime (general use).

Yoroshiku onegai itashimasu よろしく お願いいたします
Literally: I beg your kind favour.

Yukata 浴衣 An unlined cotton summer kimono, worn in casual settings such as summer festivals and to nearby bathhouses. Originally worn as bathrobes, they are a common sight in Japan during summer.

Thank you . . .

I would like to thank all those without whom this book would not have seen the light of day.

- To Reuben Grace, content and media co-ordinator at OMF UK headquarters, and his team for their encouragement, editing and practical help in many ways from the start.
- To Colin Waterman, Director of Fabulahula Publishing, for his voluntary contribution of countless hours of unstinting hard work in editing, formatting and publishing. Without his meticulous, painstaking work, *Utterly Amazed* would not have been published in its present form.
- To Mary Grace Sy (Meg), who despite the demands of a highly pressured job, volunteered many hours and her artistic skills to produce the cover design and wonderful illustrations. Thank you, Meg, for your patience and willing perseverance over several months despite my many requests and some rejections.
- To Michael and Sue Carter who lent me their holiday home in the New Forest for three one-week stays when I first attempted to write with the aim of seeing if there was any future in it. It was in their home that I sensed God's leading to press on with writing.
- To all those who encouraged me, proofread early drafts and gave advice: in particular, Elisabeth Sawle, Sue Lyon, Paul and Jackie Butcher, Liz Lister, Chris Idle and Becky Chevis.

- To all who read a draft for the purpose of writing a review.
- To all my prayer partners and financial supporters for 'No man can do me a truer kindness in this world than to pray for me' (C.H. Spurgeon).[53]
- To the congregations of my three principal supporting churches over many years: Brunswick Baptist Church, Southgate Street, Gloucester; Street Baptist Church, Somerset; and St Philip and St James Church, Hucclecote, Gloucester.
- To my wonderful worldwide OMF family.
- To my parents who prayed me into faith, supported me in my journey to Japan, and lovingly kept every personal letter and every prayer letter I ever wrote (an immense help in checking facts, and reordering faulty memories)!
- And above all to God. 'I stand in awe of your deeds, O LORD' (Habakkuk 3:2).

---

[53] https://www.azquotes.com/quote/814301 Accessed 30 March 2021